YOUR HOLIDAY IN
YUGOSLAVIA

B

YOUR HOLIDAY IN YUGOSLAVIA

by

ERNEST WELSMAN

LONDON

ALVIN REDMAN LIMITED

By ERNEST WELSMAN

YOUR HOLIDAY IN YUGOSLAVIA

By GORDON COOPER *and* ERNEST WELSMAN

YOUR HOLIDAY IN IRELAND
YOUR HOLIDAY IN EUROPE

By GORDON COOPER

YOUR HOLIDAY IN BELGIUM, HOLLAND AND LUXEMBOURG
YOUR HOLIDAY IN ITALY
YOUR HOLIDAY IN FRANCE
YOUR HOLIDAY IN SWITZERLAND
YOUR HOLIDAY IN GERMANY

First published in Great Britain by
ALVIN REDMAN LIMITED
4 Fitzroy Street, London, W.1, England
1954

MADE AND
PRINTED IN GREAT BRITAIN BY
MERRITT & HATCHER LIMITED.
HIGH WYCOMBE AND LONDON

CONTENTS

CONTENTS

6

PART V. SOME SPECIAL INTERESTS

LIST OF ILLUSTRATIONS

8

Plates 7, 12, 21, 22, 23, 27, 28, and 32 from photographs by the Author. Plates 41 to 45 kindly supplied by the Tourist Association of Slovenia, and the remainder by the General Administration of the Travel and Catering Industry of Yugoslavia. The map was drawn by Mr. N. Vincent.

INTRODUCTION

DURING THE past two or three years my advice has often been sought by people who have wanted to visit Yugoslavia, the new holiday-land in the Balkans. Since the end of the war large numbers of tourists from Britain and America, and also from the Dominions, have spent their holidays in France and Switzerland, Italy and Austria and the other conventional holiday countries of Europe. Now they are beginning to feel the desire to visit lands which are less accessible and which give more opportunities of getting off the beaten track.

That is why Yugoslavia as a holiday country is coming into its own. It is new to most people—and therefore it is exciting and romantic. This impression is heightened in most minds by the political character of the country, which has the unique status of being a Communist state but outside the Iron Curtain. Some, too, remember travellers' tales from the years before the war of the beauties of the incomparable coast of Dalmatia, of the loveliness of the great ranges of mountains and of the countless islands, and of the Turkish character of many towns and villages of the interior.

These tales were not exaggerated, for Yugoslavia is indeed a land of great natural beauty, of historic interest and of contrasts. Variety is one of the keynotes of the Yugoslav scene. The sun-drenched coast, with the mountain-sides sheer to a sea which is studded with islands, contains not only some of the finest stretches of golden sand in Europe but also towns and villages which are living monuments of past ages, when Rome and later Venice and Ragusa established trading posts and fortress ports all along the Adriatic. There are mountains everywhere, but how different are those of Slovenia, in the north, from the rugged wilderness of Montenegro where the clansmen fought for centuries against the Turks, or from the barren limestone of the Dinaric Alps running parallel to the coast for hundreds of miles. The centres of population, too, exhibit the greatest variety of colour and of architectural styles. Those of the north are akin to Austria and other parts of western Europe, but in central and southern Yugoslavia the graceful minarets of the mosques bear witness to the fact that little more than forty years have passed since this part of the land was still subject to Turkey, and had been so for centuries.

The purpose of this book is not to tell of my personal travels in Yugoslavia, though my own experiences are mentioned from time to time when they are likely to be of practical use or interest to the reader. Nor have I set out to produce a "Baedeker", giving detailed information about every village, museum and monument. My aim has been rather to present practical advice of the kind which every traveller needs to have if he is to get the best out of his holiday—a good deal of background information of a general character, and recommendations of the best places to be visited by people whose holidays are inevitably too short to see the whole of the country, and who want to feel that their time will not be wasted and they will not miss something delightful which is just round the corner.

Information, then, is the keynote of this book and I think that it is sufficiently comprehensive to enable the reader to plan a very full and varied holiday. I have not overlooked, however, the interests of the prospective visitor who does not want to travel widely, for there are many places in Yugoslavia where a delightful holiday can be spent just sitting in the sun by the sea or by the side of a lake, often with a range of mountains as a colourful and impressive background.

A warning must be given concerning prices. Those mentioned in this book are, of course, subject to change and you should make enquiries from a Yugoslav National Tourist Office about the current range of charges. However, the Yugoslavs are badly in need of foreign currency and likely to be in this position for many years yet; they therefore look upon the foreign tourist as a valuable economic asset and they are not likely, I feel sure, to deter visitors by raising their charges steeply. Certainly, at the moment, Yugoslavia is one of the least expensive of all European countries for the holiday-maker from overseas.

A word must be said to those who feel that in this communist country they will be subjected to all kinds of regulation and supervision. This is very far from the case, for there are few countries in which one is less troubled by red tape. Your passport will be collected by the hotel proprietors, who have to register your arrival, but there is none of the constant form-filling which one finds, for instance, in Spain or even at times in Italy. You can go anywhere you like by rail or bus, steamer or plane and you will seldom be asked why or where you are going. The people themselves are amongst the most friendly in Europe, always anxious to guide and assist the foreigner and with a specially helping hand to those who were Yugoslavia's

13

allies during the war. There is no touting and hardly any tipping, and people who help you nearly always refuse to accept any monetary reward.

You will not be expected to speak Serbo-Croat or one of the other national languages, which are very difficult to learn. Many people have been to Yugoslavia without even knowing how to say "Please" and "Thank you" and they seem to have fared well nevertheless; but in the belief that one ought to know at least these two words and a few other essentials I have included as an appendix a short list of everyday phrases. When your needs take you beyond these phrases and English does not help, try German, Italian and French, in that order. A policy of "pidgin-everything-you-know" can work wonders.

Finally, a word about Putnik. This is the magic name for visitors to Yugoslavia, an "open sesame" to all kinds of interests, a ready help in time of trouble, a guide, counsellor and friend. Putnik is the national tourist organisation and there are offices everywhere, very often with an English-speaking member of the staff. They will do anything for you. If you want a room in a hotel or if you need to change currency, if you want to go on a coach-trip or motor-boat excursion or to buy theatre tickets, if you lose your way or your wallet or your wife, go to the Putnik office, and they will help you. Their staffs are usually young, always helpful, invariably enthusiastic. Sometimes their exuberance overruns their technical ability, a facet of Slav character which is not confined to Putnik. You will soon learn to recognise this Ruritanian characteristic and to laugh at it, but it can be exasperating the first time you encounter it; so although you should note all the advice and information that Putnik can

14

give you, it is well to check it when the opportunity arises.

In the course of preparing this book I have made many journeys to Yugoslavia and I have received much help from Yugoslavs of all kinds, officials and men in the street. I have also had the opportunity of discussing with many British visitors their experiences and impressions. I have done my best to be accurate in matters of detail, but Yugoslavia is a country of rapid change and the field is so wide it is difficult always to be accurate. Should the reader note any details which require correction, or have suggestions for improvements in future editions, I shall be most grateful if he will send a note to me in the care of the publishers, thus rendering a service to others who may use this book in the future.

ERNEST WELSMAN

PART I

WHAT YOU SHOULD KNOW BEFORE LEAVING HOME

(i) PLANNING YOUR HOLIDAY IN YUGOSLAVIA

HAVING DECIDED to go to Yugoslavia, the reader will find, I hope, that my description of the various towns and regions will help him to make the next decision, which is where to go within the country. Before deciding where to go and what to see, however, he should first make up his mind about the kind of holiday he wants.

You can spend your holiday at one centre, by the sea or on a lake-shore; you can ramble through the mountains; you can explore a limited area by means of local excursion coaches; or you can undertake more extensive travel through the country, staying a night or two at each of the main places of interest. All these types of holiday, and many others, are possible, and you should make up your mind what kind of vacation you want, and then prepare your travel plans.

Unless you have several weeks and plenty of dinars to spend, you certainly will not be able to "do" Yugoslavia completely in one visit. By European standards it is a big country; by the same standards its trains and buses are not at all speedy, even on the main routes, and connections are seldom good. It is not a country for the impatient traveller, anxious to dash from place to place with the minimum of delay. On one of my recent visits to Yugoslavia my compartment on the Simplon-Orient Express was shared with two American ladies, who had been told, when in Venice, to " make an excursion to Yugoslavia ". So they had lopped a few days off their Italian trip and were now on their way. They had heard that the Dalmatian coast was fine, especially Korčula and Trogir and Šibenik and Bar; they felt that they ought to go to Macedonia to see the costumes; and Sarajevo, too, had been recommended to them as a place to visit. So it went on; and it was my sad duty to disappoint them. It was in the early spring, before the daily service of steamers had commenced along the northern part of the coast and I explained that it would take them a full week to visit the four coastal places alone—and at the end of the week they would be near the Albanian frontier and then have to come back to Dubrovnik before going inland.

No, you must have an intelligent and carefully prepared plan of travel, unless time doesn't matter to you. When you have decided on the type of holiday you want, consult the time-tables of trains and steamers, planes and buses and work out your personal schedules, leaving a few days in hand for unexpected whims and fancies—and for missed connections. Of course, if your aim is more limited—just to spend all or most of your time at one place, for instance—you will not be so concerned with time-tables and travel problems. Your aim will be merely to get to your destination and back again as efficiently and pleasantly as possible; but even then, the pitfalls of Yugoslav travel being what they are, careful planning is important.

Even for the person who wants to see as much as

possible there is a lot to be said for concentrating on one area and seeing it properly, rather than making the vain attempt to cover the whole country in one holiday. Yugoslavia is a land in which the intelligent traveller, content to move about slowly, will find as much to interest him in the byways and in villages which are never mentioned in a guide-book as in the popular tourist resorts. Each of the republics that make up Yugoslavia can alone provide a very full holiday, whatever your tastes and interests may be: and it is better to spend your time in one district—say the Dalmatian Coast, with time to visit some of the smaller islands as well as Split and Dubrovnik, or Macedonia, getting off the beaten track to mountain villages like Galičnik or Lazaropole—rather than to attempt to cover the whole of Yugoslavia on one holiday.

I realise, of course, that despite these warnings many of my readers will want to see as much as they can. Life is short, the countries of Europe alone are many. We cannot all be specialists and connoisseurs. I shall therefore pander to the tastes and needs of those who want to get a brief glimpse of many parts of the country by suggesting some extensive itineraries. (See Appendix B.)

Whether you decide to stay at one or two centres, to range widely and swiftly over the country, or to explore one region more thoroughly, read as much as you can about Yugoslavia before you go. It is important to acquire some background against which to measure the sights and scenes which await you. Unfortunately there are comparatively few books on Yugoslavia—and fewer good ones. You will find a suggested reading list on pages 46 and 47 but your own librarian may have other suggestions. Be sure to include in your reading something about the struggles of the last war and, in particular, Fitzroy Maclean's "Eastern Approaches". The pattern of Yugoslavia today owes much of its character to the events of the war of 1941-45, which wrought great changes in the social structure in town and country alike.

I shall give some information, too, about maps which are available. Get a good general map of the country, preferably one indicating the relief and, if they are available, more detailed maps of the districts in which you will be spending most of your time.

So far I have assumed that you will be doing your own planning and that your holiday in Yugoslavia will be an independent affair and not a conducted tour; but there are, of course, a number of travel agents who specialise in Yugoslavia and who will be very willing to give you their advice and assistance—from just providing your travel tickets to working out your whole itinerary and making all the arrangements for your travel and accommodation. Some, too, organise escorted tours, by public rail and steamer services or in private motor-coaches and these can be recommended to people who want everything "laid on" in advance; though you won't get so much out of your holiday when travelling in the company of a large number of your own compatriots, and in private coaches, as you will if you adopt a more adventurous plan.

There are, of course, a number of voluntary organisations which provide informal party holidays in Yugoslavia, usually youthful in outlook, travelling fairly adventurously and certainly not staying at first-class hotels; they provide good company and an excellent holiday spirit and their charges give excellent value for money, but you must be prepared to take the rough with the smooth.

Whatever help you decide to seek from a travel agent, be warned and make sure of the *bona fides* of the firm you intend to patronise. Check up and see if they belong to one of the professional associations, the Institute of Travel Agents, the Association of British Travel Agents or the American Society of Travel Agents. There are many "mushroom" firms who are not members of any of these bodies and, even if their prices appear to be cheap, they are best avoided.

(ii) THE BEST TIME TO VISIT YUGOSLAVIA

Avoid July and August everywhere—if you can. They are the hottest months of the year and it can be *very* hot in Yugoslavia in summer. This is especially true inland, at places like Belgrade, Sarajevo and Skopje, whilst in the mountains and at some of the higher lakeside resorts the temperature is pleasanter. If you have to visit Yugoslavia in high summer, remember that the heat will make you want to rest a good deal, especially in the middle of the day; though on the coast the midday heat is often tempered by a cool north-west breeze.

May is the pleasantest month in most parts of the country. There is little to choose between the spring and autumn in the matter of temperature, but the landscape is greener and more colourful in the earlier season.

Walkers and mountaineers will find that in a normal year most of the snow will have disappeared from the passes by the beginning of June, even in the Julian Alps and the other ranges along the northern frontier. The Dinaric Alps, lying parallel with the coast of Dalmatia, and inland ranges like the Lovćen of Montenegro and the Macedonian Šar Planina are very hot in summer even at high altitudes. The day's walk or climbing should be commenced at dawn and finished by noon if you want it to be enjoyable and not an endurance test.

At most of the tourist centres, especially on the coast, the hotels reduce their charges by 10% to 20% outside the months of June to September and this is another advantage of spring and late autumn holidays. It must be noted, however, that many of the excursions organised by the local travel offices do not begin until early May and cease during October.

Winter in Yugoslavia is cold inland but very pleasant by the sea, though there are rainy periods. The average winter temperatures along the Dalmatian coast are a good deal higher than those of the Côte d'Azur and the Italian Riviera, but a fierce wind called the Bora occasionally blows from inland. The mountains of Slovenia and those near Sarajevo and Skopje all have good centres for winter sports, though the season is not a long one by usual Alpine standards. To be sure of good snow conditions it is best to go during the latter part of January, February or the first half of March.

(iii) HOW TO REACH YUGOSLAVIA

(a) *By Rail*

There are three main rail routes to Yugoslavia:—
   The Tauern Express Route: via Dover, Ostend, Brussels, Cologne, Munich and Salzburg.

The Simplon Route: via Paris, Vallorbe, Lausanne, Milan, Venice and Trieste.

The Northern Swiss Route: via Calais or Boulogne direct to Basle, or via Paris to Basle, changing there to the Adria Express via Zurich, Innsbruck and Schwarzach St. Veit.

The Tauern Express Route. At the time of preparation of this book this is the cheapest route to Yugoslavia. There are through coaches every day from Ostend to Belgrade and on some days of the week all the way to Athens, which means that you can travel as far as Macedonia without changing trains. On this route you reach northern Yugoslavia (the Julian Alps, Ljubljana, or Zagreb) on the evening of your second day of travel from London or Ostend. You will thus have to spend one night in the train. German sleepers are available in all three classes and they are quite inexpensive by comparison with usual Wagon-Lit charges. They are consequently in great demand in the summer, especially the third-class berths, and very early application has to be made for them. Apart from the cost, the through coaches and the sleepers, the Tauern route has my recommendation for another reason, and that is that the journey itself is most interesting because you cross the Alps in daylight in both directions. The Tauern Express carries restaurant cars the whole journey. Coupons for the meals can be purchased in advance, an important currency-saving device for British tourists. The Belgian meals are rather expensive, whilst those in Germany, Austria and Yugoslavia are cheaper.

If you plan to take the steamer down the whole of the Dalmatian Coast, you should alight from the Tauern Express at Ljubljana and spend the night there.

22

Next day[1] you can travel on to Rijeka (visiting the grottoes at Postojna *en route*) and commence your coastal journey from there.

Another way of reaching the coast is to continue on the Tauern Express to Zagreb and take the connecting overnight train from there to Split, arriving early the following afternoon; or to spend the night in Zagreb, going on by train to Split next day. You can break your journey to see the Plitvice National Park. The Tauern connections to Sarajevo and thence to Dubrovnik are not so good. It is best to spend a night in Ljubljana, travel on to Zagreb the next afternoon and take a night train from there direct to Sarajevo.

For Belgrade you stay on the Express itself for an extra night, arriving early next morning. For Macedonia you travel still further south on the main line, some days of the week changing at Belgrade, on other days staying in your through coach all the way to Skopje, which is reached during the afternoon of the third day of travel.

The Simplon Route. On this route you first cross to Paris. There are several cross-channel services available, from the Newhaven-Dieppe ferry, which is the cheapest if you are travelling third-class, to the Golden Arrow Pullman service via Folkestone-Calais and the night-ferry via Dover-Dunkirk, with through sleepers. You can also go to Paris by air, quite cheaply if you travel on one of the tourist or "off-peak" flights.

If travelling second or first class, you can go all the way from the Gare de Lyon in Paris to Yugoslavia on

---

[1] A new development has just been announced (Feb., 1954). The Tauern Express now has through coaches from Ostend to Rijeka.

the Simplon-Orient Express. You will have the satis-
faction of travelling on one of the best-known trains in
the world, following in the wake of the famous and the
notorious. Even Hercule Poirot has passed this way
before you!

The train has no third-class accommodation[2]. It
carries sleepers, but they are expensive ones; if, however, you are passing only one night on the train you
need book a sleeper only from Paris to Milan. There
are restaurant cars on the Simplon-Orient Express all
through its long journey, but the meals are expensive.

The train reaches Yugoslavia on the evening of the
second day, and there are connections to the coast. You
can change at Pivka (formerly known as St. Peter and
still indicated by that name on many maps) and reach
Rijeka the same night; except in the summer you have
to wait a few hours at Pivka for the local train and it
will be nearly midnight before you reach your hotel at
Rijeka. The S.O.E. reaches Zagreb late in the evening and connects there with the overnight services to
Split and Sarajevo, with a further connection to Dubrovnik from the latter. By remaining on the Simplon-
Orient you reach Belgrade on the morning of your
third day of travel and Skopje the same afternoon.

The Simplon route can also be used by people who
are travelling third class. In Paris they can catch the
Direct-Orient Express, which leaves after the Simplon-
Orient and eventually runs several hours behind it.
After they have spent two nights in the train they reach
Ljubljana and Zagreb early on the third morning and
Belgrade the same evening. It is far better, however,

---

[2] Commencing with the summer of 1954 the Simplon-Orient
Express *will* carry third-class coaches between Paris and Milan.

to break the journey at Verona or Padua or Venice, travelling on next day in the Simplon-Orient Express, second class of course.

With either the Simplon-Orient or Direct-Orient you can reach Venice on some days of the week in time to catch an overnight boat to Rijeka.

The Northern Swiss Route. If you travel by this route you first have to reach Basle, either by direct train from Calais or Boulogne, via Paris, or by air. There are cheap night excursion flights from London. The through coaches of the Adria Express to Ljubljana and Rijeka leave Basle early in the morning and a change can be made to a sleeping car at Schwarzach St. Veit. It should be noted that this service operates for only two months of the summer season.

(b) *By Air*

There are direct air-services to Zagreb and Belgrade from Frankfurt, Munich and Paris, all operated by Yugoslav Air Transport (JAT). There are also direct flights between Yugoslavia and Zurich, operated by JAT and Swissair, and between Belgrade and Athens. No other national air corporations at present have direct flights, but a private company, Eagle Aviation Ltd., runs a scheduled service between London and Belgrade.

It is to be expected that there will soon be a considerable development of air services between Western European countries and Yugoslavia, and direct flights from the United States may also be operated in the near future.

(c) *By Steamer*

At present there is only one regular passenger-steamer service to Yugoslavia, and that is the weekly sailing of the s.s. "Partizanka" from Venice to Rijeka, continuing the length of the Dalmatian coast. Even this service is operated only in summer. It is probable, however, that there will be more vessels on this route in the near future. There has also been talk of direct sailings between Ancona and Dubrovnik.

(iv) PASSPORTS: VISAS: CUSTOMS: MONEY

Everyone travelling to the continent must, of course, have a passport.[3] It is also necessary to have a Yugoslav visa. To secure this, you first have to obtain and complete the application forms. These are easy to fill in as all the questions are translated into English. One of the questions asks about business connections in Yugoslavia, but no references are required for tourist visas and to this you should, therefore, answer "none". When the forms are completed, they must be sent, together with your passport and two photographs (preferably of passport type) and a fee of 11/- to a Yugoslav Consulate. (For addresses see Appendix G.) Any travel agent will see to the formalities on your behalf. This saves you time and trouble and the small fee which is charged is generally not much more than your own out-of-pocket expenses. Some agents charge as much as 7/6d. or $1.50 for obtaining a visa, but such a high charge is not justified by the expense involved. I know of agents who charge less than half these sums for their services, and this is quite adequate.

Holders of United Kingdom and United States passports do not need transit visas for any of the countries they are likely to pass through on the way to Yugo-

---

[3] See Appendix A on how to obtain a British passport.

26

slavia. Persons of other nationalities, including holders of British Dominion and Colonial passports may, however, need transit visas and they should make enquiries from travel agents or in some cases from their own banks.

When you have your Yugoslav visa, check it as follows: —

(a) It should be stamped "Turistička Viza". This is important because of travel concessions which I shall mention later.

(b) After the words "Ulaz u FNRJ do" will appear the date up to which you may enter the country.

(c) After the words "Boravak u FNRJ" will be inserted the number of days the visa permits you to stay in Yugoslavia.

* * *

The Customs formalities for foreign tourists are not very irksome. You can take with you all the personal effects you need but it is as well to declare at the frontier such things as cameras, portable radio sets or typewriters, sporting-guns and fishing-tackle. They will be noted in your passport and you will then have no difficulty in taking them out again.

You are officially allowed to take into Yugoslavia forty cigarettes or about 1½ oz. of tobacco, but in practice there is some small tolerance over these quantities.

Remember that when you return home, whether to Britain or the U.S.A., you will be called upon to declare everything you have obtained abroad and that customs duty, and in some cases purchase tax, too, is payable on most articles. It will perhaps be useful, in this connection, to mention for the benefit of British

27

tourists the regulations concerning the importation of tobacco, wines and spirits. There is a common belief that a Briton has a right to bring back with him certain quantities of these commodities duty-free. This is in fact not the case, but there are concessions which customs officers are authorised to make at their discretion. In practice these concessions are made in all normal cases, but it is important to note that they cannot be demanded as of right.

Under these concessions the following quantities are normally permitted duty-free:—

> 200 cigarettes or $\frac{1}{2}$ lb. tobacco.
>
> One half-bottle of liqueur, brandy or other spirits.
>
> Half-a-pint of perfume.
>
> One bottle of wine.

Tourists who are domiciled outside Europe can bring into Great Britain double the above quantities of spirits and cigarettes or tobacco. If the amounts in any of the categories indicated above are exceeded, you will probably be called upon to pay duty on the whole quantity—and British tobacco and alcohol duty is very heavy.

You may bring up to 50 lbs. of food with you to Britain, but not more than 10 lbs. of any one type of food. The import of uncooked meat is prohibited. Provided that you declare them, the customs officer will usually not make any charge on small souvenir or gift items, a couple of pairs of nylons, a shirt and so on; but as these concessions vary much from day to day and between port and port, it is safest to assume, when making your purchases, that you will be called upon to pay duty upon them.

The import regulations into the United States are

very complicated. There is a general duty-free concession of goods to the value of $500, but there are many exceptions, the most important relating to wines and spirits.

British subjects intending to take abroad foreign cameras and accessories, field glasses, etc., should be sure that customs duty was originally paid on them. A receipt showing that such articles were purchased from a reputable dealer is usually accepted as evidence that duty was paid when the apparatus was first brought into Great Britain.

*   *   *

The unit of currency in Yugoslavia is the dinar and there are 840 dinars to the pound sterling and 300 to the U.S. dollar. There are notes for 1, 5, 10, 20, 50, 100, 500 and 1,000 dinars and coins for 1, 2 and 5 dinars. Occasionally one may see coins of 50 para (half a dinar) also. There are some out-of-date notes in circulation and if you are given a note of an unusual pattern, especially if it is a dirty one, make immediate enquiries to assure yourself of its validity.

You should take your currency to Yugoslavia in the form of travellers' cheques. It is doubtful if your bank will have any actual dinars in the till but you should note in any event that a person is allowed to take into Yugoslavia not more than 500 dinars, and no notes of denominations exceeding 50 dinars. You need not be worried if you go to Yugoslavia without any dinars in your pocket because a "Putnik" official is available to exchange cheques at every frontier point.

When you enter the country you will be given a certificate of the various monies in your possession and another certificate will be presented each time you exchange your cheques. These certificates should be carefully kept as they may be asked for when you leave Yugoslavia. You can exchange travellers' cheques and any foreign notes at branches of the Yugoslav National Bank or, usually more conveniently, at any of the Putnik offices. Small deductions will be made for expenses. Sleeping-car and restaurant-car attendants will also exchange foreign notes.

You are not allowed to take out of the country more than 500 dinars and, again, no notes of denominations over 50 dinars. In any event, you will find that your bank at home will be unwilling to take back any surplus Yugoslav currency. You should, therefore, be sure that some of your travellers' cheques are of the smallest denomination obtainable and you should retain these until the end of your holiday. There is nothing more annoying than to have to change a large cheque on your last day in the country.

If you follow this advice, your currency problems will be few. In fact, it is easier to conduct exchange operations in Yugoslavia than in most other European countries, and there is less red tape.

(v) COSTS IN YUGOSLAVIA

The cost of your holiday in Yugoslavia depends a good deal on your tastes and outlook, but whatever your ideas you will find that Yugoslavia is an inexpensive country.

The tourist who wants luxury hotels will find them only in a few places—Belgrade, Zagreb, Ljubljana, Dubrovnik and Opatija. The highest prices for a single room with private bathroom at the most expensive hotel in Yugoslavia, the Mažestik in Belgrade, is about 2,250 dinars a day, with excellent meals and all tips and taxes included in the charge. At the few other luxury hotels the all-in cost of a day's full board and accommodation is under 1,600 dinars.

The more modest grade of hotel, known as category B, provides a higher standard of comfort and service for between 750 and 1,200 dinars a day than you get for the same price in most other countries. The charge varies, roughly within these limits, according to the popularity of the place. In a favourite resort like Dubrovnik or Split, Bled or Sarajevo, you pay about 1,000 dinars a day for what you find at smaller places, Budva or Hvar, Bohinj or Ohrid, for example, for 800 dinars or even less.

You can economise by using category C hotels where they are available, the charges being roughly 200 dinars a day less than category B hotels in the same town. You need not be afraid that at category C hotels you will have dirty rooms and poor food. I have stayed at C hotels all over Yugoslavia and have found only one thing to complain about, and that is the sometimes slow and rather inefficient service.

I have quoted "all-in" prices for hotels, but many people will prefer just to pay for their room and buy their meals at restaurants. This is a far more interesting way of eating when on holiday abroad, but it is nearly always more expensive. At the luxury hotels your room will cost about 800 dinars a night; at "B" and "C" hotels from less than 250 dinars up to 400 dinars, seldom more. Eating *à la carte* in a medium-class restaurant will cost you about 50 dinars for soup, 200 to 250 dinars for a main course with vegetables and another 50 to 80 dinars for sweet or cheese. This is a total of about 350 dinars, but you can obtain as good a meal, still *à la carte,* for 250 dinars or lower, in a less pretentious place. Most restaurants and hotels, of all categories, have fixed price menus, which are usually very good value and range from 150 or 200 dinars at the quieter and less-visited places to 400 dinars or more at the luxury hotels. 250 or 300 dinars is a reasonable average figure to estimate. Breakfast (coffee and bread and jam, usually with butter but not always so when off the beaten track) costs from about 50 to 150 dinars, again according to grade of hotel and popularity of the resort.

There is a tourist tax everywhere in the country and this is added to your room-bill (not to what you pay for meals). The tax varies from 10 to 40 dinars a night, the popularity of the town again being the deciding factor.

These notes on hotel costs can be summarised by saying that if you avoid the luxury hotels, don't spend all your time at the big and fashionable places, ask for pension terms sometimes and at other times eat *à la carte,* you will find that you will do quite well on 1,000 dinars a day, including the service charge and taxes, and you should have something over towards your drinks. If you are very careful and insist mainly on "C" category pension rates, you can cut this figure by 250 dinars or even more.

Drinks are cheap, especially wine and beer. Soft drinks and coffee are rather more expensive. Cigarettes are very cheap by British standards. Ice-cream is inexpensive, too. Souvenirs, to be found in "arty-crafty" shops in most of the big places, are quite reasonable in price. Clothes are dear and of poor quality. Manufactured articles, such as razor blades, toilet soap and camera films, are either expensive because they are imported or of poor quality if made in Yugoslavia.

Travel of all kinds is cheap and I shall have more to say about this when dealing with the internal transport systems of the country. Admission fares to cinemas and theatres, etc., are ridiculously low by British standards. For example, seats for the opera in Ljubljana, the capital city of Slovenia, cost from 150 dinars for the stalls down to only 10 dinars for the gallery! In most places you pay to go on to the bathing beaches (except in spring and winter!) but the cost is quite small and it includes the use of a box for changing.

Excursion trips, whether by coach or motor-boat, cost roughly the same as in most other countries. I shall give some examples when dealing with the various centres at which excursion programmes are organised.

When thinking about the cost of a holiday in Yugoslavia, and especially when you are there, you will wonder how the Yugoslav people themselves live, and what they earn. For the vast majority of them the cost of living is very high in relation to their wages. A school-teacher and a clerical worker, say in the civil service, will get about 8,000 to 10,000 dinars a month, supplemented by generous family allowances. A University professor or a man in an executive position in commerce may receive up to 15,000 to 20,000 dinars a month, but that is about the limit. There is no direct taxation but most prices are fixed by the State in such a way as to produce a good deal of revenue. There is a system of national health insurance, but only for wage-earners and their dependants. There are, of course, many self-employed people in Yugoslavia—

farmers, small-holders, small shop-keepers and craftsmen for the most part. They are often much better
off than those who are paid fixed wages. There are
also many co-operative enterprises, which have a
periodical share-out of the part of their profits which is
not needed for expansion or development, or for state
levies.

Wherever you go in Yugoslavia you will see people
on holiday, spending far more than seems justified by
these figures. The chief reason is that holiday costs
are subsidised by trade-union and other state organisations. For a large proportion of the population the
cost of the annual holiday travel, accommodation and
meals is very low by comparison with what the foreign
tourist has to pay—especially outside the high season.
The average Yugoslav, too, sets great store on his
holiday and will save up for it throughout the year and
even sell some of his possessions to make up for his
low wages—and have an exceptionally good fling when
his holiday time comes round.

(vi) PUTNIK

The word "Putnik" comes from the verb "putovati"
—to travel. As I explained in my Introduction, Putnik
is the national travel agency, formerly centralised in
organisation but with branches all over the country.
Since 1952 there has been decentralisation, and now
each region has its own group of Putnik offices,
operated under the "workers' co-operative" system.

To quote an official publication—"Putnik arranges
hotel accommodation, sells railway, steamer and air
tickets, organises excursions, exchanges money and

gives all kinds of information to tourists." In fact, Putnik does far more. In this country of difficult communications and with a language you can hardly be expected to understand, the Putnik offices are havens of reassurance to foreign travellers. However trifling your enquiry and however irrelevant it may be to the normal business of a travel agency, you will find that you will always receive the utmost help and courtesy from Putnik.

There are nearly a hundred Putnik offices in Yugoslavia, situated in the main towns and in all the tourist centres. At eight places—Belgrade, Dubrovnik, Ljubljana, Rijeka, Sarajevo, Skopje, Split and Zagreb —there are separate offices, with multi-lingual staff, for travellers from abroad. Even at the smaller places, however, there is usually someone who speaks German, French, or English. A few of the offices are closed during the winter months, and in these cases you will have to rely on your hotel manager for information.

Putnik's offices are usually opened at 6 a.m. or 7 a.m. and closed for a siesta at noon. They are re-opened at 5 p.m. and finally closed at 7 p.m.

Wherever you go in Yugoslavia, make use of Putnik. Their organisation will certainly help to solve your travel problems and will ensure that you get the best out of your holiday.

Since the decentralisation of the Putnik organisation a few other local travel bureaux have been opened. They, too, can be relied upon to give good service, and special mention must be made of the "Turist" agency in Belgrade and the "Kvarner Express" office at Opatija.

(vii) ACCOMMODATION

Yugoslavia is better provided with hotels than any other country in the Balkans, and this is true not only of the tourist resorts on the coast and the main centres inland but also in out-of-the-way places. It is, indeed, on the coast that it is most difficult, in the season, to obtain accommodation; the small inland village always seems to have room for you in its simple inn or hotel.

I hesitate to recommend all my readers to go to Yugoslavia without booking hotel accommodation in advance through a travel agency. It can be done, and quite often easily, especially outside the summer months, but whether or not you will enjoy going "freelance" depends very much on you and not on Yugoslavia. If you are prepared to take the rough with the smooth you can go off the beaten track into the heart of the country with an easy mind.. You will never fail to find a bed for the night and in an out of the way village, if the inn is full, there will always be an hospitable peasant to give you a welcome and plain but wholesome food in his home.

This type of accommodation is, however, not likely to come your way often and for the most part you will find a hotel of B or C category with room for you. Even so, in remote parts of the country you may have some surprises. The last time I was in Skopje, the capital of Macedonia, I was shown into a room with three beds in it in a hotel which ranks as one of the best in the town. Being a sound sleeper, I was not disturbed during the night; but when I woke up in the morning I saw, to my amazement, that the other two beds had been occupied by strangers. They were strangers to each other, too !

Of course, this was Macedonia and when you have travelled so far south you will find that things can happen which the more " civilised " Croat or Slovene doesn't even dream about. You are not likely to find a strange person in your bedroom at any of the resorts along the coast. In fact, my experience can be counted as exceptional—unless you travel to unusual places. (Even the capital of Macedonia is little visited by comparison with the coast and the north.)

If you go " unbooked " along the Adriatic the tendency will be for you to have to spend more rather than less for your accommodation as many hotels are full in summer. Even this is by no means a rule, for in some places, Split for example, the local Putnik office often directs people to private houses when the hotels are fully booked. By and large, however, the ordinary tourist will be using the hotels of B category, or C hotels if he insists on cheapness. This is true whether he books in advance before leaving home or finds his accommodation on the spot.

I have mentioned "categories" of hotels several times and now I must explain in more detail what this means. Before the decentralisation of the tourist industry took place in 1952 the hotels were graded A, B, C and D. There were less than a dozen first-class or A hotels in the country; B hotels were comparable with good second-class hotels elsewhere and in the C category appeared the more simple and homely type of hotel or pension, of the kind that would be run by the proprietor and his family in other continental countries. D hotels, usually very small, were the simple country inn or the few rooms over the village café. This is only an approximate description of the four categories and sometimes one stayed at a place which seemed to have been the subject of a typing error in Belgrade; but the classification was a fairly satisfactory one and reasonably reliable.

In those days the great advantage was that the prices in each category were exactly the same wherever you went in Yugoslavia. A room with a private bathroom at an A hotel cost 1,050 dinars a night whether it was in Ljubljana or Dubrovnik; dinner at a C hotel in Bled cost 120 dinars, the same as in Belgrade or Budva. The tourist knew exactly where he stood with prices, as long as he had "pension" meals and did not eat *à la carte*. This system has been abandoned, but it remains a useful one to know about for the hotels are still known by their old category letters, which are used in many lists of accommodation prepared by the various provincial tourist offices or local Putnik bureaux. When asking for accommodation you can therefore specify the type you want or can afford, with some assurance of finding the standards you are seeking.

What grade of hotel should you choose? This depends very much on yourself. The average middle-class Englishman will find all the B's and most C's quite satisfactory and will not think the extra cost of the A hotels worth paying. He will not use D category places unless he is hard up and must make every dinar do the work of two. If he wants to meet his compatriots in Yugoslavia he will find most of them staying at B hotels; if he wants to avoid them he can be fairly sure of doing so by concentrating on category C. The real difficulty is to obtain, outside Yugoslavia, full information about all the hotels of the lower grades that exist, as the Putnik offices frequently omit the cheaper places from the lists which they publish. So much for the Englishman in Yugoslavia. The average American tourist will want in this country, as elsewhere, something rather better than the poorer Briton and will not often be satisfied with C hotels; for him it should always be at least B, and A (with private bathroom) when he can get it.

Charges now vary from place to place and the old system of national price-fixing is, unhappily, a thing of the past. Today the prices have regard not only to the category of hotel but also to the popularity from the tourist standpoint of the place in which it is situated. When you leave the popular tourist centres you will find that charges are very low indeed. A motorist who pulls up for the night at a roadside inn or at a small agricultural village without any special tourist attraction may pay a mere 100 dinars or even less for a plain and simple room and he can often stop for the best part of a week, with all food provided, for what it costs for one full day at the "Mažestik" in Belgrade. I must emphasise, however, that places where such exceptionally low rates can be found are not likely to be of much interest to the ordinary tourist; indeed, they are only of use to the motorist or cyclist as resting places on their journeys.

Towels are supplied at hotels of all categories except D, although at C places you sometimes have to remind a forgetful manager. Soap is not provided even in A hotels, so you should take your own. Toilet paper seems to run out more quickly in Yugoslavia than elsewhere and it is wise to take a packet in your bag.

Hot water is a great luxury. The hot tap often runs hot in A hotels, but only occasionally in summer in those of lower categories. Sink-plugs seem to have suffered the ravages of war throughout the country, and

I always include a large cork in my pack when I am travelling in Yugoslavia. Most hotels have baths, even those in C category and very many D's, but again you will have to get used to cold water. The summer temperature is often such that cold baths are no hardship.

The tourist who has to make every economy need not scorn the offer of accommodation in a private house, especially at the more expensive and crowded places. When your steamer pulls in at Split or Dubrovnik you will usually see a crowd of women, especially in summer. They are not all awaiting friends off the boat; they are there to offer travellers rooms in their houses. As the passengers file down the gangway and crowd across the quayside, you hear the women say "Soba; soba; soba. . . ."—which is Serbo-Croat for "room". If you care to take a chance, you can always inspect the room you are offered and assure yourself that it is clean and comfortable. To this must be added that by no means all private rooms offered *are* clean and comfortable, and if you are the more conventional type of tourist you will go straight to the Putnik office and ask them for a room in an hotel.

There are mountain huts in some districts. In Slovenia a large number of these huts were established in Austrian days and many more in the years between the wars. There are forty of them in the Julian Alps alone and others in the Karawanken, Savinje (or Kamnik) Alps, the Pohorje and other ranges. A large proportion of the huts are open all the year round, especially in the Pohorje, which is easily accessible for skiers from Maribor and other towns; in the Julian Alps about half of the huts have full-time guardians and meals can be obtained. It will be found, as in Austria, that many huts have rooms with one or two beds as well as a common dormitory (skupno ležišče) with straw-filled mattresses. The charge for sleeping is very modest indeed, but meals tend to be dearer. If you reckon on spending about 750-800 dinars a day you should not be far out in your calculations; but nobody objects, of course, if you take your own food. A list of the huts in Slovenia can be obtained from any Yugoslav National Tourist Office or from Putnik in Ljubljana.

There are a few huts in the mountains south of Belgrade and in the Šar Planina range in Macedonia. There are also several in the mountains south of Sarajevo, organised by the Planinarska Društvo Bjelašnica, the leading climbing and ski-ing club of Bosnia.

There is no youth hostels association in Yugoslavia, but some holiday arrangements are made by the travel department of the Youth and Students Organisation. They run camps at Novi Vinodol and Baška Voda on the Adriatic Coast, and a holiday centre at Dubrovnik. The camp charges, including food, are about 550 dinars a day, whilst to stay at the Dubrovnik centre costs about 750 dinars a day and so is not cheap by youth hostel standards elsewhere. The same organisation runs reception or transit centres at other places, such as Ljubljana, Zagreb, Belgrade and Sarajevo, the cost of a night's stay (without food) being about the same as at a category C hotel, or in some cases rather more.

Finally a word about camping. People with their own tents will find little difficulty in securing sites, and every help is given to campers from abroad. The southernmost part of the Dalmatian Coast, beyond Dubrovnik, is found most attractive by campers:

41

magnificent sites, excellent sandy beaches and plenty of wood. Water is not plentiful everywhere and this usually makes it necessary to camp near a village or one of the small towns. In most of the mountain areas there is plenty of water to be found, of course, and Slovenia is another most attractive region for the camper.

(viii) LUGGAGE: CLOTHES: PHOTOGRAPHY

On the assumption that you are going to travel in Yugoslavia by rail and steamer, with perhaps an occasional journey by public bus, my very strong advice to you is: "Travel light." If you can carry your own luggage you will save quite a lot of money; not only will you be free of porters but you will also be spared the expense of taxis. Indeed, it is often essential to carry your own bags for porters and taxis are not always available, especially at out-of-the-way places.

The Latin word for luggage is "impedimenta", and many a Briton and most Americans seem to pack their bags in the manner of the ancient Romans. Several large trunks and suitcases, filled to capacity with articles which are never used, seem to be a necessity for most people. How often do you see people whose journeys are made miserable because they overburden themselves with too much luggage? Take warning from them and resolve to cut your needs to the minimum and to carry them in as few bags as possible.

During many thousands of miles of travel around Europe and North Africa since the war I have found my own solution to this problem. It is to use a rucksack, of the framed type, and a canvas grip. The rucksack is a comfortable article to wear, and the

42

shoulders are designed to carry much more weight than the extended arm. The grip is much lighter in weight than a suitcase of the same capacity and I use it for my spare clothes, putting the things I want most readily to hand, such as my camera, maps and guide-books, in an outside pocket.

* * *

You do not need to take smart clothes to Yugoslavia. In all the places most visited by tourists, the normal summer wear for men is flannels or a pair of shorts and an open-necked sports shirt; for women, light cotton frocks and sportswear. A light mac and a pullover should be taken, for there can be occasional wet days and cool evenings. Outside the summer months and in the mountains you will need extra clothing, of course. Some form of hat, with a brim, and a pair of sunglasses will provide necessary protection from the heat of the sun. A good sunburn cream, of the kind that really protects the skin from burning, is an essential for most people.

Two piece swim-suits for women and trunks for men are worn on the beaches; but you often see notices in hotels asking you not to go about the corridors and public rooms without a wrap. Sandals are excellent footwear, cool and comfortable, and people wear them everywhere.

For some of the long train journeys and for use on the steamers, some of which have no deck chairs, I advise you to take a pneumatic cushion of the "Lilo" type. A light-weight plastic or aluminium water bottle will also be useful when travelling, as will an aluminium sandwich box.

You can have your clothes laundered at most hotels,

and the work is done cheaply, quickly and well. This is possible even if staying at a place only one day, for the clothes dry very quickly in the hot sunshine. You need not therefore take many changes of clothing. In any event I find that clothes keep clean much longer in Yugoslavia than in Great Britain. There are the usual notices in hotel bedrooms requesting you not to do your laundry in the wash-basin but this seems to be a regulation that, as everywhere, is more honoured in the breach than in the observance, so it is a good idea to put a packet of detergent in your bag. Ladies will know that nylon garments will dry very quickly indeed in hot and sunny weather, and men should note this too, as nylon shirts and socks are cool and comfortable.

* * *

The most "photogenic" parts of the country are the mountainous districts for scenic photographs; the Dalmatian Coast for scenery and architecture; and Bosnia and Macedonia, especially the latter, for costumes. Good subjects for colour photography are everywhere. Unless you are used to taking photographs in Mediterranean countries or other regions of bright sunshine you will tend to over-expose your shots, and I strongly recommend you to use an exposure meter.

There seem to be no definite regulations as to the number of films you can take into the country, and the customs officials do not seem to bother much about a reasonable quantity. I have taken as many as ten films at a time without any difficulty. It is possible to buy films in Yugoslavia, but those of foreign makes are seldom seen and in any event are very expensive indeed, whilst the home-produced articles are reputed to be unreliable. Developing and printing is best not entrusted to local shops, but left until you reach home.

There are no general restrictions on the use of a camera, but you will be asking for trouble if you point your lens at things likely to be of military importance, such as army camps, naval vessels, airfields, and so on. Occasionally I have seen signs by the wayside indicating that photography is forbidden, for example around the naval base of Zelenika, near Hercegnovi, and the emergency oil-storage tanks near Risan on the Kotor Fjord. You may also arouse some suspicion if you innocently take a photograph of a column of marching soldiers or of a group of prisoners at work on a road. On the whole it is best to err on the side of caution and to photograph only scenes which are unexceptionable. If you do inadvertently take a shot of something you ought not to you won't be put in prison, but you might have your camera emptied and your films and time wasted!

You will find that many Yugoslavs are rather camera-shy and you may have difficulty at times in getting well-composed pictures of people in costume. Remember that in the south it is not many years since the women of the predominantly Moslem population were never seen except with their faces veiled; although this is a thing of the past it is very natural that such women should not feel at all easy before the camera of a stranger. A good deal of discretion and quick and efficient action with the controls of your camera are essential if you want to get good results without feeling that you have embarrassed your subjects.

(ix) BOOKS AND MAPS

No good general books on Yugoslavia have been published in English since the war. A few travel books have appeared but these are either discursive, extremely inaccurate or, in some cases, both. In this connection it should be noted that books published during the years 1947-1953 are certain to be inaccurate in many details (prices, hotel facilities, regulations, etc.), so extensive have been the changes which have taken place.

Many pre-war books of a topographical character are still sufficiently accurate to give the reader a general picture of the country. They are mostly out of print, but copies can usually be obtained through a public library. Among these the best, in my opinion, is *A Wayfarer in Yugoslavia* by Lovett Fielding Edwards, published by Methuen. The 1929 edition, in German, of Baedeker's *Dalmatien und die Adria* is invaluable for the tourist who is travelling far through the country, but allowance must frequently be made for the changes which have taken place. This is even more necessary with the chapters on Dalmatia and Bosnia in Baedeker's *Austria-Hungary* (English edition, 1911). A book called *Beautiful Mountains* by Mrs. F. S. Copeland, dealing with Slovenia, was published in English in Yugoslavia, but it used to be sold in Britain and may be obtainable through a library. A journey through the country shortly before the second World War is well described in Rebecca West's two-volume *Black Lamb and Grey Falcon* (Macmillan).

Books of history include *The Eastern Question* by Sir John Marriott (Methuen), Miller's *Ottoman Empire and its Successors* and Professor Temperley's very useful *History of Serbia* (Bell). The revolutionary days in Macedonia are dealt with in *Heroes and Assassins* by S. Christowe (Gollancz). A fascinating earlier book is *Through Bosnia and Herzegovina on Foot during the Insurrection, 1875* by Sir Arthur Evans (Longmans, 1877).

More recent history is contained in the remarkably interesting *Eastern Approaches* by Fitzroy Maclean, published by Jonathan Cape, a classic among the literature of the last war; and in *Tito Speaks* by Vladimir Dedijer (Weidenfeld and Nicolson).

Robert Adam's *Ruins of the Palace of the Emperor Diocletian at Spalato in Dalmatia* is a rare and valuable work. It can be seen in a few reference libraries and is interesting for its wonderful copper engravings. Gibbon's *Decline and Fall* is another historic work which tells about Split. Jackson's *Dalmatia, the Quarnero and Istria with Cettinge and the Island of Grado* (Oxford, 1887) is excellent for the art and architecture of the coastal districts.

Novels about Yugoslavia which are of interest include *Illyrian Spring* by Ann Bridge (available as a "Penguin") and *Balkan Monastery* and *St. Vitus' Day*, both by Stephen Graham.

The publishing house of Jugoslovenska Knjiga, Belgrade, produces a sumptuous quarterly journal called *Jugoslavija,* and there is an English edition. It is a mine of information about Yugoslav life, culture, folklore, architecture, art and scenery. Back numbers can often be obtained at Yugoslav National Tourist Offices.

Some booklets in English about Dubrovnik, Belgrade, Trogir, and Diocletian's Palace at Split have been published by Putnik and copies may sometimes be obtained from the Yugoslav National Tourist Offices abroad; but the supplies they receive are usually small and the deliveries from Yugoslavia are sporadic.

For walkers and mountaineers in Slovenia there is an excellent post-war guide to the northern mountains, published under the title of *Priročnik za Planince*. There is, unfortunately, no English translation, but a person who is accustomed to reading mountain guide-books will be able to make something of the information in Slovenian about the mountain huts. A small pre-war guide-book of the same area, entitled *A Short Guide to the Slovene Alps for British and American Tourists* by Mrs. F. S. Copeland is extremely useful, and you may be able to borrow a copy through your public library.

* * *

There is a great shortage of good maps of Yugoslavia. You can buy in Britain or the United States the following two maps of the whole country: —

(i) Published by the Yugoslav National Tourist Office; scale fifteen miles to the inch: distance between main towns and some villages marked in kilometres. Price in Great Britain: 7/6d.

(ii) Published in Switzerland by Kümmerley and Frey; scale fifteen miles to the inch: a rather better map than (i), but without road-distances shown. Price in Great Britain: 7/6d.

For tourists by steamer or car down the Dalmatian coast I can recommend the very interesting "Karta Jugoslavenske Obale" published by Učila of Zagreb. It is on a scale of about four and a half miles to the inch and covers the whole coast from Trieste down to the Albanian border. The same firm publish other local maps—including a few on larger scales—for

COSTUMES AT SINJ, DALMATIA   Plate 1

Women wearing colourful local costumes are seen in many parts of Yugoslavia. In the illustration above will be noted a difference between the styles
of headgear of the unmarried woman (on the right) and the two matrons.

ROOFTOPS AT RAB   Plate 2

The medieval town of Rab, on the island of the same name, has many fine
houses and palaces which were built in the days when it was an important
Venetian sea-port. To-day Rab is one of the most popular holiday resorts of
the Adriatic.

Plate 3

SPLIT

Split was founded at the end of the third century, when the Roman emperor Diocletian built his great palace there. Much of the structure still remains, and more than 3,000 people are now living within the palace walls.

INSIDE THE PERISTYLE DIOCLETIAN'S PALACE, SPLIT   Plate 4

The streets within the palace of Diocletian have changed little for centuries and many of the Roman architectural features have survived for more than sixteen hundred years. Robert Adam drew much of his inspiration from this massive building.

instance the Dubrovnik region on a scale of about a mile to the inch.

There is no comprehensive series of maps available for walkers and climbers comparable to the British Ordnance Survey sheets, but the mountain regions of Slovenia are well covered by a series on a scale of $1:75,000$ (i.e., about $1\frac{1}{4}$ miles to the inch) published by the Slovenian Mountaineering Association. The most useful map is the one of Julian Alps, but there are sheets covering the Karawanken and other ranges. The Julian Alps are also included in the Austrian series published in Vienna by Freytag and Berndt on a scale of $1:100,000$ ($1\frac{1}{2}$ miles to the inch).

Many maps of Yugoslavia, including pre-war sheets and some maps which have not been published for public sale, can be consulted free of charge at the headquarters of the Royal Geographical Society in London. This excellent map-library is supported financially by the government and so is open for public use.

(x) FURTHER INFORMATION

In writing this book I have endeavoured to give the reader all the practical information he will need for his holiday in Yugoslavia, but I cannot in such small compass provide, in advance, the answers to every question which may arise. If there is anything more you want to know, you should address your enquiries to the Yugoslav National Tourist Office in your own country. Their staff are there to help you and to advise you concerning your travel problems and they are a veritable mine of information about their land. They do not arrange holidays, book hotel accommodation or sell travel tickets, but they will recommend to you the travel agent who is most suitable for your requirements.

Motorists will, of course, be guided by the advice they can obtain from their own organisations—the Automobile Association, the Royal Automobile Association or the American Automobile Association. Cyclists should consult the Cyclists' Touring Club or the National Cyclists' Union. These bodies are usually able to advise about the state of the roads and to provide outline routes. Members of the Ramblers' Association can obtain advice from their organisation about walking tours, especially in the Julian Alps and other parts of Slovenia. When writing to any of these societies, or to the Yugoslav National Tourist Offices, list your enquiries clearly by number and you will find that this helps to produce a speedy and efficient reply.

The British-Yugoslav Society, a voluntary non-political and non-profit organisation formed to promote friendly relations between the people of the two countries, runs a series of lectures in London and these will be of interest to people who want to know more about life and work in Yugoslavia to-day. The Secretary of the Society will be pleased to send details to any person interested.

When you reach Yugoslavia your sources of future information are, of course, the Putnik offices. As soon as you arrive in any town enquire for the whereabouts of Putnik. Anyone will direct you to it or, the friendliness of the Yugoslavs being what it is, will take you there. I always make Putnik my first visit in a town, even if I know it well, so that I can ascertain what concerts or festivities there are and what excursions are being arranged. I may say, too, that it is usually easier to obtain pension terms through the Putnik offices than it is by negotiating direct with the hotel managers. If you find out everything that Putnik has to offer you will not miss much and you will be able to make the best use of your time.

PART II

YUGOSLAV BACKGROUND

(i) A BRIEF HISTORY

THE COUNTRY which we know to-day as Yugoslavia was settled by Slav races from the north in the fourth and fifth centuries. Many separate kingdoms were established but from time to time they combined against common enemies—the Austrians and Hungarians in the north, the Venetians along the coast, and the Turks. Gradually, however, the Slav lands fell under the domination of these alien powers. The Turks penetrated first into Macedonia, then into Montenegro and Bosnia; finally in the years after the Battle of Kosovo in 1389 they broke the resistance of Serbia and she too was incorporated in the Ottoman Empire. The Venetians extended their sway over Dalmatia and Austria-Hungary absorbed Slovenia and Croatia and established a common frontier with the Turks. Later Dalmatia, too, became part of the Austrian Empire, but this was the only major change in a position which remained virtually unaltered for centuries.

Politically and culturally the north and west looked to Vienna, and the people were Catholics. The south and east formed the western outpost of Asia in Europe, with an Eastern culture and many converts to the faith of Islam; the Christians were Greek Orthodox and looked to the Patriarch of Constantinople for their religious doctrine. These religious, political and cultural divisions form the background of most of Yugoslavia's history and have resulted in the antipathy between the Serbs and the Croats which has caused much bloodshed, even during the present century.

During the centuries of foreign rule a keen spirit of independence continued to exist, and the occupying powers had to maintain strong garrisons; in Montenegro especially there was constant fighting. Much Yugoslav folklore and legend is based on the struggles for independence. At the beginning of the nineteenth century the first real opportunities came and the Serbs, under Kara Djordje, had many successes. The next national leader was Miloš Obrenović, who made peace with the Turks and accepted their nominal suzerainty as the price of their recognition of Serbian autonomy, with himself as ruler.

Unfortunately the Serbs now quarrelled among themselves and the Karadjordjević and Obrenović families successively ousted each other from the dominating position in the state. It was an Obrenović who finally threw off the last vestiges of Turkish domination, but it was a Karadjordjević who regained the throne in 1903. Meanwhile Slovenia and Croatia were still part of the Austrian Empire and Bosnia, Hercegovina and Macedonia remained under Turkey, with Montenegro virtually independent.

This situation was not to last long. The current of Slav nationalism, flowing more strongly because of Serbia's successes, crossed that of Germanic imperialism, with the policy of the *Drang nach Osten,* the Drive to the East, and the scheme for a Berlin to Baghdad railway. Croatia was almost wholly a peasant country, with a feudal nobility linked with that of Hungary and with an independence movement mostly confined to the common people. Slovenia is a rich forested land, but her wealth mostly belonged to Austrians. The lot of the peasants was a poor one, with minute holdings, seldom enough food and sometimes famine. (Tito was born on the borders of Croatia and Slovenia. His father's holding was of but ten acres, and eight of Tito's brothers and sisters died in infancy). Such conditions encouraged the independence movements. In the Turkish provinces the people were strengthened in their national feeling as they saw the Ottoman power becoming weaker, and by 1912 Serbia had succeeded in clearing the Turks from Macedonia.

In the year 1878 Austria had made her first territorial move towards the east—she had sent troops into Bosnia and Hercegovina for the purpose of restoring order. Thirty years later she formally annexed these provinces, and it is from this act which stems not only all later Yugoslav history but most of the world problems of the last half-century. It had the effect of intensifying the spirit of independence and led to the assassination of the Austrian Archduke Franz Ferdinand at Sarajevo in 1914, and so directly to the first World War.

The subject peoples of all the Austrian provinces were pressed into their army and most of them fought on the Eastern front, against Serbia and Russia. They thus were serving an alien master in a war against other Slavs. At the end of the war they returned to their homelands to discover conditions of misery existing; no work, the land laid waste, profiteering and corruption. A mood of revolution was in the air, but the more influential people in Croatia had asked the King of Serbia to send troops to maintain law and order, and it was not long before he became the ruler of a United Kingdom of Yugoslavia. It was united in name only, for the rule of the Serbian King and aristocracy was unpopular elsewhere and the old Serb-Croat antipathy flared up and began to dominate the political scene.

It was at this time that the Yugoslav Communist Party was formed. Speedy action was taken to suppress it and many of the members were driven underground. Then the Serb-Croat problem was brought to a head when, in 1928, the leader of the Croat Peasant Party was murdered during a debate in Parliament. In the period of unrest which followed, King Alexander abolished the constitution and declared a royal dictatorship. There was much repression of the dissident elements in the population and some of the Communist committee members escaped to Vienna and there set up their headquarters, whilst the Croat extremists, with Ante Pavelić at their head, fled to Italy and with the support of Mussolini formed a terrorist organisation named the Ustaše, pledged to liberate Croatia. It was Pavelić who was responsible for the assassination of King Alexander at Marseilles in 1934.

One of the Communists who was imprisoned at this time was Josip Broz, later known as Tito. He had left his home in 1906 to serve an apprenticeship in a machine-shop and had joined the Social Democratic (later Communist) Party. He had served in the Austrian army, been captured by the Russians and, on returning to Yugoslavia, had begun to work actively in the Party and had been imprisoned as a result. He was released in 1934 and then joined in the formation of a Communist committee in Zagreb. It soon became apparent that the party could not be rebuilt if everything was left to the *émigré* committee in Vienna and Tito was appointed to see them and stir them into activity. They gave him the task of organising the party within Yugoslavia, but first he was sent for two years to Russia to study policy and organisation. Later the corruption of the Vienna committee was proved and Tito was appointed General Secretary. A new national committee was formed and the gradual development of the party, still a proscribed organisation, began.

Meanwhile the rule of King Alexander had been succeeded by that of Prince Paul, acting as Regent for the young Prince Peter. When the second World War commenced Yugoslavia was neutral, but she was subjected to great pressure by the Axis Powers, and in March 1941 Germany made demands which virtually amounted to requiring complete Yugoslav support. Prince Paul complied, but immediately there was a popular outcry and a military *coup d'état* deposed him, set up a new government under General Simović and established Peter as King. Within a fortnight the Axis forces invaded Yugoslavia.

They had an easy victory and soon the whole of Yugoslavia was partitioned among the enemy powers. Ante Pavelić became the quisling ruler of Croatia and his Ustaše carried out a violent suppression of the Serbs, with mass executions and forced conversions to Catholicism.

The *émigré* Simović government in London appointed a certain Colonel Mihailović, who had taken to the hills with a few of his men, to organise opposition to the enemy; but he feared reprisals against the civilian population and did little fighting, although he received arms and other supplies from the Allies. The members of the Communist committee established secret headquarters in Belgrade and in June 1941 issued a proclamation, calling on the people to rise. Their efforts gradually bore fruit and many rallied to fight with them. Sabotage of German communications led to fierce reprisals, in which the populations of whole villages were destroyed, but their resistance gathered momentum. They used guerilla tactics, for which the country is ideally suited, and succeeded in dislodging the invader from many key positions.

At first the Germans took little notice of the Partisan activities, but they soon found that they had a major problem to deal with and a series of counter-offensives began. In time the Allies realised that they, and not Mihailović and his Četniks, were the forces who were really fighting the Axis in Yugoslavia. The Partisans were very short of arms and other supplies and were bitterly disappointed when no aid came from Russia. It was, indeed, not until 1943 that the first signs of outside help and recognition arrived. It came in the shape of an investigating mission from Britain and, later, a full military mission in charge of Brigadier Maclean. The story is told in his book "Eastern Approaches". In due course an Allied base was established on the island of Vis and from here the battle for Yugoslavia was directed. Gradually the Partisans moved up through the country and finally Belgrade was liberated and the north, too, cleared of the enemy.

As it became obvious that the Communists would be in effective control when the Germans had been thrust out, a new problem arose for the Allies. What was to be done about the Royal Yugoslav Government in London? A series of negotiations took place and finally a joint government was established, but before long there was a cleavage. After an election in November 1945 the Republic was proclaimed, and King

Peter's war-time stay in Britain was turned into permanent exile.

It was only natural that the Communists should take Russia as their example and distrust the Western powers, which they believed would attempt to re-impose the Royalist *régime* on the country. They were very grateful for UNRRA aid, however, for a tenth of the population had perished, most of the bridges had been blown up, all the power stations save one were out of action and more than half the livestock had been destroyed. This was the background against which the new untried government had to rehabilitate Yugoslavia. Agreements for the exchange of capital goods for timber and other raw materials were made with Russia and other Communist states, and Russian technicians were sent to assist.

Now began the friction with Russia which later resulted in the open breach of 1948. Tito was becoming extremely popular throughout the Balkans and when a Balkan Federation was proposed it was obvious that he would be the natural leader; but this was not at all to Stalin's liking. Then it was found that the Russian technicians were expected to have a specially privileged position as investigators of state and party affairs. The trade agreements, too, revealed that the Soviet Union intended to keep Yugoslavia as a primary producer, in effect a peasant state, and under some agreements for the formation of joint stock companies the Russians claimed the lion's share of the profits. Diplomatic protests from Yugoslavia were countered by accusations that the country was not being organised in true Communist fashion. In short, Russia was not prepared to permit equality between the various Communist states, and when Yugoslavia would not submit to harsh terms and subjection she was thrown out of the Cominform.

Efforts were made to cause a split in the country but, to the amazement of everybody, the Yugoslavs stood their ground and those who had fought with Tito during the war closed their ranks at this no less critical time. The people, once they had overcome the initial shock, gave them their support and Yugoslavia stood alone—a Communist country outside the Iron Curtain.

The first years after the break with the U.S.S.R. were difficult ones, for supplies of all kinds of manufactured goods were cut off and schemes of industrial development had to be stopped. A new economy had to be created. Yugoslav recovery suffered a most severe setback, from which it is only now beginning to recover. The process of converting a substantially agricultural land, with the scantiest of technical background, into a flourishing industrial state is something which cannot be successfully completed in a few years; but the task is being carried on with vigour, and much of Yugoslavia's wealth is being diverted from the comforts of the people today to the prosperity of their children tomorrow.

(ii) THE LAND AND THE PEOPLE

The area of Yugoslavia, the largest country in the Balkans, is about 100,000 square miles, and this means that it is somewhat larger than the United Kingdom, or the States of New York and Pennsylvania combined. It has frontiers with the disputed territory of Trieste and with Italy, Austria, Greece, Hungary, Rumania, Bulgaria, and Albania. The last four of these, with nearly 80% of Yugoslavia's land frontiers, are within the Soviet sphere of influence. The country is bounded on the west by the Adriatic Sea, the length of the coast being about 400 miles in a direct line; but it is really nearer 1,000 miles, so irregular is its configuration. There are about nine hundred islands off the coast, most of them uninhabited, and many lakes of which the most important are Scutari (Skadarsko), Ohrid and Prespa, all three of which Yugoslavia shares with Albania, and Prespa with Greece as well.

Yugoslavia is a federal state made up of six separate republics and the Yugoslav "Zone B" of the Trieste region. The republic of Serbia contains two autonomous districts, one in the north and one in the south, called Vojvodina and Kosmet.

Republic	Approximate Population	Chief City
Slovenia (including "Zone B")	1,400,000	Ljubljana
Croatia (Hrvatska)	3,750,000	Zagreb
Serbia	6,500,000	Belgrade
Bosnia and Hercegovina	2,600,000	Sarajevo and Mostar
Montenegro (Crna Gora)	380,000	Titograd
Macedonia	1,150,000	Skopje

If you take a map and a ruler and join Zagreb with Sofia (in Bulgaria) it is roughly true to say that most of the land to the south and west of that line consists of mountains over 3,000 feet above sea-level; the land to the north-west of Zagreb, right up to the Austrian frontier, is also mountainous. The foothills of the high mountains stretch well to the north-east of your line, especially to the south-west, south and south-east of Belgrade.

Much of the mountain area is forested, and in Bosnia and Macedonia especially there are wide upland pastures, grazed by sheep and goats. The mountains lying roughly parallel to the coast, along the whole length of Dalmatia, are known to geographers as Karst —arid limestone with forests on the landward side but otherwise almost completely bare of vegetation. A journey by train or by air from Zagreb to Split will take you right through the Karst country and will give you some idea of the economic problems of this region.

There are vineyards in most parts of the country, except the most arid regions, and the principal districts for viticulture are south-eastern Serbia, around Skopje, the flatter parts of Montenegro, the Dalmatian coast, including many of the islands, and parts of Slovenia. The northern part of the country from the east of Zagreb to Belgrade is rich arable land, with wheat, maize and other cereals right up to the frontier. The part near Zagreb also bears much fruit. Cattle are raised in many localities in this region, especially to the north-west of Belgrade. Sugar is another important crop in Serbia, as is tobacco in Bosnia and Hercegovina, parts of Montenegro and in many districts of Macedonia. Cotton also is now being developed in Macedonia.

Before the war the system of sharecropping, under which a proportion of a peasant's produce went to the landowner, was very common and it is estimated that nearly half a million families farmed under this method. The richer peasants and big landowners accounted for only 5% of the agricultural population but owned nearly 60% of the produce. The tiny holdings which were left to the peasants were inefficient to run, there was much land-hunger, rural poverty and distress and many of the peasants were heavily in debt. It has been estimated that over much of the country there were 110 peasants working 200 acres of land, as against about 26 in Denmark and 42 in Germany. Agricultural methods were everywhere of the most primitive kind—as indeed they still are in many parts of the country.

After the war large-scale landowning was eliminated and no private individual was permitted to own more than ninety acres. At the same time pressure was put upon the peasants to join the collective farms—groups of peasants pooling their land, labour and experience and farming as profit-sharing teams instead of as individuals. It is difficult to obtain reliable statistics, but it seems that by the beginning of 1951 about a quarter of the arable land of the country was being farmed collectively, the rest still remaining in private hands.

The theory of the collective farm was not new in Yugoslavia, for in some parts of the country a form of co-operation had been practised for centuries. In the recent book "Tito Speaks", a self-portrait of Tito written by Vladimir Dedijer, we read:

' My ancestors lived in a patriarchal collective called the "zadruga". The land was tilled in common, and the whole zadruga was under the rule of the "Gospadar" (head man) who was elected. He lived in the biggest house, in which everybody ate together. When a member of the zadruga married, the zadruga would build him a special little room attached to the big house, so that the whole zadruga looked like a beehive.'

This had been a voluntary and local form of co-operation, however, and although in theory the collective farms of the post-war period were also voluntary enterprises there was in fact much moral and economic pressure on the peasants to join. In most villages the "party man" was responsible for the carrying out of the agricultural policy and individual peasants were forced to sell their produce to the state at fixed prices which were often much lower than those paid to the collectives. Thus the man who preferred to work on his own was much at a disadvantage.

During recent years there has been a change of policy and much of the pressure has been relaxed. The system of compulsory sale to the state has been abolished and, although the collectives still receive very favourable treatment, for instance in regard to taxation and the supply of feeding stuffs, large numbers of peasants have gone back to independent farming and many collectives have been disbanded. The system is far from abandoned, however, and agricultural co-operation remains the official long-term policy. In the areas of good land the collectives, using up-to-date machinery which cannot be purchased by holders of a mere ninety acres, will probably demonstrate their productive superiority over the small owner, and if the wiser methods now being employed to win over the peasants are continued there should be seen a gradual development of the co-operative system.

Until 1952 there was a high degree of nationalisation, with centralised administration and control throughout all branches of production and distribution. Then a great change took place, for most business activities, large and small, were transformed into self-managing enterprises or "workers' co-operatives" with the workers being responsible for the management and to a large extent for the policy. The surplus funds, or profits as we should say, of each undertaking are divided in accordance with fixed percentages between the state (a form of indirect taxation), a reserve for improvements or expansion, and the workers, the share of the latter being the smallest proportion. From my own observation the new system has succeeded in ridding many enterprises of a much too highly centralised and often extremely inefficient control and in putting responsibility on the shoulders of the men and women on the spot. By the yardsticks of most Western countries Yugoslavia still has to go a very long way to reach a satisfactory standard of efficiency in almost every field of business and industrial activity, but the improvements which have taken place must have been seen to be believed.

Yugoslavia is rich in minerals and is now one of Europe's leading producers of bauxite, lead and copper. There are extensive coal deposits near the Bulgarian frontier to the east of Niš, and in the inland parts of Croatia. There are many centres of heavy industry, such as the great steel "city" of Zenica in Bosnia. Power stations are under construction in many places, such as at Jablanica, on the Neretva River between Mostar and Sarajevo, and at Mavrovo in Macedonia.

The tourist who is able to visit many parts of the country will be struck by the great differences between one region and another. The north seems to be well organised, tidy, prosperous—indistinguishable in many respects from Austria. The Dalmatian coast also has an atmosphere of prosperity. Yet in Bosnia and even more in Macedonia you feel that you are not only in a different country but in a different civilisation or a different century. Here the character of the country is not of the West, and an atmosphere of poverty and neglect still permeates these former Turkish provinces.

Plate 5

HVAR

Because of its sub-tropical climate the island of Hvar is known as the "Madeira of the Adriatic". The town of Hvar itself contains many beautiful buildings from the middle ages and it is dominated by an ancient fortress.

KORČULA

Tightly crowded on a tiny peninsula is the historic and picturesque town of Korčula. The island was occupied by British forces for several years during the Napoleonic wars.

Plate 6

Plate 7

THE "VLADIMIR NAZOR" AT KORČULA

This is one of the smaller vessels of the Jadranska fleet, which maintains the services along the coast and between the islands from Venice and Rijeka to Ulcinj, near the Albanian frontier.

MAKARSKA   Plate 8

A popular sea-side resort on the mainland, between Split and Dubrovnik. It
has fine sandy beaches and is in an impressive situation, with the mountains
rising behind it to culminate in the 5,800 ft. peak of Sveti Jure.

Most tourists go only to the Adriatic coastal resorts or to the mountains of Slovenia and they do not get a true picture of Yugoslavia. If you can, go to the inland south. For colour and costume and diversity of interest you will find Macedonia one of the most attractive parts of the country and you will gain a much broader impression of the land.

Yugoslavia is a nation of many different races— Slovenes, Serbs, Croats, Montenegrins, Macedonians and so on—but all of these are Slavs, formerly belonging to separate countries and now brought together as citizens of the Federal Republic of the South Slavs. There are minorities, however, some of them not being Slav peoples. There are, for instance, Italians at several places in the northern part of the Dalmatian coast and on the peninsula of Istria, Hungarians and Turks, many Slovaks in the villages of Northern Serbia, and a large Albanian population in Macedonia. They all enjoy Yugoslav citizenship whilst forming their own social communities and speaking their own languages.

About 11% of the population is Mohammedan, the concentration being greatest in Bosnia and Macedonia. Here the minarets of the mosques are graceful adornments of most towns and many villages, often side by side with Christian churches. The latter are divided between the Roman Catholic and Greek Orthodox faiths.

I fear that I cannot, in a book which is written for holidaymakers, attempt to thrash out the thorny problem of the position of religion in Yugoslavia today. I have read much on the subject in recent years and I still have an open mind. Let this be said, however; the Yugoslav government has not suppressed religion, for everywhere in the country, on the Sabbaths, you can see

F

Roman Catholics, Moslems, and adherents of the Orthodox faith going to worship without let or hindrance. Sometimes the churches are full to overflowing, sometimes they are as empty as in many a supposedly more Christian country. The major part of the formerly extensive church lands has been expropriated, in the same way that other large estates have been split up, and there is no religious teaching in the schools. There has definitely been a falling away from religion among the younger people, but this is not a peculiarity of Yugoslavia.

Some show of assistance is given to religion and money has actually been paid by the state to the churches, but the general policy is one of passivity, which denies to religion any encouragement, refuses to give it special privileges or status, but does not interfere with the right of the ordinary citizen to worship as he pleases.

Attendance at school is compulsory for all Yugoslav children between the ages of seven and fourteen and there are about 100,000 students in the universities. The first task of the post-war government in the field of education was the fight against illiteracy, for prior to 1941 over 44% of the population could not read or write, and in some rural areas the proportion of illiterates was over 80%. The fight has been organised on a large scale, involving not only children but all age-groups, but it will take at least a generation to reach standards which are accepted as normal in countries like Britain or France.

PART III

WHEN YOU HAVE ARRIVED IN YUGOSLAVIA

(i) TRANSPORT SERVICES

(a) By Train

At least half the railway tracks were destroyed during the war and hardly a bridge remained in 1945. Much of the rolling stock was destroyed also, and the post-war Government was faced with a major task of reconstruction. The work was tackled with great energy and groups of students and other volunteers gave much of their spare time and holidays to the work of re-laying the tracks and to bridge-building.

A remarkable recovery was made and the railway system is now back to pre-war standard but, alas, this is still far below the standards of most countries in Western Europe. Let me say at once that the traveller by rail in Yugoslavia has to get used to slow speeds and poor accommodation—except on a few trains. If you demand the same degree of efficiency that one finds today on main lines in France, for instance, you certainly will not be satisfied in Yugoslavia.

The main line through the country is that over which runs the Simplon-Orient Express, from the Italian border at Sežana via Ljubljana, Zagreb, Belgrade and Skopje to the Greek frontier at Gevgeli. The total length of this journey through Yugoslavia is 815 miles and it takes the Simplon-Orient Express more than 28 hours. You will see that by the time it has reached

Yugoslavia this train has become an express in name only! The Tauern Express from Austria crosses the frontier at Jesenice, in the extreme north and, joining the Simplon route at Ljubljana, takes about the same time to cross Yugoslavia. These trains can be taken as yardsticks by which to measure general speeds throughout the country.

The tourist who expects to be doing much travelling in Yugoslavia should buy a copy of the national time-table, the "Red Vožnje". It is quite a compact book and contains details of all the train times of the country, as well as steamer, air and bus schedules. It can be obtained at most bookshops in Yugoslavia, though supplies often run out by the autumn; in England you can buy Red Vožnje through Butler's Advertising Service, 22 St. Giles' High Street, London, W.C.2. I must warn you, however, not to take anything in this time-table for granted. Changes are made quite frequently, and all times must be confirmed if you want to avoid delay and disappointment. This is particularly important in the winter and early spring, when the full summer services are not in operation.

Yugoslavia is a country with a sliding scale of fares; the longer your journey, the cheaper it is per kilometre. It is, therefore, economical to plan your travel in advance and to buy a through ticket, even if you are breaking your journey. If you are using a rail ticket bought outside Yugoslavia your journey can be broken without formality at any station named on the ticket, and four other breaks can also be made provided that you have the ticket duly endorsed at the station where the journey is broken. Yugoslav trains are divided into two categories, this system being similar to that in force in Austria and Germany. Every train is either a "brzi voz" (fast train) or a "putnički voz" (all the others) and you pay about 50% more for travel by "brzi". Generally you haven't much choice, as the time-tables of the two classes of trains are not usually practical alternatives. All the main long-distance trains are in the *brzi* class; you will rarely find it convenient to travel by *putnički* except on comparatively short local journeys of 100 kilometres or so. It should be noted that there is a minimum charge on *brzi* trains (268 dinars second class) so if you catch one of these in order to go to the next station down the line you have to pay heavily for the privilege.

These two classes of trains are clearly indicated in the time-tables, the *brzi voz* timings being printed in bold, black type. Otherwise the rail section of the Red Vožnje is compiled in the accepted international fashion, with wavy lines for trains that do not run every day of the week or are seasonal, key letters to notes, international symbols to indicate sleepers, dining-cars, through-coaches and so on.

The following words used in the time-tables, both in the Red Vožnje and in those exhibited at stations, should be noted:

Saobraća do (date)................Runs only up to (date)
Saobraća od (date)................Runs only from (date)
Saobraća samo (utorkom, etc.)...Runs only on (Tuesdays, etc.)
Direktan voz Sunja-Split.........Train has through coaches from Sunja to Split.
Samo radnim danom..............Does not run on Sundays and holidays.
Samo nedeljom i praznikom......Runs only on Sundays and holidays.

69

Kola za spavanje...................	Sleeping car.
Veze sa................................	Connects with.
I obratno	And in the other direction also.
Saobraća po potrebi...............	Runs only when traffic demands are heavy.
Svakog dana.........................	Every day.
Mesta se rezervišu.................	Advance reservation is compulsory.
Motorni voz.........................	Diesel train (autorail).

Most trains have second and third class coaches and a few of the main ones have first class accommodation also (though sometimes only one first class compartment on a whole train). Some of the trains on short local journeys are for third class passengers only. If you hold a tourist visa you can claim a reduction of 25% from the normal charge for tickets, but it is wisest to buy them in a Putnik office or from a travel agency before you leave, as some of the smaller stations have been found not to understand the system. A few specimen fares, with the 25% rebate deducted, are as follows:—

Sežana-Rijeka	330 dinars	
Sežana-Sarajevo	1824 dinars	
Sežana-Split	1702 dinars	These are third
Sežana-Belgrade	1644 dinars	class fares, Brzi
Jesenice-Ljubljana	226 dinars	Voz. Add 50% to
Jesenice-Rijeka	664 dinars	obtain second class
Jesenice-Zagreb	690 dinars	fares. Double
Jesenice-Skopje	2554 dinars	the amounts to
Dubrovnik-Sarajevo	882 dinars	obtain first class
Dubrovnik-Zagreb	1888 dinars	fares.
Belgrade-Skopje	1170 dinars	
Prahovo-Skopje	1090 dinars	

With a copy of the Red Vožnje you can work out any fares for yourself. Note the number of kilometres between the two places between which you wish to travel and, after ascertaining whether the train is a *brzi* or *putnički,* turn to the list of fares for various distances, printed at the beginning of the book, and find the charge. Deduct the 25% rebate to which your tourist visa entitles you and the net figure is the amount you will have to pay.

Most foreign tourists travel second class. So do many Yugoslavs, but the great majority go third. Except on the international trains (i.e. those which cross the frontiers) third class seats are of wood and second class ones are padded but are often hard. A disadvantage of many second class compartments is that they have very small windows, so that unless you have a window seat you cannot see much of the countryside through which you are passing. From this standpoint the third class compartments, usually of the kind with the "corridor" passing down the middle and with wide windows, have much to recommend them.

The long distance trains are generally the most crowded and, in summer, if you do not board such trains at their starting point you may frequently have to travel quite a way in the corridor until some other people get out and you can take their places. Local trains are usually less crowded. There is no queueing and you will have to push your way on to a train as the natives do, though it is often surprising what courtesy and self-sacrifice are shown when the people realise that one is a foreigner. It can even be embarrassing at times. If you want to be sure of a seat and if you are catching a train at its starting point you can obtain a reservation, either from a Putnik office or, on occasion, at the station itself.

To sum up these remarks, I will repeat what I have said before, and that is that inland travel in Yugoslavia can be quite an adventure and you must be prepared to take the rough with the smooth whatever the class of your ticket. You stand rather more chance of comfort if you travel second class, you will find third class travel more interesting and colourful. If economy is an important factor do not be put off by a travel agent or Putnik officer who insists that third class travel "isn't done". Finally, be early at the station, for however early you are you won't be the first arrival.

Many of the Yugoslav trains are narrow-gauge, but these are not usually on tourists' routes. There are some exceptions, however, for the useful and very beautiful route between Dubrovnik and Sarajevo, via Mostar, is a narrow gauge line, as are its branches to Titograd and to Hercegnovi on the Kotor Fjord. Another narrow line is the one which goes to Jajce. Finally there will be found in Macedonia the line which carries the slowest train in Europe—from Skopje to Ohrid. The length of the journey is just over 150 miles and it takes 20 hours, including a wait of an hour at Gostivar. Fortunately you can do this journey by bus!

A few of the lines carry "express" diesel cars, and on some of these advance booking is essential. A journey on a narrow gauge line through the mountains in a *motorni voz,* swaying from side to side like a see-saw, is a never-to-be-forgotten experience. It may be added that once you get used to the movement you will find travel in a *motorni voz* quite comfortable, and there is usually a buffet service on these trains for the sale of food and drinks.

There are restaurant cars on all the international trains and also on some others on the main Simplon route through the country. At present the only other restaurant cars are on the lines radiating from Sarajevo (to Zagreb, Dubrovnik, etc.) and on a few trains between Zagreb and the coast. Restaurant car meals are fairly plain, but they are good value for money— 100 dinars for breakfast and only 380 dinars for lunch or dinner. The wine served is quite good and inexpensive.

The Simplon-Orient Express carries international Wagons-Lits and there are some also on the Tauern Express. The charges for these are about the same as on the other Wagon-Lits routes. The rest of the sleeping car business in the country is administered by the Yugoslav State Railways and charges are very cheap. A second class sleeper (second class only are available) from the border at Jesenice to Belgrade costs less than 1,300 dinars and from Belgrade to Split costs about the same. For little more than 900 dinars you can have a sleeper from Belgrade to Sarajevo or Skopje, whilst from Zagreb to Split or to Belgrade the cost is rather less. Unfortunately with one exception (Zagreb-Sarajevo for 1,000 dinars) this completes the internal sleeping-car facilities which are at present available. The cabins have two berths, the normal wagon-lits arrangement, and they are clean and comfortable. The attendants are not so obviously after tips as in the usual Wagons-Lits, yet the service they give is just as efficient. You can book a sleeper at any Putnik office or at special bureaux at the main stations. The tourist reduction of 25% is, unfortunately, not granted in connection with the sleeping-car charges.

(b) By Air

The internal air services of a country are not often used by the tourist, but in this respect Yugoslavia is an exception, for the Yugoslav planes are speedy and comfortable by comparison with the trains, the cost is very reasonable indeed and the flights, in summer especially, serve many of the tourist resorts.

A few of the services run all the year round:

Belgrade-Zagreb	3,000 dinars
Zagreb-Ljubljana	1,100 dinars
Belgrade-Sarajevo	3,300 dinars
Belgrade-Skopje	3,400 dinars
Belgrade-Titograd	4,000 dinars

In the summer months, from the beginning of June to the middle of September, there are extra tourist services on certain days, the most useful being the following:

Belgrade-Ohrid (via Skopje)	4,900 dinars
Belgrade-Dubrovnik or Hercegnovi	4,500 dinars
Sarajevo-Dubrovnik or Hercegnovi	2,100 dinars
Belgrade-Split	4,500 dinars
Sarajevo-Split	1,900 dinars
Zagreb-Rijeka	1,700 dinars
Zagreb-Split	3,100 dinars
Zagreb-Dubrovnik	4,500 dinars

The charges shown are for single flights, there being no reduction for return journeys and no rebate for holders of tourist visas. It may be useful to compare the cost of air travel with that of rail on some typical journeys. If you travel from Zagreb to Dubrovnik by train you have to make an overnight journey to Sarajevo, then continue nearly a full day (11 a.m. to 9 p.m.) to Dubrovnik. Second class tickets for this journey, with a sleeper for the night section, cost about 3,700 dinars.

74

You can do the journey by air in a couple of hours for only 800 dinars more. From Belgrade to Skopje a second class rail ticket costs 1,755 dinars and the time taken is over nine hours; by plane the charge is 3,400 dinars and the duration of the flight is only an hour and a half. Zagreb to Rijeka costs about 1,100 dinars by rail or 1,700 dinars by air, the comparative times being six hours and thirty minutes. It is true that you have to add half an hour each end for the time spent in the airport coach and in the waiting about which is inexplicably associated with air travel everywhere, but even so it will be seen that air travel has much to commend it.

The planes at present in use are DC-3's; they all have air hostesses; and no charge is made in connection with internal services for the coach-journeys between the town terminals and the airports. Some of the services are heavily used in the summer and it is advisable to make your booking well in advance through a travel agency. When in Yugoslavia reservations can be made at Putnik offices.

(c) By Coastal Steamer

Before the war the cruise down the Dalmatian coast was a classic trip, undertaken by many British tourists but by far more Germans and Austrians, with whom the Adriatic was always very popular. The steamers which ran from Venice to ports in Albania and to Corfu were very luxurious, with ample berthing accommodation and a standard of comfort and cuisine which was renowned.

There are now fewer vessels to maintain the coastal services and they are generally simpler than in pre-war days, but two of them have a number of berths and other large and comfortable vessels are being constructed. The majority of the boats start from Rijeka and go no further than Dubrovnik, but one or two add to this long journey the additional stretches from Venice to Rijeka in the north and between Dubrovnik and Ulcinj, near the Albanian frontier, in the south.

The boats have two classes, generally known as first and tourist, sometimes on the slower boats as second and third. Whatever names are used the conditions and the charges are the same. Here are a few specimen singles fares, return fares being double:

	First Class	Tourist Class
Venice to Dubrovnik	2,412 dinars	1,643 dinars
Rijeka to Split	1,329 dinars	886 dinars
Rijeka to Dubrovnik	1,768 dinars	1,178 dinars
Split to Dubrovnik	961 dinars	641 dinars
Rijeka to Rab	431 dinars	289 dinars
Dubrovnik to Budva	441 dinars	294 dinars

As on the railways, the farther you travel the less the amount you pay per mile and this should be borne in mind when you are making your plans. With a ticket all the way down the coast there is no objection to the journey being broken at Split, but you could not expect to be allowed to make many stopovers, visiting successive islands one day after another, on a through ticket from, say, Rijeka to Dubrovnik.

The fares I have quoted above are 75% of the full passage rates as visitors with tourist visas are granted a 25% reduction.

Most of the boats which steam between Rijeka and Split and *vice versa* carry out the journey by night, and berth charges between these ports vary from a mere 240 dinars for a berth in a tourist class cabin (four or six berths) to 600 dinars for a berth in a double "cabine de luxe". Travellers who do not succeed in obtaining cabins can generally hire deck-chairs and blankets for about 150 dinars. The boats in summer are very crowded, however. Berths are therefore very much in demand and must be booked early and there are often not enough deck-chairs and blankets for all who want them. If one adds to this the fact that the arrangements for reserving berths are badly organised, it will be seen that one must be prepared to sit up all night on a hard seat. At present the only two vessels with berths are the "Partizanka" and the "Dalmacija", and you will do well to find out the days on which these make the journey and arrange your programme accordingly. Many people will, of course, not want to make their whole itinerary depend on the possibility of having a night lying down instead of a night sitting up and will be content to take a little hardship in good spirit; but they will be well advised to take a small air-cushion to take the sting out of the hard seats.

On one or two days of the week[1] only is it possible to travel between Rijeka and Split in daylight and you are advised, if you can, to plan your holiday so that you can use one of these day services. This problem does not arise between Split and Dubrovnik; on this part of the cruise day services are maintained all through the week throughout the year.

The steamer journey from Rijeka to Split is about fifteen hours. Dubrovnik to Split is a shorter run, the time taken being about nine hours. From Dubrovnik southwards it takes three hours to Hercegnovi, four and a half hours to Budva or about seven and a half hours all the way to Ulcinj.

---

[1] New time tables for summer 1954, received as this book is being prepared for press, announce improved services, including a daily Rijeka-Split sailing.

Meals served on the steamers cost 65 dinars for breakfast and 200 dinars for lunch or dinner. On some vessels more expensive meals costing 380 dinars are also available. The meals are adequate in quantity but the fare is usually quite simple. There are bars on board all the boats.

In addition to the places I have mentioned so far, most of the fast steamers along the coast call at Zadar, Šibenik, Hvar or Makarska and Korčula and some call at Crikvenica, Kotor and Bar. If you leave the steamer at any of these places you will usually have to wait a day for the next one, and in some cases a good deal longer. There are, however, many slower boats which run up and down the coast, connecting the smaller islands with the towns on the mainland and providing communication between the islands themselves. I cannot attempt here to give details of the various services, of which nearly fifty appear in the Red Vožnje. If you want to make a long voyage down the coast, staying a day here and a day there, visiting many of the islands including some of those which are not much frequented by foreign tourists, such as Vis, Korčula and Lastovo, you can plan a very interesting journey with the aid of these fifty time-tables. This is by far the best way of seeing Dalmatia, if one has the time to spare, and the slow, local boats are often less crowded than the fast ones which carry the tourists the whole length of the coast.

(d) By River Steamer

There are steamer services from Belgrade along the Danube in both directions and up the Sava as far as Šabac; but the only journey likely to be of interest to the tourist is the one through the famous Iron Gates and along the Rumanian frontier. This journey is best done from Prahovo (which can be reached by train from Niš) upstream to Belgrade, for in this direction a long night halt, of between six and eight hours according to season, is made at Kladovo. If the journey is undertaken in the reverse direction one misses some of the scenery, as no halt is made. If travelling upstream the total time taken on the journey, including the overnight stop, is between 28 and 30 hours. The most interesting part of the route is between Kladovo and Veliko Gradište, through the Iron Gates and the impressive gorges of Djerdap.

There is a reduction of 25% granted to holders of tourist visas and the net cost of the journey is about 960 dinars second class and 1150 dinars first class, with supplementary charges for cabins at 350 dinars and 450 dinars respectively. A few "de luxe" cabins at 550 dinars are also available. Deck chairs can be hired. Meal prices are 100 dinars for breakfast, 350 dinars for lunch and 500 dinars for dinner.

(e) *By Public Bus*

Now comes adventure indeed! Some will call it adventure, some will prefer to call it frustration. It all depends on your point of view.

There are local buses running all over the country and many of them form vital links for the tourist who wants to get off the beaten track. In some cases they provide the only means of transport between one place of interest and another, this being especially true in Bosnia, Montenegro and Macedonia; but the buses are very crowded and there is seldom any system of seat reservation—and it has been traditional in Yugoslavia since the first bus was seen in the country that he who makes the most noise and argues the loudest should, in theory, secure the best seat. Your inability to speak the language may enable you to succeed where others fail; for even when the Yugoslavs are arguing fiercely between themselves they will often extend special courtesy to foreigners. Generally, however, you have to be prepared to push as vigorously as the next man. Most long-distance buses start on their journeys at the crack of dawn and you must usually buy your ticket before that. It is essential to learn the ropes, and here your hotel manager or sometimes a Putnik man will help you. You must be warned, however, that many Putnik staff seem to adopt the attitude that if you want to travel by public bus you do not deserve to be helped!

The first problems are to find when the bus starts, where it starts from, where you buy the tickets and how early in the morning the ticket office opens. Your Red Vožnje will not help you much, for even if it contains the time-table you are looking for it is quite likely to be wrong. Even time-tables posted up outside a bus office are sometimes incorrect, as I have discovered to my cost. You must therefore ask and ask again until you are sure you have the right information. When you arrive at the ticket office, do not look for a queue, but for a large swarm of people outside a small window. State your destination loudly, especially if it is a long way, for those wishing to travel far are often given priority. It really is one of the few times when you must be firm and forceful—unless you want to stay in one place indefinitely.

Of course, it is not always as bad as that, but it does frequently happen in the way I have described. You must be prepared for the worst and, if it turns out to be not so hard, so much the better. The one real difficulty, of course, is getting on a bus at a place other than its starting point. In that case you do not have to pay

DUBROVNIK Plate 9

Dubrovnik is called the "Pearl of the Adriatic". It is certainly one of the most beautiful places on the Dalmatian coast, and its picturesque streets, historic buildings, fine beaches and the many excursions organised by the local tourist office make it an excellent holiday centre.

DUBROVNIK AND THE ISLE OF LOKRUM   Plate 10

The illustration shows the ancient harbour of Dubrovnik and, beyond it, the
wooded island of Lokrum. It was here that Richard Coeur-de-Lion was
shipwrecked on his way back from a crusade.

KONAVLI COSTUME   Plate 11

A maiden from the Konavli valley, near Dubrovnik. These costumes are worn by many of the women, who are famed far and wide as being the most beautiful in Yugoslavia.

BOWLS AT GRUDA   Plate 12

These rough bowling-alleys are common sights in Yugoslavia, and every week-end and holiday sees many men taking part in matches. This photograph was taken on May Day at Gruda, in the Konavli Valley.

your fare at a ticket office; it is simply collected by the conductor on the bus—provided you can get on. Unless you have plenty of time in hand, do all you can to avoid taking buses except from their starting point.

The buses themselves are often very old. The luxury coaches used on Putnik excursions must be the envy of many a local bus concern. Delays of an hour or more, through some mechanical trouble, are not at all unusual and punctures are not uncommon. This, of course, adds much to the interest of the journey—unless you have a connection to make! In the pleasant intervals which have elapsed on bus journeys I have gone swimming, gathered oleanders, joined in a village football-match and learned to dance the *kolo*. You certainly find opportunities of mixing with the people when you travel by public bus!

Fares work out at 5 or 6 dinars per kilometre, which at the current rate of exchange is about the sum of twopence-halfpenny or 3 U.S. cents a mile. Considering the state of many of the roads, and the fact that journeys are often across mountain passes, the average bus trip is not bad value for the money.

(f) Trams in Cities and Towns

These are generally "two piece" affairs, the tram itself pulling a trailer-car. Sometimes the trailer is open, the seating being arranged like a toast-rack. If you have a lot of luggage it is best to get in the rear car. Fares are usually on the "universal" system, which means that you pay the same however far you go, and you can even break your journey and continue later in the same direction or on a branch-line without paying again. Sometimes the period of validity of the ticket is limited to an hour, the conductor punching a hole to indicate the time you boarded the tram. The most common fare for a tram journey is 10 dinars.

(g) *Excursion Coaches*

These are very different from most of the public buses. You make your booking in advance through a travel agent or, when in Yugoslavia, through a Putnik office. There are excellent excursions organised from most of the places on the coast and from the principal centres inland, and they are invariably good value for money. The cost per mile works out at roughly the same figure as the charge made for public bus journeys, which I have mentioned above. On day-trips it is quite usual for an excursion to start at 6 a.m.

A number of British and American travel agencies organise coach tours around Yugoslavia, usually going as far as Dubrovnik and Sarajevo.

(h) *Excursions by Motor-Boat*

All the Putnik offices along the coast arrange half-day trips in small motor-boats, usually with stops at some of the nearby islands.

(i) *Taxis and Private Car Hire*

The charges for taxi rides are about the same as in Britain. There is frequently no meter and you are strongly advised to settle what the charge will be before you hire the taxi.

There is no system of self-drive car-hire but most Putnik offices can supply you with a car and chauffeur. The usual charge is 55 or 60 dinars per kilometre, irrespective of the number of seats occupied. At such a price you are unlikely to be tempted to hire a car for long journeys, but for occasional short excursions to places of interest which cannot otherwise be reached the cost is not prohibitive if four or five people can get together to share.

(j) By Car or Motor-Cycle

The roads of Yugoslavia are very poor by general European standards. Most of the main roads are surfaced, but even some of these in the south are little better than earth tracks. Facilities for repairs are few and far between and if you have a breakdown you must expect considerable delay and expense. It is well-nigh essential for you to be able to carry out minor repairs and adjustments yourself and spare tyres should be carried.

There are no restrictions on the sale of petrol and oil. You must be warned, however, that there are few pumps except in the towns and it is essential to carry cans for reserve supplies and frequently to make enquiries about the whereabouts of the next place at which you can refill your tank.

The main frontier crossings into northern Yugoslavia are:

Frontier Point	Route
Vič	Klagenfurt-Maribor
Šentilj (Spielfeld)	Graz-Maribor
Koren (Wurzen Pass)	Villach-Ljubljana
Sežana	Trieste-Ljubljana
Kozina	Trieste-Rijeka
Ljubelj (Loibel Pass)	Klagenfurt-Ljubljana
Jezersko (Seeberg Pass)	Klagenfurt-Ljubljana

In winter and in early spring some of the passes between Austria and Yugoslavia are covered with snow and are impassable. Motorists can then put their cars on a train at Rosenbach (south of Villach) and go through the long Karavanken tunnel to Jesenice. Two trains a day in each direction operate this service, and the loading station must be notified at least twenty-

83

four hours in advance. The cost is from 1,400 to 5,000 dinars, depending on the weight of the car.

Motorists are warned that some insurance companies have been known to refuse to extend their cover to journeys made in Yugoslavia. Enquiries should be made as long as possible before leaving home.

Here are a few notes on the "rules of the road". There is generally no speed limit in the country districts, but in built up areas the maximum permitted speed is 50 km. (31 miles) per hour and in the larger towns it is only 30 km. (12 miles) per hour. You drive on the right. You are not allowed to use your horn in the towns between 10 p.m. and 5 a.m. but otherwise there are no special restrictions. Indeed, in Yugoslavia you can use your horn to indicate the direction you are taking, one blast meaning, "I am going straight on", two meaning, "I am turning to the right", and three blasts indicating "I am turning left". You will not be troubled with traffic lights in Yugoslavia, as they do not exist there.

(k) *Cycling*

It cannot be said that Yugoslavia is an ideal country for the ordinary cyclist, for the state of the roads leaves so much to be desired, even in the north. If, however, you are a cyclist of the adventurous kind you will not be deterred by this warning and your bike can be used to take you to places which are off the track of all other kinds of tourists, except those with their own cars.

Make sure that your cycle has good brakes and a rear lamp. (A reflector is not sufficient). It is advisable to carry a spare tyre and inner tube with you and a fairly comprehensive repair kit.

You should make your arrangements for customs, etc., with the Cyclists' Touring Club or the National

Cyclists' Union, and they also assist members with advice and suggestions concerning cycling abroad.

(*l*) *Hitch-hiking*

If you have never practised the art of hitch-hiking it is unlikely that you will decide to carry out your first experiments in Yugoslavia. If you are a first class exponent of the arts of "auto-stop" you will have to be very patient indeed if you decide to practise them there. Road traffic is very thin indeed in most parts of the country and even on a main road, except near the towns, it is not unusual for a whole hour to elapse without one vehicle passing. I remember a recent car journey of over 120 miles during which we passed only three other cars—one of them full, one driven by a foreign tourist and the third broken down!

If you are on a lonely country road and the rare car comes along you do not usually have to "thumb" it. The driver is most likely to stop and ask if you want a lift, without any gesticulations on your part.

(*ii*) FOOD AND DRINK

Yugoslavia is a fascinating country for the gourmet. There is a great variety of food and drink which is peculiar to the Balkans; one could live for weeks in Yugoslavia having a different dish every day, all of them unknown in more western countries. Of course, the traveller who eats *en pension* at an inexpensive hotel cannot expect to discover all the unusual dishes, for many of them are expensive and take much time to prepare. The normal, plain hotel meal is, however, copious and well-cooked; there is always plenty of meat, though veal appears with a regularity which some people find monotonous. Green salads, or sometimes tomatoes, are provided with almost every meal and if you do not like an excess of vinegar you will have to ask specially to have yours served without it. Bread is sometimes white, but more often it is dark in colour and rather tasteless, though no doubt very good for you. Avoid hotel packed lunches as you would avoid the plague, for there does not seem to be an hotel in the country which knows how to make one which is palatable. (In fairness to Yugoslavia it must be said that this is a failing which seems to run right through the hotel industry of Europe, with Switzerland an honourable exception.)

From such mundane matters I will turn to the triumphs of Yugoslav cuisine. Pride of place must be given to the grilled dishes and especially, in my opinion, to ražnjići, pieces of tender lamb or pork grilled on skewers and so served on the plate. Then there are čevapčići, small rissoles of minced meat, seasoned and served with fresh onions or paprika; and whole sucking-pigs for those who have no objection to infanticide so openly demonstrated.

There are several kinds of stuffed dishes. Sarma is the name of the most common of these, consisting of fresh or pickled cabbage-leaves, or sometimes vine-leaves, stuffed with meat and rice and served with a rich sauce or with sour cream. There are various kinds of pastry dishes, such as gibanica, pastry-crust filled with cheese, eggs and cream, and then baked in the oven, and zeljanica, rather similar but containing spinach also. Halva is another pastry delicacy, stuffed with chopped walnuts and honey. Musaka, well-known all over the Balkans, is a kind of shepherd's pie with layers of minced beef or pork alternating with potatoes or aubergines, cooked in kajmak, rather like cream-cheese. An excellent thick stew is called djuveč, with meat or fish and rice, paprika, tomatoes and potatoes. Podvarak, made of turkey or chicken with sauerkraut, is another excellent dish.

Fish is plentiful along the coast, specialities being tunny, molo, orad and the tasty little barbone. Fresh sardines are a curiosity to most visitors. You will find excellent trout in Bosnia and Slovenia, the Danube sterlet in Belgrade, and lake-trout at Ohrid in Macedonia. The most famous caviare comes from Kladovo, on the Rumanian frontier, and an unusual dish is the red caviare of Ohrid, which comes from trout.

Yugoslav wines are as yet little known abroad, but they are excellent and could form a more important source of foreign currency. They are inexpensive, too. There are three main types: belo, ružica and crno which mean respectively white, rosé and black. The crno wines are really red, but the Slavs display more logic in their nomenclature than we do. The outstanding red wines are those of the island of Vis, rather like Burgundy; dingač, a claret-type from the Dalmatian coast; and the wines from the district of Negotin, in Serbia. There are excellent rieslings from around Fruška Gora and the most famous rosé, flavoured like a delicate muscat, comes from Smederevo. The Dalmatian prošek is a fine, sweet dessert wine and the place of port as an after-dinner wine is taken by Karlovački Bermet, heavy and with a subtle flavour of burnt almonds. This list does not pretend to be complete and there are many others, including some good wines from Montenegro and Slovenia.

The social drink of Yugoslavia is šljivovica, a colourless plum brandy which is drunk at every hour of the day, especially when people meet together "for a quick one". There are many qualities of šljivovica, the best being reserved for export. You will find it rather fierce at first, but it improves on acquaintance. I doubt, however, if you will become accustomed to drinking it at six o'clock in the morning when it sometimes appears on the breakfast tray!

There are many other spirits and liqueurs: ljuta, rather like šljivovica but even stronger; komovica, another strong drink, made from vine-shoots; maraschino, a cherry brandy from Zadar and elsewhere; and even such strange spirit as orohovača and pelenkovac, distilled from unripe walnuts and wormwood respectively. Most Yugoslav beer (pivo) is good, especially when served ice-cold. Malina is a rather thin non-alcoholic raspberry drink which is obtainable everywhere. An unusual drink is boza, a refreshing non-alcoholic beverage made from maize, vanilla and sugar.

A word must be said about Turkish coffee, which is very strong and sweet and always served in little metal jugs, with long handles, called džezve. People who like black coffee will find it an excellent drink but others may take some time to acquire the taste for it. If, like myself, you dislike sugar, you must say so when ordering your coffee; the password is "bez šećera".

Finally, the names of the meals: they are doručak—breakfast; ručak—lunch; and večera—dinner.

(iii) SOME THINGS TO NOTE

(a) Tipping

Your hotel bills invariably include the service charge, though it is never specially indicated by a percentage addition in the way which is common in most lands.

Prices on the menus in hotels and restaurants also include service. As a result of this, the system of tipping is not customary in Yugoslavia and nobody will think you mean if you do not leave a tip after your meal. The same applies to the driver of your excursion bus, the guide who takes you round some ancient monument, the steward in your sleeping car and so on.

Most foreign tourists are hardened to the system which prevails elsewhere and they find it embarrassing not to leave tips in Yugoslavia. It is best, however, to make your routine tips really small ones; if you have something to spare, give it to those who render really special help or service. Indeed, it can be said that Yugoslavia is a country where tipping is what it ought to be—a personal token of appreciation of extra services freely rendered.

This is unique in Europe and it will be a great pity if it is spoiled. Unfortunately there are already signs that it may not be long before the tip becomes a routine operation for in places like Dubrovnik, which are visited by many foreign tourists, one has begun to notice some of the waiters hovering around at the end of the meal in a manner which is so easily recognisable.

(b) *Mail*

It is wise not to have important letters forwarded to you in Yugoslavia, for the post is very slow indeed. It seldom takes less than four days for a letter to reach the country from Britain and to the south it can take more. Every Putnik office has many uncollected letters from abroad, almost certainly addressed to tourists who have long since departed.

Putnik is the best *poste restante* for foreigners. To claim a letter from a Putnik office is far simpler than from a post office; in fact, you usually merely look through the rack yourself and pull out your own mail.

The postage on letters sent from Yugoslavia to addresses abroad costs 40 dinars and an extra 30 dinars is charged for air-mailing of letters weighing up to about half an ounce. A postcard can be sent for 17 dinars. It will be seen that the person who has to send many postcards to friends at home will run up quite an account with the post office! The standard of the picture postcards is extremely low, as you will soon discover. You will hardly believe it, but they are nevertheless infinitely superior to what they were a year or two ago. Postage stamps can be bought from newspaper shops and tobacconists as well as from post offices.

(c) Newspapers

British and American newspapers are seldom obtainable in Yugoslavia. In Belgrade and Zagreb you may sometimes obtain them at the larger (Grade A) hotels. I have also bought them, when in Belgrade, at Jugoslovenska Knjiga, 17 Knez Mihajlova. German newspapers can sometimes be purchased in the larger towns.

In smaller places and in the south you would be cut off from the news, unless you can speak the language of the country, were it not for the excellent News Bulletins published daily by the Information Department of the British Embassy. These bulletins are sent out to many parts of the country and are often to be found in the Putnik offices.

(d) Smoking

Tobacco products are a Federal monopoly and the revenue must contribute handsomely to the funds of the state. It is not often possible to buy British and American cigarettes in Yugoslavia (though the Category A hotels sometimes have small supplies) but the local brands are quite satisfactory and comparatively cheap.

The most popular cigarette is " Morava " costing 45 dinars for a packet of twenty. They are rather loosely packed but otherwise are quite pleasant. Some imitations of American cigarettes (such as "Prilep") are on sale, costing about double the price of Morava. The latter brand is packed in a variety of cartons, differing according to the factory where they are made, but I have not detected any difference between the contents of one and another. There are plenty of shops selling cigarettes and they can also be bought in most hotels and cafés.

Not being a pipe smoker, I cannot speak with authority about pipe tobacco, but I have been assured by friends that it is quite satisfactory and equally economical. In fact, you very seldom see a Yugoslav smoking a pipe, though the type of cigarette-holder which is in the form of a miniature pipe, with the cigarette standing up vertically in the tiny bowl, is common.

There is no country in Europe, in my experience, in which the smoker is stopped so frequently by strangers and asked for a light. This is an index of the general poorness of the people. Fifty free lights means a box of matches saved, and a box of matches costs money.

If you have a lighter, fill it with petrol and see that it is in working order before you go.

(e) *Shopping and Office Hours*

Banks and offices are open from 7 a.m. to 2 p.m.

only and are closed on Sundays and public holidays. The business man works these seven hours at a stretch and then has the rest of the day to himself—in theory, at any rate. Most shops are open from about 7 a.m. to noon and are then closed until 4 p.m. or 5 p.m., when they remain open for two or three hours and then finally put up their shutters. In the winter months they are usually opened rather later in the morning and the staff have a shorter sièsta. Many of the food shops have even stranger hours, opening at 5 a.m. for about four hours and then again at 4 p.m. for three or four hours more.

There are no restricted hours for the purchase of drinks and in the cafés and restaurants the day starts at about 6 a.m. and continues till about 11 p.m., or sometimes until midnight. The Putnik offices are usually open from 6 a.m. or 7 a.m. until noon and again from 5 p.m. until 7 p.m.

In Slovenia and inland Croatia the midday break tends to be shorter, and evening closing hours for shops and offices are more like those of western countries.

(f) *Public Holidays*

1st January, 1st and 2nd May, 15th May, 29th and 30th November are public holidays throughout the country. In addition each of the republics has its own national holiday:

Slovenia	27th April	Croatia	27th July
Serbia	7th July	Bosnia and Hercegovina	27th July
Montenegro	13th July	Macedonia	2nd August

Many of the towns and villages also have their own traditional holidays and days of festival.

It is on these days that one sees most people in their colourful costumes, for not only is it brought out of the cupboard and donned by people who do not usually wear it, but the peasants, for many of whom costume is everyday dress, flock into the towns to join in the celebrations.

If you are in Yugoslavia at the end of April you will see nearly every shop window decorated for Labour Day, 1st May, with gaily coloured banners and signs and with photographs of Marshal Tito and the president of the local republic. Everywhere you read the slogan "Živio Prvi Maj"—"Long Live the First of May".

(g) *The Time—and Getting Up*

The official time in Yugoslavia is Central European Time. This is the same as British Summer Time, but the clocks are not changed in spring and autumn. The 24-hour system is used in railway and other time-tables, but otherwise the 12-hour system is used. There are very few public clocks in Yugoslavia.

You will have gathered already from some of the information I have given that this is a country in which things start very early in the morning. Most of the population are at work by 7 a.m. and the streets are as full of people before that hour as those in Britain are at nine. Buses and steamers normally start their journeys at six o'clock or even before, so you have to become accustomed to getting up much earlier than you probably do at home.

In my experience Yugoslavia is the country *par excellence* for the early morning call. In a small hotel in France one often gives instructions to be knocked at a certain hour, only to wake half an hour later to find that one's instructions have been forgotten. In Yugoslavia you will not only be awakened at 4 a.m., if you so request, but the porter or manager or whoever it is will come back two or three times to make sure that you have really heard him and that you are out of bed! That, at least, has been my invariable experience. It sounds too efficient to be true in Yugoslavia—so I still carry a small alarm clock as well!

(*h*) *Health*

Present-day Yugoslavia is a fairly healthy country. There used to be many infectious diseases such as typhoid, smallpox and fevers, but with the aid of various United Nations and relief organisations they were brought under control at the end of the war, and now standards are fairly normal. Malaria used to strike thousands of Yugoslavs every year but the infested areas were sprayed with D.D.T. and the disease has virtually disappeared.

You may possibly suffer from stomach pains and diarrhoea for a day or two and feel like doing nothing except rest. This is really a minor kind of dysentery and it is common to all the countries bordering the Mediterranean, including much of France for instance. You can cure it by taking sulfaguanadin, a sulfa-drug which can be purchased in many places, at the old chemist's shop in Dubrovnik, for example.

You can safely drink water in hotels and restaurants in all the tourist resorts, but if you get really off the beaten track it might be wiser to give up drinking water and concentrate on wine.

Please, please be careful to get brown slowly! The burning power of the sun is extremely strong, even when a cool wind is blowing; and unless you want a very painful holiday it is essential not to expose your untanned skin for long periods.

If you are British, remember that your National Health Scheme does not cover you whilst in Yugoslavia. It is possible, for a very modest premium, to insure against the risk of having to incur medical expenses arising from illness or accident abroad, and this is a wise precaution to take.

(i) Old and New Names of Towns

A large number of places in Yugoslavia are still referred to in old guide-books and on maps by names which have now been changed. Some used to be Italian or Austrian, other have been changed for sentimental or traditional reasons. In view of the scarcity of up-to-date books about the country the following list is given of the most important changes:

Old Name	New Name	Old Name	New Name
Abbazia	Opatija	Marburg	Maribor
Agram	Zagreb	Monastir	Bitola
Antivari	Bar	Podgorica	Titograd
Arbe	Rab	Postumia	Postojna
Cattaro	Kotor	Ragusa	Dubrovnik
Cherso	Cres	Sebenico	Šibenik
Curzola	Korčula	Spalato	Split
Fiume	Rijeka	Trau	Trogir
Laibach	Ljubljana	Üsküb	Skopje
Lesina	Hvar	Veldes	Bled
Lissa	Vis	Zara	Zadar

PART IV

SEEING YUGOSLAVIA

(i) A SHORT GENERAL SURVEY

BEFORE DESCRIBING the various regions of Yugoslavia in detail I must make a brief general survey of the country as seen from the standpoint of the tourist. This outline will be filled in when I come in later sections to describe the principal centres and the main routes of interest and scenic beauty throughout the country.

The coast can be conveniently divided into three parts—the Istrian Peninsula in the extreme north, the coast and islands from Rijeka to Split, and finally the remaining part of the coastline from Split to the Albanian frontier. Istria, which I shall deal with in the section on Slovenia, is less scenically interesting than the rest of the coast, but it has a few popular seaside resorts. On the section from Rijeka to Split one passes the majority of the islands, the most interesting of them being Rab. There are several popular resorts in this part of the coast, but only two places, Zadar and Šibenik, are of historic interest. Split itself is one of the most fascinating places on the whole coast and well deserves the special section I shall devote to it.

The southern part of the coastline, beyond Split, is much more scenically attractive than the northern part, because both the mainland and the islands themselves are more mountainous. There is more historic interest,

Plate 13

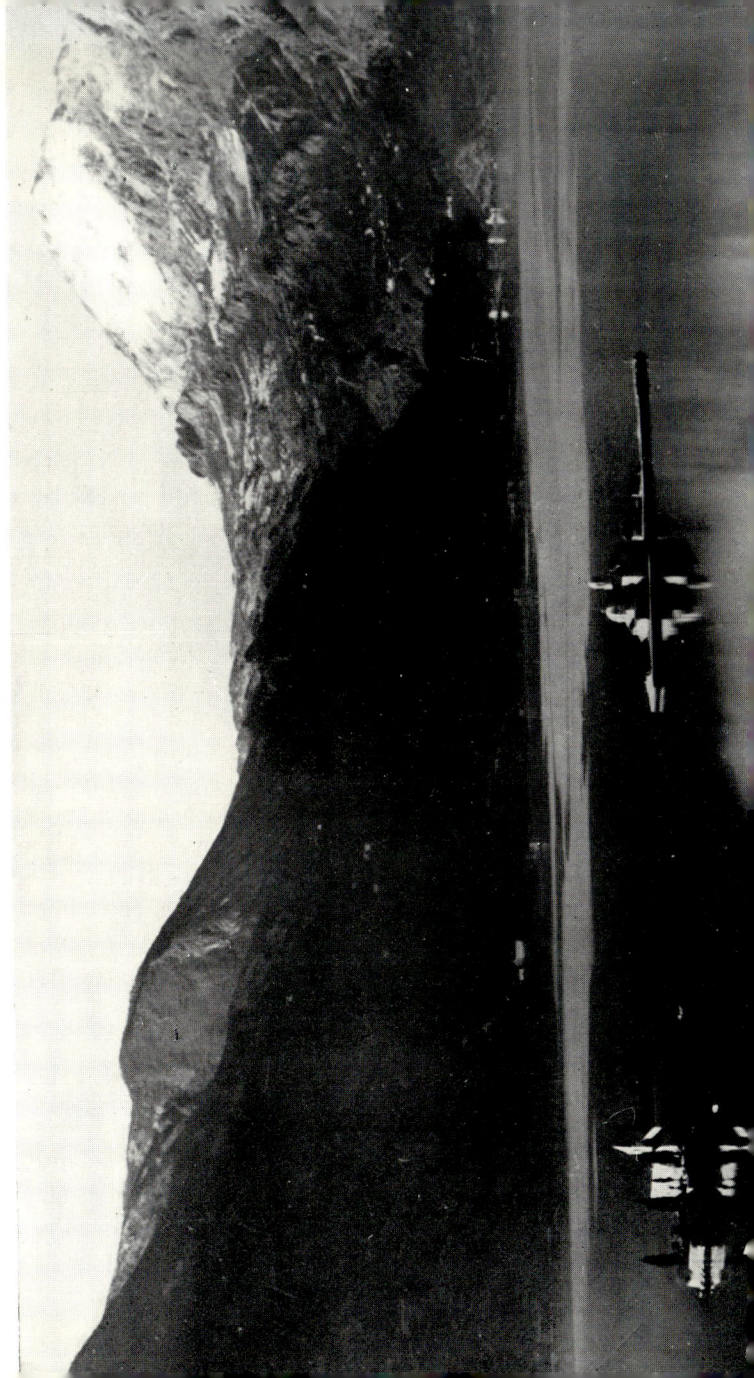

THE CHURCHES OF PERAST

These two churches, one Roman Catholic and the other Greek Orthodox, lie off the town of Perast in the Gulf of Kotor.

BEACHES NEAR BUDVA

These sandy beaches are typical of hundreds which can be found on the coast of Montenegro, the southernmost stretch of the Adriatic sea-board of Yugoslavia.

Plate 14

Plate 15

BUDVA

Budva, on the Montenegrin Littoral, was once an island and the isthmus which now connects it with the mainland was constructed centuries ago by the inhabitants. Budva's situation, in a wide bay with mountains rising high above, is magnificent.

SVETI STEFAN

The little island of Sveti Stefan (or St. Stephen), now connected to the mainland by a narrow strip of gravel, is one of the most interesting places in the country. After many years of neglect, it is now being restored by the Government.

Plate 16

too, in the islands off this stretch of the coast, especially Hvar and Korčula.

Dubrovnik is by far the most popular place on the whole of the coastline, and its claim to be more beautiful than Venice has much to support it. To the south of Dubrovnik there are no islands, but the coast here, with the magnificent Kotor Fjord, is the loveliest of the whole of the Adriatic.

The Republic of Slovenia is mostly mountainous. It contains not only the Julian Alps, but many other fine ranges. Ljubljana, the Slovenian capital, is an interesting city. There are many charming inland spas and such natural wonders as the Grottoes of Postojna and the well-known lakes of Bled and Bohinj.

When one leaves Slovenia for Croatia one also leaves the northern mountains. Inland Croatia is not outstandingly attractive from the tourist's standpoint, and although Zagreb is a pleasanter city, in many ways, than Belgrade it is still not a place in which the holiday-maker will wish to stay for long. One of the most beautiful districts of the whole of Yugoslavia is, however, contained in inland Croatia, namely the National Park and Lakes of Plitvice.

Bosnia and Hercegovina are wild and comparatively little visited regions, with communications by rail and road which are generally very poor. For the tourist who is able to get off the beaten track, travelling in his own car for example, a journey through Bosnia and Hercegovina takes on something of the nature of an exploration. The tourist who is not so mobile can, however, find much of interest in this republic, as Mostar and Sarajevo, still retaining much of their old charm, can easily be reached either from Dubrovnik or Zagreb, and even such characteristic Moslem towns

97

as Travnik, Jajce and Banja Luka are served by narrow-gauge railways.

Montenegro is another remote district with few roads, and with hardly any railways at all, but it has regular bus connections with Dubrovnik, and with other places on the coast. A journey by this means through Montenegro, from the Adriatic to Titograd and on to south Serbia, is strongly recommended.

Belgrade, the capital of Yugoslavia, has little of attraction to the tourist, apart from its ancient fortress. It serves, however, as a good base for the steamer trip down the Danube, through the magnificent Djerdap Gorges and the Iron Gates.

Southwards from Belgrade there are two main routes to Macedonia, each of them traversing beautiful mountainous regions as far as Skopje. This city, the capital of Macedonia, combining old Turkish quarters with industrial development, seems to typify the difference between Macedonia itself and much of the rest of Yugoslavia. The lakes on the southern boundary, the many fine Orthodox monasteries and the fascinating town of Ohrid are among the outstanding interests of Macedonia.

(ii) THE DALMATIAN COAST FROM RIJEKA TO SPLIT

Rijeka is the place from which most visitors commence their journey down the Adriatic coast and it is the largest port in Yugoslavia. It was formerly known as Fiume and it became a free city after the 1914-18 war, but it was later seized by d'Annunzio and remained part of Italy until 1945. It is now of great commercial importance to Yugoslavia.

Like most modern ports, Rijeka has little of interest to tourists and its value to them is merely as a convenient transit place. There are many hotels, the best situated in relation to the railway station and the port being the Bonavia (category B). Across the river which formed the old Italian-Yugoslav frontier is the suburb of Sušak, connected with Rijeka by bus services, and here is the rather less expensive Hotel Continental, of the same category. When the Yugoslavs could no longer use Fiume they built a new port at Sušak, and now that the two towns are connected again there are very extensive docks and harbours.

Although Rijeka itself is of little interest to the holiday-maker there is a good deal worth seeing in its surroundings. The suburb of Trsat, on a hill overlooking the port, can be reached by a great flight of 412 steps from the main square of Sušak. Trsat was the stronghold of the Frankopans, a branch of a Venetian family which settled there. They were more powerful than kings, and at one time they commanded much of the northern coastline. You will find their ruined castles all through this district, and the church at Trsat contains some of their tombs. This fifteenth-century church, dedicated to the Madonna, was built to celebrate a miracle. Legend has it that in the year 1291 angels brought here from Nazareth the house of the Virgin Mary and deposited it on the hillside. Three years later, however, they decided to move it again, but Trsat still remains a place of pilgrimage in memory of these miraculous occurrences.

Although Opatija is on the Istrian peninsula, which I shall deal with in a later section, it is so near to Rijeka that it will be more convenient to describe it here. Opatija, which was known as Abbazia until it became

Yugoslav in 1945, was built by the Austrians as a fashionable seaside resort, such as one finds on the Italian and French Riviera but which are rare along the coast of Yugoslavia. For people bent on an ordinary seaside holiday with excellent hotels, restaurants and cafés, with good bathing beaches and plenty of bright lights and dance music, Opatija is certainly a fine place. They can enjoy its sophisticated life and its excellent climate, they can walk in its parks and promenades and enjoy a typical, smart Riviera holiday—at half the price they would pay on the Rivieras of France and Italy. For a quieter holiday of the same kind there is Lovran, a few miles away. Both Opatija and Lovran have many hotels of categories B and C and at Opatija is the *de-luxe* Hotel Kvarner which attained international fame in Italian days under the name of Quarnero.

Two inland places near to Rijeka deserve special mention. The first of these is Fužine, a beautiful resort about thirty miles from Rijeka on the main railway line to Zagreb. Its altitude is 2,500 feet above sea-level and it is an excellent centre for a country holiday of the simple kind, with walking and fishing. The one hotel, the Bitoraj (category C) is very inexpensive. The second centre is in the wooded highlands of Platak, fifteen miles from Rijeka and at an altitude of over 3,600 feet. There are nearby mountains rising nearly 1,400 feet higher, and the simple category C hotel Dom na Platku is managed by the Mountaineering Association of Rijeka.

We now return to the coast and, going southwards from Rijeka, we shall have a look at Bakar, Kraljevica, Crikvenica, Selce, Novi Vinodol and Senj. All of these are connected by steamer services with Rijeka but they are more easily reached by the regular bus services along the coast.

Bakar, the first of these places, is only eight miles from Rijeka and it lies at the inmost point of a small gulf or fjord. It is a small, medieval town with only 1,600 inhabitants and is built on a spur of hills which descends to the water's edge. It is extremely pictures-que, with its old houses and its narrow streets of steps climbing steeply from the sea. The very inexpensive hotel is the Jadran (category C). Kraljevica, situated at the entrance of the same gulf is less picturesque than Bakar itself. Both these places have sandy beaches.

Crikvenica, about ten miles further from Rijeka, is a much larger and better-known seaside resort. It lacks the simple charm of Bakar—indeed, it has some of the sophistication of Opatija. It possesses a Putnik office which organises, in the summer season, a wide range of excursions. These vary from full-day coach-trips to the Plitvice Lakes or the Postojna Grottoes, at a cost of 1,500 dinars, to steamer and motor-boat excursions up and down the coast and to various points on the islands of Krk and Rab for from a mere 50 to 250 dinars. Crikvenica is a good place for children, as there is a shelving sandy beach nearly three miles long. It has several hotels of categories B and C, most of them situated on the sea-front. Almost adjoining Crikvenica is the quieter resort of Selce, also with hotels of these two categories.

Next along the coast is Novi Vinodol, another hilly town with a long history. Here is one of the castles of the Frankopans, an impressive edifice. It was in this castle that, in the year 1266, there was signed the Vino-dol Code, a charter from which stems the beginnings of legislation in Croatia. The original code is still in

existence and is thought to be the oldest secular manu-
script in Yugoslavia. The Yugoslav students' organisation run a camp at Novi Vinodol and there are several
category B hotels and one, the San Marino, of category
C.

Senj is picturesque and has an interesting history, but
it is a place at which I strongly recommend you not
to stay. It is in a very exposed position, facing the
gap between the islands of Krk and Prvić, and when
the Bora wind blows it hits Senj as nowhere else on this
coast. Much of the history and legend of the town is
woven around its stormy weather and the adventures
of its mariners, but its most famous period was in the
sixteenth century. It was then the stronghold of a warlike tribe called the Uskoks who made a valiant stand
to preserve their town from the Turks and who fought
far afield, not only in the Slav countries but in lands as
distant as Egypt and Cyprus.

Krk is the largest of the Yugoslav islands and it has
a number of coastal resorts. They are mostly on the
western side, for the shores that face the mainland are
generally steep and wild. The town of Krk itself has
been left almost untouched by modern development
and is still surrounded by its medieval battlements. It
has a fine thirteenth century cathedral, some churches
nearly as old, a castle of the Frankopans, narrow,
winding streets and many lovely old houses. The
hotel of Krk is the Jugoslavija, category C.

In the north-western part of the island are Malinska
and Omišalj. The first of these is a quiet little resort,
with sandy beaches and several hotels. Omišalj,
almost at the northern tip of Krk, is little more than
eight miles from Rijeka and it is situated at the landward end of a deep bay. The old part of the town

is built on a hill dominating the coast but there is a newer part along the seashore. Here is the Hotel Jadran, category C. At the other end of the island of Krk is Baška, a very pleasantly situated resort, with the lower slopes of the hills which rise steeply behind it covered with vineyards and orchards. The fact that its long foreshore is of gravel and not of sand probably accounts for the lack of modern development. The hotels—the Baška, Jadran and Velebit—are all of category C, and inexpensive.

Cres, the long island farther out into the Adriatic, was an Italian possession until 1945, when it passed to Yugoslavia with the Istrian peninsula and the isle of Lošinj. For me, it remains to be explored. From the map it looks very interesting, for in some parts it is only two or three miles across and the hills rise to over 3,000 feet above sea-level. There are hotels in the town of Cres itself and at Osor, in the south of the island, but as they do not appear in any official lists which I have seen they are probably very simple places. Lošinj, which is connected with Cres by a bridge, is a better-known island, though the fact that all the hotels in its twin towns of Mali Lošinj and Veliki Lošinj are of category C indicates that they are comparatively quiet places. Lošinj enjoys a very mild climate and abounds with vines and lemon- and orange-groves.

Rab, four hours by sea from Rijeka, is the best-known and most interesting of the northern islands. The principal town, also called Rab, is one of the most delightful places in Yugoslavia and has a character which is similar to that of Dubrovnik. It is crowded on to a little peninsula and the general lay-out of the town was established well before the coming of the Venetians. In the same way that the Statue of St.

Blaise, in Dubrovnik, carries a model of his city as it was in the fifteenth century, so here at Rab in the church of St. Anthony, at the extreme point of the peninsula, is an ancient picture of the Rab of an even earlier epoch. You can trace many of the streets and pick out several of the buildings, just as they are today.

Rab was an important place even in Roman times, when it was known as Neoparis. Its cathedral dates from the twelfth century and its belfry is one of the four which dominate Rab and give it such a unique character when seen from the surrounding hills. The town walls, once a strong defence against invasion from the sea, are mostly still standing. It is, however, the Venetian style of architecture which is the town's most distinctive feature—narrow, paved streets, fine old residences with beautiful terraces and balconies, and decorated windows and gateways with the Lion of St. Mark, the national symbol of Venice, frequently to be seen.

On the eastern side of Rab is a wide quay and it is here that most of the modern hotels have been built, forming an amazing contrast to the ancient town which lies behind them. For Rab is a very popular holiday resort and has plenty to offer to the visitor apart from its beautiful old buildings and other medieval survivals. Its harbours are full of sailing vessels, small and large, many of them being used to take holiday-makers to the sandy bathing-beaches, and there are sub-tropical parks and gardens, with palms and cedars. The Putnik office arranges motor-boat excursions to Lopar, at the northern end of the island (itself a small resort and the birthplace of the founder of the Republic of San Marino), to Jablanac on the mainland and to the island of Lošinj, which I have mentioned earlier. The cost of these trips varies from 100 to 250 dinars. It is also possible, quite inexpensively, to hire motor-boats to take you to the villages along the coast, such as Barbat (famous for its lobsters) or Matovica. Canoes and sailing-boats can also be hired.

The attractiveness of Rab has made it very popular with the Yugoslavs and this, in turn, has inevitably led to fairly high prices and to some difficulty in obtaining accommodation in the high season. The main hotels are the Imperial, Istra and Villa Danica of category B and the Miramare, Park and Slavija of category C. In addition there are many private lodgings, arrangements for which can be made on the spot.

Southwards from Rab and Lošinj there are only three places of note until one reaches Trogir, not far from Split. These three are Zadar, Biograd na Moru and Šibenik, all on the mainland. The islands along this stretch of the coast are almost countless and the majority of them are little more than rocks projecting from the sea, making navigation of the channels a very skilful task. Most of the islands are uninhabited and many of those which have a settlement or two are off the routes of the passenger steamers. The average tourist will have neither the time nor the desire to spend his holiday in this wild medley of land and water; the connoisseur of islands can devote a fascinating month or more to making his way from one to another, relying on the fishermen to take him if no more conventional means of transport is available.

Zadar, by contrast, is one of the easiest places to reach in this part of Dalmatia for all the steamers from Rijeka to Split make a call there. Strictly speaking it is only when one reaches Zadar that one enters Dalmatia, for the part we have so far covered, from Rijeka southwards, is really the Hrvatsko Primorje or Croatian Littoral and not part of Dalmatia at all. The term "Dalmatian Coast" is, however, one which is commonly used to describe the whole of the Yugoslav Adriatic region and so, whilst it is not strictly correct from a geographical standpoint, it is the form I have used for the convenience of the reader in the text and chapter-headings of this book.

Zadar was once the capital of Dalmatia. It is still a large and important town, Yugoslav only since 1945. In the years between the two world wars it belonged to Italy, forming an *enclave* which caused considerable resentment to the Yugoslavs despite the fact that most of the inhabitants were of Italian stock. The town is built on a peninsula, in a similar fashion to Rab, and its fortifications have long been used as promenades. Zadar contains many interesting monuments from past ages. The church of St. Donato, now used as an archaeological museum, was constructed in the ninth century on the foundations of a Roman temple, the base of which can still be seen. The Romanesque Cathedral dates from the fourteenth century. The church of St. Simeon contains a wrought silver coffin with relics of the saint, the patron of Zadar. Other interesting buildings include the Municipal Loggia, formerly used as a court of justice, and the old guard-house with its Venetian-style clock-tower, now containing a collection of national costumes.

Zadar has a Putnik office which arranges coach excursions in the summer, the most interesting being to the Krka waterfalls and to Obrovac. The latter can also be reached by service bus and from it a steamer can be taken, through the impressive gorges of the river Zrmanja to Jablanac and Senj or all the way to Rijeka.

The hotels of Zadar are the Beograd, category B and the Zagreb, category C.

Biograd na Moru is eighteen miles south-east of Zadar. It commands the narrow channel between the mainland and the island of Pašman and through this channel, in the early days of sail, all ships had to pass during the winter months. It was therefore of great strategic value and became the most important place in the Croat Kingdom. For most of the ninth and tenth centuries Biograd dominated the Adriatic, but it fell under the power of Venice after a great sea battle in the year 1000. In 1123 it was completely razed to the ground and nothing can now be seen of its ancient glories. Today it is a pleasant seaside resort, with a sandy, pine-sheltered beach and a category C hotel, the Europa, on the harbour-front.

Šibenik, forty miles by steamer from Biograd, lies in a broad basin formed by the River Krka before it cuts through a narrow channel to the sea. It is an important naval and commercial port and is connected by rail with Zagreb and Split. There is extensive modern development around the town but the old part is of much interest. The crowning glory of Šibenik is its magnificent cathedral, constructed in the fifteenth and sixteenth centuries. It is a mixture of many styles but so skilfully are they blended that they merely add to the harmony of the whole. Every part of the building is of stone, even the dome and the roof; it is said to be the largest church in the world to be entirely stone-constructed. Not only the main architecture but also the details and decorations are of outstanding interest and beauty. You will see the Lion Doorway, the delicate carvings of foliage and flowers, the beautiful cupola and, perhaps finest of all, the frieze of human heads round the outer edge of the apse, representing men and women of all ages, ranks and races. To appreciate all the wonders of this outstanding triumph of art and architecture you must read Jackson's *Dalmatia, the Quarnero and Istria* (see my note on page 47).

There are other fine buildings to see—the sixteenth-century Venetian Loggia, the three castles which dominate the town, the Church of St. John, and many fine and gracious houses. You can also make an excursion to the Krka waterfalls, ten miles up the river, and you can include a visit to the Franciscan convent on the island of Visovac. Šibenik is worth a day or two of your holiday and you should be able to find accommodation without difficulty at the Hotel Krka, category C. There is a Putnik office to help you during your stay. All the fast steamers down the coast call at Šibenik and from the latter to Split is a journey of about three hours.

(*iii*) SPLIT AND ITS SURROUNDINGS

Until the summer of 1953 every tourist going up and down the Dalmatian Coast had to break his journey at Split, for all the steamers used to berth for a night in the harbour there, completing the journey along the other half of the coast the following day. Now many tourists do little more than catch a glimpse of Split from the decks of the vessels that sail the whole way from Rijeka to Dubrovnik without a break. This is indeed a pity, for Split is one of the most remarkable towns in Europe. Today it is an important port but its chief claim to fame and its main interest for the tourist is the great Palace of Diocletian. The story of the Emperor and of his palace is a fascinating chapter of history.

This part of the coast came under the sway of Rome between the years 35 and 33 B.C. and the port of Salona, five miles to the north of Split, became the military and commercial capital of Dalmatia. Many roads were built along the coast to the interior, and Salona was a place of great importance. The city was at the height of its prosperity when Diocletian was born in a village nearby. The father was a freed man; the son was destined before he reached the age of forty to sit on the throne of the Caesars.

He reigned in Rome from 284 A.D. to 305 A.D., an absolute monarch with the whole of the great Empire under his sway. Many must have been the times when, surrounded by courtiers and seekers after office and overburdened with the affairs of state, he thought of his lovely homeland of Dalmatia. Like a city man who longs to escape from the toils of business and buys his plot of land in the country long before he reaches the age of retirement, so Diocletian, about the year 295, chose an attractive coastal site a few miles from his boyhood home and ordered a great palace to be erected there. Then, in the year 305, when the building had been completed, he voluntarily renounced his imperial honours and retired to spend the remaining years of his life at his coastal palace, which was known as Spalato. For nearly ten years folowing his abdication he lived there in peace and solitude, giving his advice when need be to those in Rome but with the cares of mighty office thrown off his shoulders.

I never think of Diocletian's Palace as being in Split, but rather of Split as being within the Palace. The town has grown much during the last century or so, but throughout medieval times all the inhabitants of Split lived entirely inside the palace walls, which even today encompass the dwellings of 3,500 citizens.

Diocletian decided that his enormous residence should be as magnificent as his resources could make it—and the resources of a Roman Emperor were boundless. The side facing the sea, a wall over 500 feet in length with the waves then lapping at its feet, was surmounted by an imposing loggia traversing it from end to end. There was but one small sea-gateway the whole length, for Diocletian knew that the power of Rome was not on secure foundations and his home had to be a fortress as well as a place of beauty. The remaining three sides of this great palace-city, for indeed it was that, faced on to the land and were penetrated by only three gateways. Sixteen great towers, spaced along the walls, added to its defences. The whole area was over seven acres.

Although much of this mighty work has long since disappeared, enough was left in the middle of the eighteenth century to attract Robert Adam, the great British architect. He wrote a massive and fascinating work entitled *Ruins of the Palace of the Emperor Diocletian at Spalato in Dalmatia,* and embellished it with many beautiful drawings. More important, his sketches became the basis of the style of architecture he adopted and later practised so extensively in England. Many of the stately homes of our country owe their beauty and grace, as well as many of their adornments, to the inspiration which Adam drew from the Palace of Diocletian. The face of London would be very different today if Robert Adam had never visited Spalato.

The palace has suffered from the ravages of time and from neglect since Adam's day, but very much is left for you to see. The eastern gate, the so-called Porta Argentea, has been carefully restored in recent years and the western one, the Porta Ferrea, is well preserved. The peristyle, which formed the centre of the palace, is very graceful, and the mausoleum, converted into a cathedral in the seventh century, is an interesting building with fine decorations.

I will not attempt further to describe the Palace of Diocletian, for you can obtain detailed brochures from the Putnik office in the town. Sometimes, even, supplies are sent to the Yugoslav National Tourist Offices abroad. It is my strong recommendation, if you want to get the best out of your exploration of the palace, to hire a guide or to join one of the organised visits which are arranged by Putnik every day, except in winter. Many of the guides, whose office is in the peristyle, speak English. Even if architecture normally holds no interest for you, I think that you will agree after you have been round it with one of these guides that Diocletian's Palace is something with a difference.

Inside the palace are now many mean and narrow alleys which would have shocked the Emperor's architect, but which add colour and interest to the scene. Yet as you wander leisurely through the old part of the town you will sometimes catch a glimpse along a passageway stretching half-way through the palace, and it is then that you suddenly realise how spacious and magnificent this great edifice must have been in the days of the man who conceived it.

As evening approaches, I like to wander through the western gateway to the main square, the Narodni Trg, with the tables outside the cafés surrounded by people drinking and with the Korzo in full swing. The Korzo is one of the most interesting social customs in

Yugoslavia. Early each evening, in every town and most of the villages of the country, the people come out into the open air and start to stroll along a certain stretch of road. Up and down they go, in their twos and threes, always turning when they reach the end of the accepted Korzo, then back again to the other end, to and fro for an hour or more. Nobody seems to be first to start and nobody seems to be the last to decide it is time to go home. In a big city (which has many a minor Korzo too) there may be thousands of people passing their time in this way every evening, busily engaged in conversation as they walk up and down, steering past one another as if by instinct.

Instinctive the Korzo is, of course. Its origins are wrapped in mystery, though perhaps it was formerly the only opportunity there was of boy meeting girl. Certainly today there is no obvious flirting on the Korzo, though people of every age take part. Perhaps nowadays the couples prefer to go off to quieter places, and shun the publicity! In any event, for the visitor this can be one of the most exciting and colourful social customs of Yugoslavia, especially if many of the women are in costume.

Costumes are seldom seen at Split, but it is distinguished by having a second Korzo, along the harbour-front beneath the southern wall of the palace. The harbour itself is palm-fringed in this part and is gay with many small craft. The modern commercial quays are fortunately farther away from the old part of the city.

The Putnik organisation at Split is efficient and helpful. There are two offices, one of them being for the reception of foreign tourists, and this will be found on the west side of the old town, outside the walls. Some

PEASANTS AT STARI BAR   Plate 17

These are typical Montenegrin peasants, descendants of the fierce clansmen
who for centuries held out against the Turks and maintained the virtual
independence of their small country.

PRIZREN IN KOSMET   Plate 18

Kosmet is part of the Republic of Serbia, but has special status as an autonomous district. In all its towns can be seen evidence of the centuries of
Turkish occupation, and many of the inhabitants are Moslems.

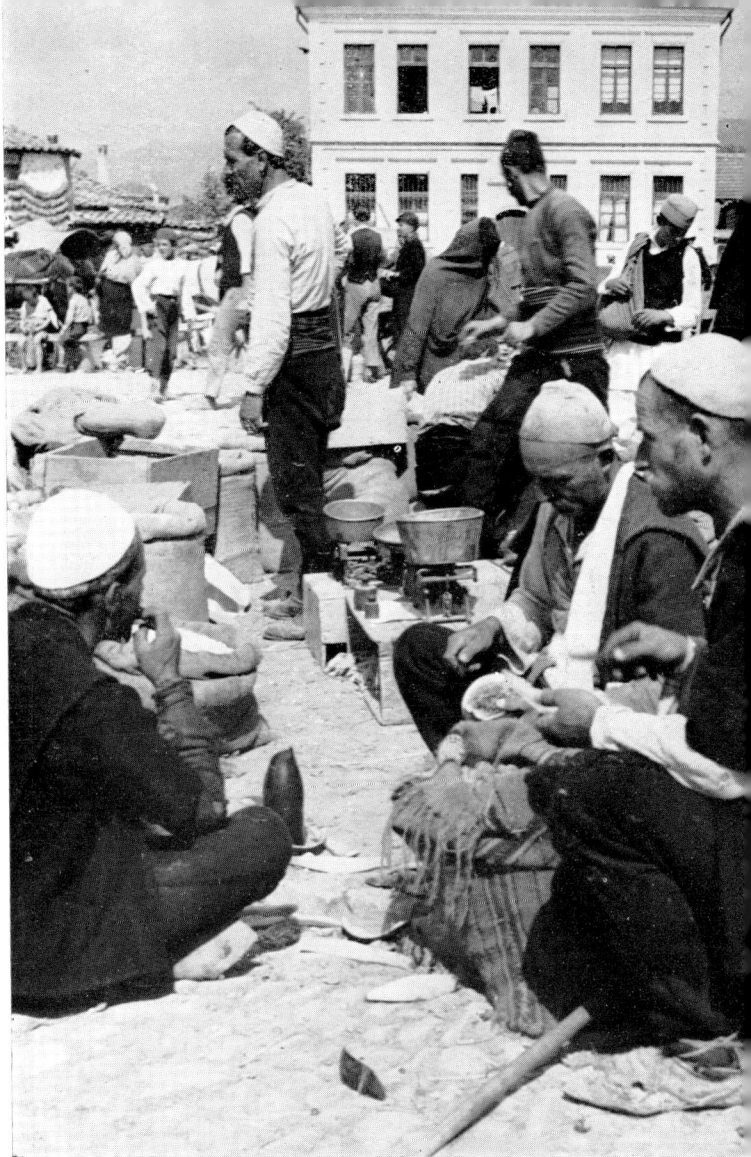

A MARKET AT SKOPJE   Plate 19

In the chief city of Macedonia two civilisations can be seen side by side.
On one side of the River Vardar lies modern Skopje, with its new factories
and commercial buildings; a few minutes away is old Skopje, with narrow
streets, many mosques and with people wearing costumes of many designs
and colours.

DETAIL FROM THE SCREEN, SVETI SPAS, SKOP

Sveti Spas, the church of the Holy Saviour, contains a fine wooden iconostasis. It was made by men from the village of Galičnik—and the illustration shows that they have included a portrayal of themselves at work on the carving. On the left is St. George, a popular saint in eastern Europe.

Plate 20

of the staff speak English and will advise you what to see and how to make the best use of your time. An information office is open during the summer months just outside the railway station and facing the quay on to which you disembark from the steamers. At this office you can book accommodation in an hotel or even in private rooms.

For Split is very short of hotels. A very large number of tourists stay there in summer for a night or two, and it also has its visitors who stay for a week or a fortnight. The authorities are well aware of the seriousness of the situation and it will not be long before more hotels are available. When I was last in Split I was told that building work was actively in hand. In the meantime most foreign tourists stay at the Park Hotel, in the eastern suburbs. The surroundings are very modern and one regrets being away from the old city, but the hotel is comfortable and up-to-date. It is in category B, as is the Bellevue, which in many ways I prefer. This is a stone's throw from the western wall of the palace, a position which is more in the spirit of Split. A third hotel, the Central, is in the Narodni Trg and is a category C place which can be recommended. There is a little hotel just inside the eastern gate which I have not tried yet, but which has one quality at least, that of being delightfully situated.

There is another C hotel, the Bačvice, well away from the town but overlooking the sandy bathing-beach of the same name. Here there are cabins, shower-baths and the other accessories of a popular *plage*. There are several other similar bathing-beaches nearby, but if you go further along the coast you will discover many less frequented small, sandy coves.

Split is dominated by Marjan, a hill rising to nearly

600 feet above the sea. It is on the peninsula that juts into the Adriatic to the west of the town, and to climb to the top is well worth the effort. Steps lead all the way up, as they did in the days when Diocletian took his guests hunting there. If the day is clear you will be able to pick out the cathedral of Trogir to the west and the islands of Šolta and Brač well out to sea. Looking inland you will see the great mountain barrier, cut only by the narrow pass of Klis. The fortress guarding this pass was one of the strong points in the defence of the coast against the Turks. After it fell to them, in 1537, the frontier between the eastern and western worlds for nearly two centuries was merely the tiny river, a bare couple of miles from Split, which you will see when you go to Salona.

A railway line now climbs through this pass and goes as far as Sinj, nearly thirty miles from the coast. It makes a very pleasant trip, but the trains are slow and the services infrequent, and it is better to go by coach if an excursion is being organised by Putnik. It it a very scenic journey, as the coach winds up many zig-zags to the pass of Klis, through a deep gorge, and then across the arid *karst* to Sinj.

This is a small agricultural centre which springs to life one day each year, on August 17th, when a great national festival takes place. It is the festival of the Alka, which celebrates the re-capture of Klis from the Turks in the year 1775. The culminating spectacle of a day of festivity is one of the most interesting and colourful folk-survivals of the country. It is a contest in which the competitors, dressed in the brilliant costumes of knights of the early eighteenth century, gallop their mounts and, riding at full speed, tilt with lances at a target. The richly caparisoned horses, the exquisitely fashioned costumes of the riders, the trumpets which hail each of them as he takes his turn, all make one realise the thrill of the tournament days of centuries ago. Make a special effort to go to Sinj if you are in Dalmatia in the middle of August.

An excursion from Split which is interesting any day of the year is to Trogir, a small islet about twenty miles to the west. It is sandwiched between the mainland and the island of Čiovo. The history of Trogir dates back to the third century before Christ, when it was colonised by the Greeks. It was a place of importance to the Romans and to the Byzantine Empire; then it was ruled by Croat and Hungarian kings until, in 1420, it came under the sway of Venice. The Austrians captured Trogir after the fall of the Venetian republic in 1797 and the French occupied the town in 1806, and stayed for eight years. The Austrians were back again for just over a century, until Yugoslavia was established after the first world war.

Trogir today is a living museum of these many changes, but the imprints of the thirteenth and fifteenth centuries are the most marked. The town gates, the Loggia, the town hall (unfortunately damaged during the last war), the monasteries and above all the beautiful thirteenth century cathedral—these are among the outstanding features of Trogir; but narrow streets with old stone-built houses, hardly changed for four centuries or more, give the town its real character. Without a doubt Trogir is one of the most delightful places in Dalmatia. If you can find the time to spend a day or two there you will become more and more fascinated by this little town; tourists seldom devote more than an hour or two to it, and when their coaches

and motor-boats have taken them back to Split, Trogir
will be yours.

The Seven Castles along the coast between Split and
Trogir are famous to the Yugoslavs as a kind of Riviera
and there are good bathing-beaches, but for me they
have been spoiled by the industrial development at the
end of the bay nearer Split and I do not recommend
them. There are so many more interesting, more
beautiful places in Dalmatia.

Only two miles from Split is Solin, the ancient
Roman city of Salona, from which the sea has re-
ceded, leaving it some way inland. "Diggings" have
been going on here for more than half a century and
there are some interesting remains. If you are a
student of archaeology, a visit to Salona will be something of a pilgrimage; if not, have a guide to explain
the excavations to you.

There are many other excursions which can be made
from Split, with the aid of Putnik's services. You can
go to Omiš, southwards along the coast, or even
farther to Makarska. Coach trips are sometimes
arranged to the waterfalls of Gubavice. There are
motor-boat excursions to several places on the island
of Brač and to Stomorska on Šolta, an island noted for
the quality of its wine and honey. You will find plenty
of opportunities, too, for swimming and sailing—or just
looking at the people as they walk through the streets
and in the squares and the colourful market-place.

(iv) THE COAST AND ISLANDS FROM
SPLIT TO DUBROVNIK

The fast steamers from Split call at Hvar or
Makarska and at Korčula, but otherwise they usually

do not stop on their way to Dubrovnik. If you want to visit other places, either on the mainland or the islands, you will have to use one of the local services, and you must remember that many of them are not operated every day.

The first island southwards from Split is Brač and it is the largest one in Dalmatia proper. It is a hilly island, rising to about 1,500 feet above sea-level at its highest point. Its largest town is Supetar, on the northern shore, with a pine-sheltered bathing-beach. It is a very quiet resort but there are others even smaller at Bol, Sumartin and Milna, each with small hotels. The one at Sumartin was formerly a Trade Union holiday centre (now category B): at Milna, my favourite place on the island, is the tiny Hotel Val (category C). These towns are connected with Supetar by occasional buses. The island is a fertile one, with many vines, figs and olive groves, but the coast is wild and rocky. It is not a place to visit if you are seeking excitement and opportunities for excursions, but for quiet, simple holidays it is ideal, especially if you like walking.

Farther from the mainland is Vis, an island which has two very different connections with Great Britain. In 1808 it was occupied by a British naval force, as part of the operations against the French, and it was then used as a base from which to smuggle British goods into Europe, even as far as Germany. Napoleon decided that this must stop, and he sent a strong fleet to take the island; but in a battle which took place in March 1811 the French were defeated by a British fleet only half as large, under the command of Admiral Sir William Hoste. A monument at Vis celebrates this victory. The British remained in occupation of the island until the year 1815, when it was transferred to the rule of Austria. They then had no connection with Vis until the last war, when it was one of the head-quarters of the Military Mission to Tito's Partisan Forces and was the place to which the British Navy delivered military and medical supplies. Some of the events which took place on Vis are recounted by Fitzroy Maclean in "Eastern Approaches".

The town of Vis itself and Komiža on the west coast are the two main centres of population, but both are very small. They can be reached from Split or Hvar on several days of the week. They are friendly little fishing centres, quite colourful without having anything specially beautiful in the way of architecture. The island is a hilly one, rising from sea level to 1,000 feet, and is noted for fruit and grapes as well as for fish. Indeed, the wine of Vis is renowned throughout Yugoslavia. It is certainly of excellent flavour—and strong! A day or two on Vis is an interesting exper-ience, and there are some very pleasant walks. You can ramble right across the island from Komiža to Vis in a few hours, if your boots are strong and you are used to stiff, uphill work.

Off Vis lies the tiny islet of Biševo. I have been told that the vines which grow here are of very old stock. A deadly scourge called phylloxera once wiped out the vines all over Europe and even reached Vis. Biševo was one of the very few places this side of the Atlantic to escape and it still bears the old vines, whereas most of the rest of Europe was re-stocked from America.

The next island to the south is Hvar and it is much more visited by holiday-makers than the last three I have mentioned. The main town is Hvar itself, one of the most beautiful places on the Dalmatian coast. It has a cathedral which dates from the twelfth century and a Franciscan monastery of the fifteenth century and it is dominated by a fortress on a hill above the town. After a climb to the top you can see the whole of Hvar laid out before you, like a map. It is a very attractive town, with many hotels of all grades, the one most visited by foreigners being the Imperial, which boasts nearly two hundred beds. There is an efficient Putnik office which arranges excursions by motor-boat and also by coach to smaller places on the island, such as Starigrad and Jelsa. Hvar is a good place to visit if you want to stay at a busy, lively resort that retains some of its old-world character, but it is very crowded in summer and therefore very prosperous, and it suffers from the inevitable result—charges which are high and a reception which is efficient but not as friendly as one finds in smaller places. It claims to be the "Madeira of the Adriatic" and that gives some key to its advantages and disadvantages as a tourist resort. There are, of course, several smaller places on the island. I have already mentioned Starigrad and Jelsa and there is also Vrboska—all charming and colourful townlets and much cheaper than Hvar itself.

Before the coastal steamers on the way to Korčula and Dubrovnik turn around the Point of Sućaraj, at the eastern end of Hvar, they pass some very attractive places on the mainland. The first of these is Omiš, about fifteen miles south-east from Split. It is a small port and a seaside resort in an attractive situation at the mouth of the River Cetina. The steep sides of Mount Mosor rise above it and add to the beauty of its situation. It has fine ramparts and palaces dating from the Middle Ages, for Omiš was a place of importance in bygone days. It was an independent republic right through the centuries until its ancient privileges were usurped by Napoleon and, although it has long since lost its political and commercial importance, it still bears the signs of its former prosperity. A wide and gently sloping sandy beach is excellent for bathing. There are a number of small boats which carry passengers between Split and Omiš and it is also served by several buses, which complete the journey in an hour and a half. The main hotel is the Dinara, a very comfortable place but included in category C, and therefore inexpensive. Omiš can be recommended to those who want to stay at a quiet resort which is seldom visited by foreigners, but it does not make a good centre for excursions to the other parts of the coast.

Farther down the coast are Brela, Makarska, the sandy Tučepi and Podgora, all of them dominated by the great mountain range of Biokovo. Brela is a quiet little town, crowded along the sea-shore and flanked by a forest of pines. It has some sandy beaches and several hotels, of which the Brela and the Soline, both category B, are situated on the sea-front amidst pine trees. Makarska, a fine natural harbour, is better known and easier of access because the fast steamers down the coast call there on several days of the week. I have never stayed at Makarska and so I can only speak from the experience of others, but I must say that it looks delightful. It is very popular with the Yugoslavs, has several hotels and good sandy beaches and as there is a Putnik office a large number of excursions are possible. Most of these are by motor-boat, to the places up and down the coast and on the islands of Brač and Hvar, but coach journeys inland are also organised, even as far as Mostar in Hercegovina. You can have a sailing-boat, with boatman, for a mere 150 dinars per head an hour, and canoes can be hired at even cheaper rates. The energetic visitor can climb up a well-made track to the highest summit of Biokovo, the 5,800 ft. Sv. Jure. Almost at the top is the mountain hut of Dom Biokovo, where you can spend the night.

A few miles from Makarska is the new 320-bed hotel of Tučepi, with a long stretch of beach; such a large place is a veritable town in itself and many amusements, dancing and motor-boat trips are organised every day in the summer months. Seven miles or so from Makarska is the seaside village of Podgora. It has a small hotel of the same name, a rather stony beach and a more recent claim to fame than most of the places on this coast, for it was here that the new Yugoslav Navy began to be formed during the last war.

As the steamer sweeps round the tip of the island of Hvar and quickly changes its course from south-east to south-west one realises the navigational difficulties of a coast with so many islands. The lighthouse here is one of hundreds which the Yugoslavs have to maintain and without which these narrow channels would be very perilous. Even the name of Hvar is said to be derived from the Greek word for a lighthouse—Pharos. If you now look at a map you will see that the shores on the port side are not on an island at all, but are part of the mainland. This is the peninsula of Pelješac. When it is joined to the mainland proper, near Ston, the isthmus is only two miles wide, yet Pelješac juts out into the sea for nearly forty miles.

The steamer again makes radical changes of direction as it passes another lighthouse, on Lovište, the furthest point of Pelješac, and then the island of Korčula comes into sight. I consider Korčula to be one of the most attractive islands of Dalmatia, with its wooded hills, rising to over 1,850 feet above sea-level, its extremely jagged coastline, the hundreds of lovely bays and miniature fjords and the interesting and beautiful town of Korčula itself.

Before describing this town, however, I will make a suggestion for the benefit of the visitor who has a day or two to spare, and is not in too much of a hurry to reach Dubrovnik. At the western end of the island is Vela Luka, a beautiful small town which the average tourist never sees, for none of the main steamers touch it, though it is served by smaller vessels from Split three or four days of the week. It has an atmosphere of calm and beauty, but is a busy work-a-day place too, and I think that one of these days it will become a popular resort. In the meantime, you can have Vela Luka more or less to yourself and there is no lack of simple accommodation to be found. A bus runs daily from Vela Luka to the town of Korčula, from end to end of the island. The hilly terrain makes the journey exciting at times, but always beautiful. You are still among the hills when the fact that your fellow-passengers are starting to gather their goods together makes you realise that you must be nearing Korčula— and suddenly there it is right below you, a huddle of houses, tightly packed on a little peninsula, towering up to the culminating point of the cathedral in the centre.

It is an historic and picturesque town. Every tourist who sees Korčula from the steamer (and one of the fast boats between Split and Dubrovnik, in each direction, calls there every day) is intrigued by it and thousands of photograph albums, all over the world, must contain views of Korčula taken from the decks of the steamers, with the quay crowded with people waiting for the vessel to tie up, the round fort dominating the harbour-front and the old town climbing up steeply above. It has an interesting history, too. It was for long centuries, like so much of this coast, under the rule of the Venetian Republic. It was the scene of an epic naval battle between the forces of Venice and Genoa and it is famous as the birthplace of Marco Polo, a scion of one of the rich Italian families who settled here and some of whose graceful houses still stand. The imprint of Venice is everywhere in Korčula and the Lion of St. Mark is seen frequently decorating the buildings. I have already mentioned how Vis came to be occupied by the British, early in the nineteenth century, and Korčula was under British rule at the same time. You can see, near the newly-constructed Park Hotel, an inscription which was carved to record the thanks of the townsfolk to one of the English governors.

You will climb up the cool, narrow streets and alleys, which often change into flights of steps, to the highest point of Korčula—and suddenly you come upon the great cathedral, a small open square before it. It has fine stone carvings, including some of elephants, and there is a local legend which connects these with stories which Marco Polo brought back from the East. High above the town rises a steep hill, covered with shrubs and bushes, with here and there a few tall cypresses asserting their personality. You can have pleasant walks not only in the town itself but on the nearby hills and along the coast, with many a delightful cove for swimming.

The Park Hotel, which I have mentioned, was still being completed when I was last on the island but it must now be ready to receive guests. It is of category B and I had the impression that it would be a pleasant place at which to stay. It certainly has a good position, with a terrace commanding fine views. The hotel I have stayed at is the Hotel Korčula on the quay—a simple place with very plain rooms and with "jugs and basins". I should add that an inadequate water-supply is one of the civic problems of Korčula, and there must be many occasions in summer when it has to be severely rationed. The shortage of water is, indeed, a problem on many of the islands and the quantity available for consumption per head varies in inverse ratio to the success of a town in developing itself as a tourist resort.

Korčula has no Putnik office, but a few enterprising folk connected with the hotels have banded together to form an information bureau and to organise excursions. This service was just being established on the occasion of my last visit, and I gave my help in translating into English a notice to be exhibited in several languages drawing the attention of visitors to the facilities available for guiding and excursions. The enquiry desk will be in the office of the shipping concern, the Jadranska Linijska Plovidba, in the loggia at the southern end of the quay.

The day of the year in Korčula is July 29th. This is the day of the Moreška. I have heard and read much of this traditional dance and when I found myself travelling over-night from Zagreb to Split recently on *June* 28th I was misled by two old guide-books into believing that if I went straight on to Korčula I would arrive in time for the Moreška. You can imagine my chagrin when I found everyone going about his business as usual. I had arrived a month too soon! You will not make this mistake, for I have checked carefully since then and I am assured by all the people who ought to know that July 29th is the correct day. The Moreška dates from the early years of the twelfth century. In the colourful dance the town of Korčula is represented as a bride, called Bula. Moro, King of the Moors, has captured her and, clad in a black parody of Moorish dress, he does battle with the red-costumed forces of the Ottoman Sultan Oman, to whom Bula is betrothed. The soldiers clash their sabres together and finally Moro and Osman fight in single combat. The dance ends in the victory of Osman, and Moro surrenders Bula to him. The rhythmical motions of the dance and the clang of the weapons, together with the gorgeous colours of the costumes, must make the Moreška a thrilling spetacle.

Korčula is not a place for those who are seeking sophisticated amusements, but rather for the connoisseur of the picturesque, who is content with simple scenes of man-made and natural beauty. It is a pity that so many people pass it by, yet for the few who do remain on Korčula this in itself is perhaps one of its attractions.

Across the narrow channel which separates Korčula from the Pelješac peninsula are several small seaside resorts—Viganj, Kučište and Orebić. The peninsula is a very mountainous one; the barren *karst* rises to a height of over 3,000 feet above the sea, although in this part Pelješac is barely four miles broad. As a result there is only a very narrow coastal strip which is suitable for cultivation; yet the peninsula is a rich one and is famous for its fruits and wines—especially a dark wine of the claret type known as Dingač. The names of some of the villages are interesting: Viganj,

Nakovanj and Kovačevići mean "bellows", "anvil" and "smoke", and the blacksmith's trade in Yugoslavia is a gypsy one. The people of these villages are known as Firauni, or Pharaohs, a name by which gypsies, or "Egyptians", are known in many lands. Probably in some distant age a colony of gypsies settled here and turned from their nomadic life to the production of fruit and wine, their origins being perpetuated in the local place-names.

Orebić is the most important place on this coast. I have not been able to visit it yet, but from Korčula I have seen the lights of Orebić blazing at night and I have had pointed out to me which are the hotels. I am told that it is an attractive place. It has poor connections with the rest of the coast and is best reached from Korčula, from which it is not difficult to hire a motor-boat to take you across.

On the other side of Korčula, well out to sea, is the small island of Lastovo which formerly belonged to Italy. Its two villages are Sv. Petar, a sheltered little harbour on the west coast, and Lastovo itself. The costume of the islanders, still seen on days of festivity, is very unusual. Crimson and black, with gold braid as decoration, are worn by both sexes and the strangest features are the bowler hats and bow ties of the men and the broad yellow "postman's stripes" down their trousers. Lastovo can be reached three or four days of the week from Split and there are two services a week from Dubrovnik. If these are inconvenient you can make arrangements at Korčula to be taken in a motor-boat.

The next island to the south-east is Mljet and it is the last one of any size down the coast of Dalmatia. You can reach it once a week by steamer from

Dubrovnik, landing at Sobra (also called Sovra) or Luka Polače. The vessel goes on to Korčula and Lastovo and returns the next day, so you can have a full day on the island. Excursion boats from Dubrovnik also sometimes go to Mljet. It is a very rugged island, twenty-five miles in length but less than three miles broad, with several hills rising to well over 1,000 feet and the highest to 1,700 feet above sea level. Mljet disputes with Malta the claim to be the island on which St. Paul was shipwrecked on the journey to Rome.

" But when the fourteenth night was come, as we were driven up and down in Adria, about midnight the shipmen deemed that they drew near to some country . . . And when it was day, they knew not the land: but they discovered a certain creek with a shore, into the which they were minded, if it were possible, to thrust in the ship . . . And when they were escaped, then they knew that the island was called Melita. And the barbarous people shewed us no little kindness."

Then follows the story of how the viper "fastened on his hand" but did not harm him; and the strange thing is that the ancient name for Mljet was Melita—and not many years ago the island was still so infested with snakes that the mongoose was imported to kill them!

(v) DUBROVNIK AND ITS SURROUNDINGS

Dubrovnik is always talked of in superlatives. "The loveliest place God ever made"; "the fairest gem in the crown of imperial Venice"; even Bernard Shaw is quoted as saying, "Those who are looking for an earthly paradise should come and see Dubrovnik".

The most recurrent epithet is "The Pearl of the Adriatic"—and like all pearls it has a price, for it tends to be more expensive than other places on the coast. But do not let this deter you, for although the Argentina and Excelsior are among the dearest (but also the most comfortable) hotels in Yugoslavia, Dubrovnik has also very many cheaper places at which to stay.

It is one of the most fascinating and picturesque towns of Europe, enclosed by magnificent ramparts within which every street is a gallery of art and architecture. Sculpture adorns a high proportion of the houses and history is written in every stone. The subtle interplay of light and shade along narrow alleys and stairways and the quietness of streets through which no vehicle passes give to Dubrovnik a beauty and atmosphere which are rarely equalled.

First, however, you must have some practical information and discover how to get your bearings. Unless you arrive by bus from the south, or by air, you will enter Dubrovnik by way of Gruž, the industrial and mercantile suburb on its north side. It is a disappointing approach, for Dubrovnik itself is hidden by the hill of Boninovo and though Gruž was in former times a beautiful and graceful place, as the neglected but once stately houses testify, now it is no more than an important port, with the usual collection of customs sheds and warehouses. The terminus of the narrow gauge railways from Sarajevo and Titograd is also situated at Gruž.

Putnik coaches meet all the important steamers and trains and taxis can also be hired, but most of the Yugoslavs scorn the luxury and take a tram. Putnik charges 150 dinars to take you from Gruž to the Pile

A MOSQUE AT RESEN   Plate 21

Every town and village in Macedonia has its mosque, and the graceful, white minarets are features of every scene. Most of the mosques are still used by the Faithful, but this one at Resen has been neglected and has fallen into disrepair.

POTS FOR SALE

Pottery is still a peasant craft in most parts of Yugoslavia and the scene of this photograph, which was taken at Resen in Macedonia, is one which the traveller frequently meets with.

Plate 22

Plate 23

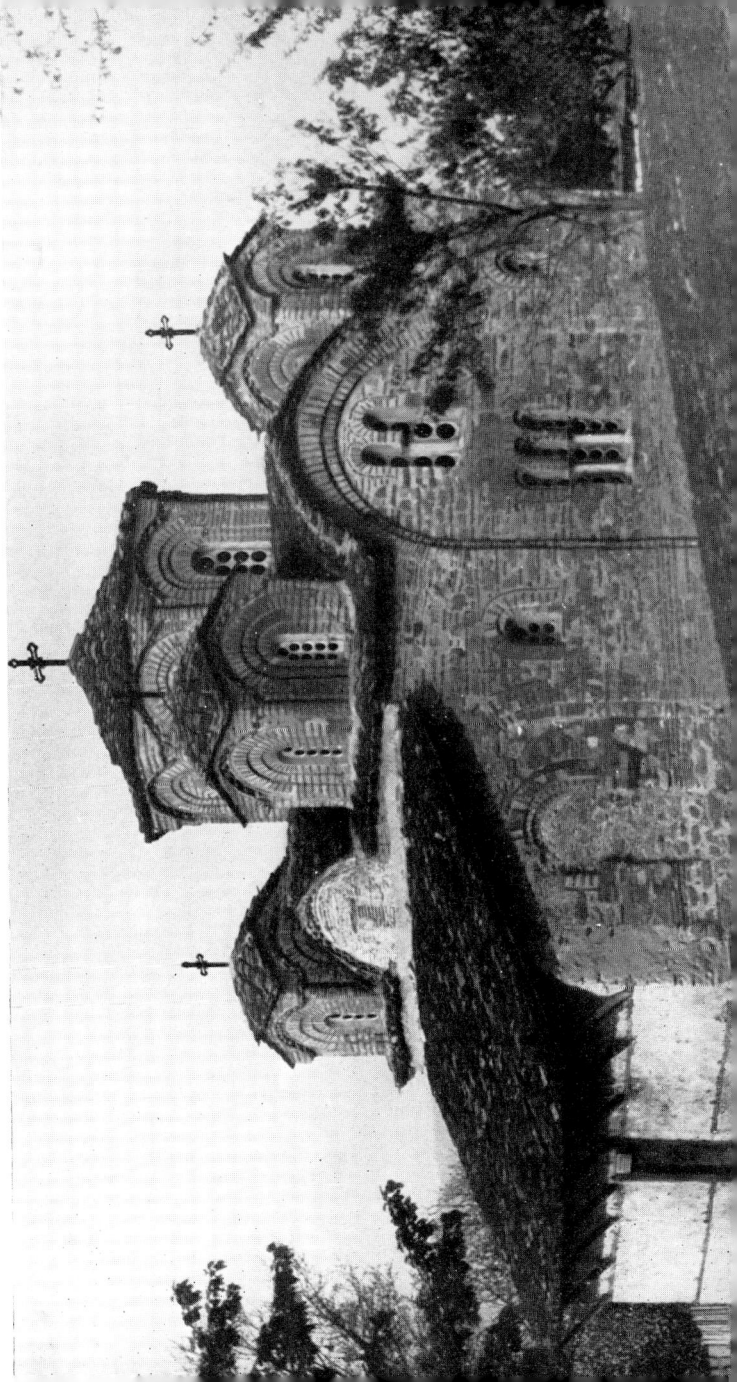

THE MONASTERY AT NEREZI

Built in the twelfth century in the hills overlooking the Vardar valley, not far from Skopje, is the little monastery-church of Nerezi. It is famous for its fine frescoes.

SVETI NAUM

Plate 24

This is one of Yugoslavia's oldest monasteries and is also one of the most beautifully situated. It stands by the side of Lake Ohrid near to the Albanian frontier.

gate of Dubrovnik; you can do it by tram for only 10 dinars. Whatever means you use to travel from Gruž when you first arrive, you are certain to be using the trams later, so I will say something about the system here. There are two lines, the first of them running from the railway station past the port, then over the hill of Boninovo and down to the terminus at Pile, just outside the walls of the old town. About half way along, at the end of the quay, is another line which joins the main one with the Lapad peninsula, its terminus being at the bathing-beach there. Shuttle-services only are maintained on both lines, so you always have to change near the quay if you are transferring from one to the other, but your 10-dinar ticket is valid right through. It is a delightfully simple system and you certainly have your money's worth if you go the whole way, say from Pile to Lapad. The trams are generally in two parts, the front car closed and the trailer-car open. You just climb in at the side of the "toast-rack" wherever you will, but if you have luggage it is best to get in at the back, where there is more room, and stand. Many passengers never trouble to sit down, just as in a London tube train. The journey is quite a short one, taking ten to fifteen minutes from Gruž to Pile and about ten minutes for the ride out to Lapad. The service is frequent, but except in the summer months the last trams run at about 10.30 p.m.

You will not want to stay at Gruž unless you are desperately hard up, when you could do worse than to book a "soba" in the house of one of the landladies who beset you as you descend from the steamer. More is to be said for staying at Lapad, which is well provided with hotels and pensions, generally less expensive than those near the heart of Dubrovnik. Lapad has

129

K

an excellent sandy *plage,* with changing cabins for hire, and you pay a very modest charge for using it. The swimming here is certainly the best available anywhere around Dubrovnik. The main hotels are the Splendid (category A and as expensive as those at Ploče, of which more anon), the Zagreb (category B); the Elit (category C, a simple pension in a remarkable situation, with its own jetty down below among the rocks, but a fairish walk from the tram terminus); and the Sumratin (category C) a comfortable place which I can recommend. It is a couple of hundred yards short of the tram terminus and the charges are very reasonable. The disadvantage of Lapad is that a good deal of time can be spent going to and from Dubrovnik on the trams —and they don't run all night! If you stay at one of the Lapad hotels it is a good idea to have half-pension only, which saves you the bother of going back for lunch. The Splendid runs its own bus service to Pile, but even so you are tied to a definite schedule. This sophisticated hotel has dancing every night in the season; you pay 100 dinars to go in but it is deducted from what you spend on drinks. Many of the Yugoslav visitors to Lapad who want to dance do so at the Dom Admora (near the tram terminus) which has a much jollier and more informal atmosphere.

There are a few hotels at Boninovo, much nearer to Dubrovnik proper. The situation is an excellent one and it isn't a long walk if you miss the last tram. The pleasantest hotel here is the Bellevue, which has a magnificent position, a beautiful terrace on which meals are served most days of the season and steps leading down to the rocks below. It is small and unpretentious, being in category C.

As the tram from Gruž runs down the hill from

Boninovo, between stately villas whose gardens of oleanders and flowering shrubs are a riot of blossom, you pass the modern post office on your left and the hospital (*bolnica*) on your right and soon reach the terminus of Pile. Here is a lively square, one of the focal points of Dubrovnik. The many trees give shelter from the heat of the sun, and under them are innumerable café tables. One side of the square is a terrace overlooking the sea, with a fine view of the town walls and of the great fortresses of Lovrjenac and Bokar. This cheerful little square, in which a band plays in the evening, is the favourite meeting place in Dubrovnik for the townsfolk and tourists alike, and the visitor must be rare indeed who has not drunk coffee or sipped šljivovica or eaten ice cream outside the Café Dubravka.

Here are the Hotel Pošta, which I cannot recommend because of its noisy situation—the trams immediately outside start before five in the morning—and the Imperial (category B), the largest hotel in Dubrovnik and the one where the majority of foreign visitors stay. It charges rather more than hotels of the same category elsewhere, but this is true of most things in the town, a result of its enormous popularity. The Imperial, which ranked before the war as one of the most fashionable hotels in Europe, is busy and comfortable and very conveniently situated, but naturally it lacks the atmosphere of a smaller place. Meals at the Imperial in summer-time are generally taken in the tree-shaded courtyard, where there is also an open-air dance-floor which is nightly filled with Yugoslavs and visitors. In the square at Pile are also found the Air Terminal and the Putnik office for foreign tourists. The airport for Dubrovnik is at Gruda, in the Konavli valley, and between the beginning of June and mid-September there are daily connections with Zagreb and Belgrade and a weekly one with Sarajevo. The airport is closed for passenger traffic the rest of the year.

The Putnik office of Dubrovnik is a busy one, with staff speaking several languages. They are rushed off their feet in the summer months, when there is a constant coming and going of visitors buying tickets, booking for excursions, changing money and asking every question under the sun; at that season they have little time to spare for the friendly exchange of conversation one often enjoys at some of the Putnik offices elsewhere, but they are not to be blamed. This is busy Dubrovnik, and the folk in the Putnik office have to concentrate on essentials if they are to get through the day's work and give everyone his fair share of attention. They could now do with larger premises* and more staff; indeed, this will be essential if the number of summer visitors to Dubrovnik continues to increase.

Within the walls, on a corner of the market place, near the Rector's Palace, is the Dubravka Hotel, a low-priced category B. It has a few rooms with private baths, is open all the year round and is chiefly used by the Yugoslavs themselves. It is a very old hotel, probably the first in Dubrovnik, and is mentioned in old Baedeker guides as the Hôtel de la Ville.

Outside the old town on the eastern side is the suburb of Ploče, once upon a time a busy market where the caravans from the East delivered their rich cargoes. Many hotels and villas have been built here during the last few decades, including the luxurious Argentina and Excelsior. These two hotels, much patronised by

---

* I understand that arrangements have been made for a new Putnik office on the ground floor of the Hotel Pošta.

foreigners who can afford it (but by very few Yugo-slavs), rank as the best on the Dalmatian coast. Their cuisine is very good, and they have their own private beaches. Despite the comfort and the service offered, the top price for a room with a private bathroom is very reasonable by international standards. In Paris, Rome or Brussels, or on the Riviera, you would pay far more for the same type of accommodation.

Your first walk in Dubrovnik will probably be from the Gate of Pile, along the main street called the Placa and out through the walls at the other end on to the quay which overlooks the attractive harbour, formerly the town port. (Now Gruž has taken its place, of course). On this short walk you will have passed many buildings of outstanding interest. First, the Gate itself, still with its drawbridge, a stern but handsome construction dating from the sixteenth century. Once inside the gate you descend a graceful flight of steps and go through a smaller portal—and the wide Placa is before you. This is without doubt one of the finest streets in the world. The standard pattern of the small shop-fronts is, to me, one of its chief delights; it is a motif I have seen repeated so extensively only once elsewhere—in the *souks* or market place of Tafraout in the Anti-Atlas mountains of southern Morocco. Placa is busy in the morning when the shops are open, but nearly deserted in the early afternoon when the shops are closed, the visitors at lunch and the inhabitants enjoying their siesta. It comes into its own at eventide when it is the scene of Dubrovnik's Korzo.

Just inside the smaller gate, on the right, you will see Onofrio's Fountain, built in 1438 by Onofrio de la Cava, an architect from Naples. It is a monumental work, erected to celebrate the completion of an aqueduct which vastly improved the town's water supply, so often a problem in Dalmatia. Behind the fountain is the ancient nunnery of St. Clara and on the left is the Renaissance church of Sveti Spas (Holy Saviour), with a fine façade, built by local architects in 1520. Next door to Sveti Spas is the Franciscan's church and, behind it, their monastery. This has very beautiful cloisters surrounding a quiet garden where a fountain plays. At the end of the narrow passage between the two churches is one of the oldest chemist's shops in Europe, dating back to the year 1317. Here can be seen the ancient porcelain jars, the weights, balances and instruments—but it is efficient and up-to-date in its work today. You can even buy sulfa-drugs to cure the mild form of dysentery which I have mentioned on page 94.

There is an inexpensive restaurant on the corner facing Sveti Spas, and Placa also has two good booksellers and a number of shops full of souvenirs which are unfortunately rather expensive. There are several jewellers, too, some of them selling silver bracelets of filigree designs which are reminiscent of Egypt or French North Africa.

At the eastern end of Placa is the belfry, built in the fifteenth century and restored far too obviously in 1928. It is now very much out of keeping with the other buildings nearby, though the inhabitants are proud of it. The clock has an hour hand only and if you want to know the exact time you find it indicated in figures in a square opening below, the numbers changing at the end of each minute. At this end of Placa there are many of the famous buildings of the town. The Dvor or Rector's Palace is the finest of them. It dates from the twelfth century, but most of the work you see today is from the late Gothic and early Renaissance periods. Its supreme features are its loggia and the graceful staircase which leads from the arcaded inner courtyard to the first floor. I consider that the bust of Miho Pracat is jarring, but otherwise the beauty of this palace is perfect. Another fine building here is the Sponza, the old customs house which dates from the early sixteenth century.

Facing the Sponza is the baroque church of Sv. Vlaho or St. Blaise, the patron saint of the town. By the general standards of Dubrovnik this is a recent building, as it was constructed in the eighteenth century. It stands on the site of another church four hundred years older which was destroyed by fire in 1706. The only thing to be seen today which was salvaged from the fire is a small statue of St. Blaise over the main altar. He holds in his hand a gilded model of the town, dating from the fifteenth century, and you can see in it a number of the buildings which still stand today. The general plan of the town is the same, with the ramparts, the main street along the middle and the harbour at the eastern end.

It is amazing that so much of present-day Dubrovnik dates from the middle ages for it has suffered from many fires and several earthquakes. The severest of the latter was in 1667, and though much of the town was reconstructed during the years which followed, it must have been the smaller domestic buildings which suffered most for many of the palaces and larger buildings are far older. There were once, however, more than 150 churches and monasteries in Dubrovnik and most of these were destroyed in 1667. The Dominican church and monastery, near the gate that leads out to Ploče, survived the earthquake and so today we can see the delightful fifteenth century cloister, in Renaissance style. Beyond these buildings the footway winds towards the eastern gate, with a charming view across the harbour to Fort St. John.

Another interesting walk of well over a mile is around the walls of the town. These are in the form of a horseshoe with entrances and exits at the two ends, by Ploče Gate and the harbour, and in the centre, by the side of Sveti Spas just inside Pile gate. To save retracing your steps you should enter at one of the first two points mentioned. The views from the walls are impressive—over the town, along the coast and out to sea—and one can realise the strength of Dubrovnik in the days of its medieval prosperity. The walls tower above the sea but they rise high above the town too, and one looks down on to rooftops and into little gardens and courtyards. On the landward side the town was further protected by a deep moat and there are three great forts—Lovrjenac on a steep promontory outside the city, imposing Minčeta on the northwest corner, and Bokar and St. John overlooking the sea.

Fort St. John (Sv. Ivan in Croat) now houses the town museum and there is an Art Gallery near the Gate of Ploče. Another museum is at Rupe, a fine building which was once an enormous granary. For most people the streets of Dubrovnik themselves form a living museum and they find it sufficient to wander through Placa to the bustling market place and up and down the narrow alleys, here and there catching a glimpse of the walls or coming unexpectedly upon a stately mansion where once lived a proud patrician family.

The history of Dubrovnik is as interesting as the

town itself. It originally contained two distinct communities, separated by Placa, which was then a narrow strait of the sea, and not a street. In the seventh century the south side, then an island, was settled by refugees from Epidaurus, an ancient Greek colony which had been destroyed by Slav marauders; later a Slav settlement was founded on the north side, the mainland. By the end of the twelfth century the strait had been drained and the two communities merged into one, but the families who lived in the more ancient settlement, retaining some tradition of Greek culture and organisation from the days of Epidaurus, became the dominant figures in the town. Although rich newcomers were occasionally admitted to equal status with them, these families for the most part formed a closed order of patricians. They alone were members of the councils of the state, which were all-powerful in Ragusa (as Dubrovnik was then called), regulating the commerce, making the laws and having all the rich public offices in their hands. At the height of Dubrovnik's prosperity, in the fourteenth century, this select circle included perhaps no more than two hundred families, whereas the total population at that time has been estimated at eight thousand, with another twenty thousand in the possessions inland and along the coast.

The main rival of Dubrovnik was Venice. The two maritime powers had developed together, their merchants contended for trade in the same markets and commercial treaties made by one often interfered with the ambitions of the other. At first the patricians of Ragusa looked upon the Venetians as elder statesmen, even requesting them to send one of their citizens to act as arbitrator in their own domestic quarrels, an arrangement which lasted for nearly one hundred and fifty years; but they made treaties with other powers and, most important, obtained the protection of the powerful King of Hungary. The Ragusan merchants were found all over the Turkish Empire in the latter half of the fourteenth century, and the coffers at home were overflowing with riches. They traded with all the countries of the Mediterranean and were closely connected with Spain; even the Armada had some of their sailors in its ships. Our own word "argosy" is derived from the name Ragusa and this is an indication of the riches which their vessels carried.

It is difficult to say for certain when the decline began. Some date it from 1520, when many thousands of the population and more than sixty patricians were killed in an earthquake. Others put it later, in the seventeenth century. There is no doubt, however, that the greatest disaster was the earthquake of 1667 when more than two-thirds of the population perished and Ragusa lay in ruins. Even some parts of the massive walls were shattered, and for weeks there were fires and pillage. Although a new city soon arose from the ruins of the old, Ragusa never regained her old prosperity. The eighteenth century was largely a a period of economic depression and it was heightened by the fact that much of her trade was with Turkey, whose power had also begun to decline. Internal quarrels became more serious, too, between the patricians themselves as well as between the ruling families and the people, and it was a much weakened republic which succumbed to the forces of Napoleon in the year 1806. She hoped to regain her independence when the French were finally defeated at Waterloo, but the Congress of Vienna gave her to the Austrians whose troops had entered her walls, replacing those of France, in 1814. From then until the first world war, when Yugoslavia was formed, she was merely a provincial outpost of the Austrian Empire.

We must turn back from this page of history to the Dubrovnik of today. We have had a brief glance at the finest of her interesting monuments, which all visitors must see, and now we will look for other things to do. They are certainly plentiful. You can swim at the bathing beach below Ploče, a fine stretch of sand, and there is a smaller one below the fort of Lovrjenac. Another beach is that of Danče, below the park of Gradac. The park itself, which is near the post office, is very charmingly situated and the townsfolk are very proud of it. I have already mentioned dancing at the Imperial and the Splendid. You can also dance at the Gradska Kafana, a large café beside the clock tower in Placa, with a terrace overlooking the old harbour.

There is an open-air cinema at Boninovo and an indoor one by the clock tower, at both of which foreign films are often shown. There are several theatres; most of the plays are from the traditional and modern Yugoslav repertoire, but foreign plays, including those of Shakespeare, are occasionally acted. There are symphony concerts and recitals of chamber music, sometimes in the beautiful setting of the Rector's Palace. Dubrovnik in summer is a festival town and there is no lack of cultural activity.

The Putnik office has a comprehensive programme of excursions by coach and by motor-boat—indeed you can go on a trip every day if you wish. The shortest and cheapest trip is to Lokrum, the wooded island just off the coast. It was here that Richard Coeur de Lion was shipwrecked in the year 1190, on his way back to Britain from a crusade. It is a very pleasant place for

a lazy day of swimming, but I should warn you that
except during the main tourist season there is nowhere
on the island where you can buy refreshments. Other
half-day motor-boat excursions are to Mlini and Cavtat
(which I shall describe later), to Trsteno, a pleasant
seaside village north of Dubrovnik, and to the little
island of Lopud. A further half-day trip is along the
Rijeka, a deep fjord which enters the sea near Gruž;
this is a beautiful excursion, and it can be made at
night, too, though you will not see much unless the
moon is full. None of these motor-boat outings costs
more than 250 dinars, except the night one along
Rijeka.

There are three coach tours which are organised on
several days of the week. The first is a very long
journey, through the Konavli valley to Hercegnovi,
around and across the Kotor Fjord to Kotor, over the
Lovćen pass to Cetinje, the old capital of Montenegro,
from there to Budva on the coast, returning to Kotor
and thence the same way back again to Dubrovnik.
I have been over this road several times, in one direction or the other, but its magnificent scenery never fails
to excite me. You have to leave Dubrovnik at 6 a.m.,
but having travelled so far south in Yugoslavia you will
by now be getting used to early rising. It is a marathon
of a journey, but well worth while. It costs 1,800 dinars
and can be paid for to a travel agent in advance, before
leaving home. (British tourists can thus save some of
their foreign currency allowance.) I shall not describe
this excursion in detail, as the places visited will all be
mentioned later.

The second coach excursion, a half-day one, is inland
to Trebinje. It costs 500 dinars and should be undertaken on a Saturday, which is market-day there. It is a

pleasant ride over hilly country. Trebinje has a castle, the Mosque of Osman Pasha (into which you are permitted to look) and some quaint little streets. I have heard on good authority that a marriage-market operates in the main square, but I have not seen signs of this myself. This excursion gives the tourist who has been confined to the coast an opportunity of seeing an inland town. Dalmatia in its holiday dress is far different from most other parts of Yugoslavia but here at Trebinje you are much nearer to the everyday life of the rural parts of the country. You will see the peasants marketing their vegetables, primitive wooden ploughs being sold and you can buy a distaff if you are looking for an unusual souvenir of your holiday. Trebinje is also connected to Dubrovnik by rail and it has a newly-constructed hotel, so it is possible to stay for a few days to explore the nearby hills and countryside. The river here is an unusual one; after running for many miles and bringing prosperity to a string of villages, it suddenly runs underground and disappears completely.

The Putnik office at Dubrovnik also organises a full-day coach excursion to Mostar, the principal town of Hercegovina. This is a beautiful journey along the Neretva river and it costs 1,800 dinars.

There are, of course, many walks in the neighbourhood of Dubrovnik. A large-scale map of the district, stretching from Ston at the beginning of the Pelješac peninsula to Cavtat, is due for publication and this will be very useful to people who want to explore the coast and the islands with some degree of thoroughness. One walk which I can remember is up the hills behind Dubrovnik to Srdj, the fortress which dominates the town from high above, and from there down to Komolac at the beginning of the Rijeka, where the river Ombla emerges fully-grown from a cleft in the rocky hillside. It is a beautiful spot, it has a good restaurant, the Tete Jele, and there is a regular bus service to the town.

Now I must leave Dubrovnik and continue the journey southwards down the coast. I have lingered longer there than at anywhere else in Dalmatia because it is the most fascinating place we have reached so far, and so excellent a centre. It casts its spell over you, and however widely you have travelled, you always think of Dubrovnik with nostalgia and affection.

(vi) THE COAST FROM DUBROVNIK TO THE ALBANIAN FRONTIER

In the foregoing sections we have covered nearly three quarters of the coastline. Except for a few islets, hardly more than rocks breaking the surface of the sea, we have left the islands behind us and now the view is always to the land. Yet in my opinion this is the most attractive part of the Dalmatian cruise, especially when the steamer has rounded Oštri point, at the entrance to the Fjord of Kotor.

The first place of interest after leaving Dubrovnik is Mlini, about nine miles away, an attractive little seaside resort with a sandy beach. It is in a very picturesque situation, with many olive groves and cypresses, and surrounded by pine woods. The main hotel is the Pension Mlini, category B and with nearly 150 beds, but there are several smaller ones.

If you look southwards from high points in Dubrovnik or from the island of Lokrum you can see a white dot amidst the brown and green landscape across the bay of Župski. This is the Račić Mausoleum which stands above the little town of Cavtat. The name comes from the Latin word "civitas", for nearby was the site of the ancient Epidaurus, a famous Greek city and the place from which refugees went to found Dubrovnik, as I have recounted. It is thought that the final destruction of Epidaurus, already sacked and fired by savage tribesmen from the interior, was due to an earthquake. The boatmen of Dubrovnik say that the ruins of the ancient city can be seen beneath the waters but that they are visible only at certain periods of the year, and then at dawn before the sun has risen high enough to reflect across the surface. I have never met anyone, except a boatman, who has seen the columns under the sea but it is an interesting story and one therefore hopes that it is more than just good salesmanship.

Cavtat itself needs no selling, for it is a delightful place. The old town, a warren of picturesque narrow streets, climbs up from a very sheltered harbour and it is full of quaint houses with their gardens blossoming with exotic flowers and lemon trees. There are two hotels, the Cavtat, category B and the Supetar, category C; they are pleasantly sited on the harbour and look across to the cypress-covered promontory on which stands the mausoleum. This was designed by the famous modern sculptor Ivan Meštrović. Wherever you go in Yugoslavia you will come across the works of Meštrović, who for many years dominated the national school of sculpture. His genius is a source of great national pride to the Yugoslavs, but much to their disappointment he settled in America.

The Račić Mausoleum was built for the rich and cultured family of that name, most of whom lost their lives during the influenza epidemic which swept Europe soon after the first world war. The monument is simple but impressive; the bronze doors depicting four Slav saints, a mosaic pavement and a figure of St. Rok with his dog are superb work of art.

Cavtat has a lesser claim to fame, but one which is a tribute to its peace and beauty. It used to be a favourite holiday place of the Duke and Duchess of Windsor and of the late Duke of Kent and the Duchess of Kent; and the local inhabitants will be sure to point out the villa in which they stayed if they discover that you are British.

When I was last at Cavtat I saw one of the groups of orphans one meets so frequently in Yugoslavia. There are probably more orphans in this country than any other in Europe, a sad result of the enormous loss of life during the war, when every ninth person in Yugoslavia was killed. The unfortunate children seem happy enough and they are well cared for, and the authorities have picked pleasant places for many of their homes. Cavtat is delightful; so, too, is the Kotor Fjord, east of Hercegnovi, where I saw another colony. Another was at Budva, but the children here have grown up and dispersed to adult homes and work and the former orphanage has recently been converted to a new use. It is now an hotel.

One of the most colourful sights to be seen in Dalmatia is at Ćilipi, a village five miles from Cavtat on the road to Hercegnovi. It is here that, every Sunday morning, most of the women of the village and many of the men attend mass at the Roman Catholic church in the picturesque costume of the Konavli. You can reach Ćilipi by taxi from Dubrovnik or you can take a motor-boat to Cavtat and walk from there to the

A FISHERMAN PREPARING HIS NETS   Plate 25

A common scene in any of the fishing towns and villages along the coast and also on the shores of the large lakes of Ohrid and Prespa in the southern-most part of Yugoslavia.

FISHING ON LAKE OHRID

Plate 26

The lake of Ohrid is rich in fish of many kinds and is famous for its excellent trout and for the red caviare,

A high proportion of the people of Macedonia wear local costume and the many races, including Albanians and Gypsies, each have their own style. This photograph was taken at Ohrid.

OHRID—OLD HOUSES AND THE CASTLE   Plate 28

Ohrid is dominated by a ruined castle, which guarded the approaches to the town for many centuries. It commands extensive views along the lake and across it to the mountains of Albania.

village. It is a hot and dusty pilgrimage but you will be well rewarded by the colourful scene in store.

Inside the church, surprisingly large for so small a place, you will find the men on the left and the women on the right, with the matrons of the village in the front and the unmarried girls behind them. When I was last there the long service was interrupted by a procession around the church. The men came out first, then the children, then the women. They gathered kneeling in a wide circle, with the village priest in a brilliant red cope in the centre, carrying the Host beneath a silken canopy. Then they went back into the church, which was full almost to overflowing, to finish the service. When it was over the women gathered in picturesque groups on the broad terrace of the church and beneath the trees in the village square, gossiping with each other and seemingly oblivious to the picturesque scene they were creating.

The excursion coaches from Dubrovnik on their way to Kotor and Cetinje pass by Ćilipi and go through the Konavli. This is a rich and lovely valley, with vines and other crops on its lower slopes and pines and cypresses higher up. Many of the women of the valley still wear the picturesque local costume, the matrons with wide starched bonnets, gleaming white in the sunshine, and the maidens with little red pork-pie hats. You sometimes see the same costumes in Dubrovnik, for the women of Konavli go to town in all their finery, but it is in the valley itself that you see it at its best. A few of the men also wear costume but it is mostly among the older ones that this has survived; indeed, this is true in most parts of the country. The men are rugged, typical peasants with their brown weather-beaten faces, but the Konavli women have a grace and

145

beauty which are renowned throughout the Balkans. It is said that the blood of the Greeks of Epidaurus runs in their veins, and this it is easy to believe.

The road runs up the valley and the land becomes poorer as you reach the pass through the hills of Sutorina, which divide Croatia from Montenegro. Then it descends steeply with many windings and with the great Fjord of Kotor far below. This great stretch of water, the Boka Kotorska, to give it its proper name today, cuts deeply into the jagged *karst* mountains and all around its shores are towns that were once important strongholds, usually dominated by castles. The entrance to the Boka was also guarded by two fortresses that must have been well-nigh impregnable. You will see from a map that there is an outer bay, about eight miles long and that then there is a narrow passage to a wider inner basin (called the Tivatski Zaljev) which is as long again; next there is an even narrower channel, less than half a mile wide, and it was across this that chain-booms were once stretched as defence against marauders. Finally is reached the innermost part of all, the bays of Kotor and Risan, ancient seaports which are very far from the open Adriatic. The Boka is surrounded by mountains which rise to several thousand feet, sometimes sheer from the water's edge.

Whether you come over from the Konavli by road or enter the Boka from the sea, you first reach Hercegnovi. The old name was Castelnuovo, signifying "new-castle" or "new town". It *was* new in 1382, when it was founded by the King of Bosnia as a salt depot to compete with Dubrovnik's monopoly of this commodity. Since then it has had a long and eventful history. The Spaniards were in possession for many years and the Turks held Hercegnovi for more than a century, and two forts, known as the Spanish Fort and the Saracen Fort, bear witness to their rule. Later it was taken by Venice and finally it passed into the hands of the Austrians.

Today it is a popular seaside resort, with hotels built on the terraces from which you descend to the little quay by a flight of one hundred steps. The climate of Hercegnovi is very equable. Cold days are rare even in mid-winter and there are many shady palms and colourful bougainvillaea. The main hotel is called the Boka, a good category B with a dining-terrace overlooking the water. There are several cheaper places at which to stay, including the pleasant Hotel Rudnik, and there is a Putnik office which organises many excursions by coach and by motor-boat. The town can be reached by steamer or bus from Dubrovnik or by the narrow-gauge railway which connects with the line from Sarajevo (a speedy direct diesel-car runs direct from Sarajevo and Mostar in summer; but you must bear in mind that you cannot travel by this unless you book a seat in advance). Finally, the airport of Gruda is nearer here than it is to Dubrovnik and on certain days of the week in summer airport coaches serve Hercegnovi.

The road around the Boka Kotorska is well-made, by southern Yugoslav standards, and runs the whole way along the shore, first through Zelenika, an important naval base where you can see trim little corvettes through a screen of brown sardine-nets hanging out to dry (and where, incidentally, you are not allowed to take photographs), next through Denović and Baošić and Bijela, sleepy little fishing villages— and then, if you are travelling by excursion coach you have a surprise. The coach stops, the passengers all

147

alight and the vehicle is driven on to one of the most insecure ferries I have ever seen; it is merely some planks laid across two small boats, and the big Putnik coaches just about fit it. You can stay in the coach (but nobody does!) or you can find a small area of plank which is not covered by coach and stand on that, or you can sit on the edge and dangle your feet in the water. It is all very unusual and exciting and you reach Lepetane on the opposite shore all too soon.

This is the short cut to Kotor. The public buses have to serve several villages yet and the rest of their journey is more than twice as long. They turn sharply into the Bay of Risan and you can see the twin churches of Perast ahead; then they make for Risan at one of the innermost points of the Boka. Along this stretch the barren hills descend steeply to the water, and in summer the masses of oleander blossom are a magnificent sight, pink against the grey-white limestone. Risan itself is of little interest, though I have heard some magnificent folk-singing there. As you pass it you will a see a large building that is a sanatorium (for tuberculosis has always been one of the scourges of the Balkans) and then you pass an important oil depot. Again, no photographs, please!

The next village is Perast, a fascinating place that is usually passed by on the bus but really deserves a visit. It used to be an independent principality and its sea-captains and sailors were reputed to be the most courageous and skilful of the Adriatic. The houses were once very beautiful and their shapely windows and balconies and the many coats of arms reveal the fact that Perast has had a rich and glorious past. The Venetians, too, have left their imprint on this lovely village, for in later years they built their summer villas

148

here and gave the navigators of Perast pride of place in their fleets. Just as Plymouth created the mariners of England, so did Perast those of the Adriatic, and rulers from lands as far off as Russia competed to enrol them in their navies.

Perast is now inhabited by fewer than a hundred people and most of the buildings are in ruins. It is a strange place; some may even think it macabre. In summer, when the pomegranates and azaleas are in flower and blossoms of subtler hues are competing with them to hide the ruins, it is indeed a beautiful place—but a sad one.

Off the shore at Perast are two tiny islands, a church on each of them, one Roman Catholic and the other Orthodox. These are the islands of Sv. Djordje and Gospa od Škrpjela. The Catholic church is topped by a spire, whereas the Orthodox one is domed. There is an interesting legend attached to the island of the Gospa. It is said that this was once but a piece of rock projecting from the waters and that to this a fisherman from Perast clung throughout one long stormy night, after his boat had been wrecked. In fear of losing his hold, he prayed to the Virgin Mary to save him and vowed that if she did so he would build a church for her on the rock. When the day came and the storm had subsided he was rescued by his friends of the town and they decided to assist him to fulfil his vow. Month after month, between their hours of labour, they rowed across to the rock with cargoes of stone in their small boats, and turned them into the water until they had made an island large enough to build the spired church which can be seen today.

The town of Kotor is a complete contrast with Perast. It is bustling and lively, always full of activity in its market-place and narrow stone-paved streets and on the harbour-front. It is an interesting town at which to stop for a day and there is one large hotel (the Slavija, category B) but it is not a town in which to spend a long holiday. Kotor has a famous cathedral of St. Tryphon dating from 1166 and is surrounded by walls two-and-a-half miles round. Three gates only lead through the battlements into the town itself, a warren of alleys in which you will often lose your way. You cannot even depend upon the sun to give you direction, so narrow are the streets and so numerous the carved, overhanging balconies of the houses. The shade is welcome, however, for Kotor can be a very hot place and it is too sheltered to have many breezes.

Above Kotor towers the mighty Lovćen, nearly 6,000 feet of mountain rising almost sheer from sea-level to twin summits which retain the snow for many months of the year. It appears to be difficult enough to climb on foot, yet if you look carefully you can discern the scores of windings of a road and, on a day when the air is clear, you may even see a bus descending the serpentines, clinging like a fly to the mountainside. This is the famous Lovćen road, without a doubt one of the most outstanding feats of road-engineering in the world. You can also discern, about half-way up, the white building that was the guard-house on the frontier between Austria and the Principality of Montenegro.

It is here that the road divides today. The left-hand branch begins to wind in ever more exciting spirals as it climbs to the Lovćen Pass, whilst the other descends more directly to Budva, by the sea. I will first take you over the mountains and then return to continue the journey down the coast.

I doubt if any tourist has yet succeeded in counting the number of hairpin bends there are on the road from Kotor to the top of Lovćen. I have started to count them three times at least, but the view is so breath-taking that on each occasion I have soon forgotten to count. The road itself is breath-taking, too, for most people! You peer down almost directly to the waters of the Boka below, first on one side of the bus and then on the other, until you seem to lose all sense of time and of direction. Finally, you reach the summit-pass and have one more look at the picture beneath you before the road drops again towards Cetinje. There is Kotor, now so tiny, far below and you can see Perast too, with its two island-churches, and far-off Hercegnovi, and the wide sweep of mountains all round the Boka. It is a view in which land and water compete for the favour of your interest, and one that you will always remember.

The road now drops into the fertile valley of Njeguši from which came the clansmen who became the princes of Montenegro through many generations. They established their capital at Cetinje and, rallying the fierce tribesmen against Turks and Austrians alike, maintained their little country's independence and ruled for more than two centuries. During the long period when the whole of present-day Yugoslavia was under the yoke of foreign powers, Montenegro was a symbol of South Slav freedom. The most famous son of the Petrović-Njegoš family (or perhaps I should say "nephew" for the succession always passed from uncle to nephew and not from father to son) was Prince-Bishop Petar, who was born in 1813. He is famous today not for his work as ruler but for his poetry. He is regarded as the greatest poet of the Yugoslav languages and his "Mountain Wreath", a poetical drama, glorifying the struggles of the Montenegrins to maintain their independence, has been translated into many languages, including English.

I will now leave inland Montenegro and return to the road to Budva, which we left at the guard-house high above Kotor. The journey from there to the coast takes you through an arid valley, though below on a broad, flat plain, stretching to the shores of the Boka, you can see some rich fields. This is the plain of Župa and I was told that it was one of the country's most prosperous and successful co-operative farming enterprises. Soon Budva comes in sight, a fishing-village on a spit of land projecting into the sea. It was once an island and the isthmus connecting it with the mainland is artificial. The old village is encircled by high defensive walls and is another maze of tiny streets, like several I have already described.

Outside the old Budva a new one has grown up in recent years. The finest hotel is the Avala (category B), comfortable, excellently maintained and with a magnificent terrace commanding wide views of the coast. Unfortunately its modern design does not blend at all well with the medieval village. There are other hotels and pensions, of course, but the standards are nothing like so good as those of the Avala.

In my opinion the stretch of coast between Budva and Bar is the finest in the whole of the Yugoslav littoral, and Budva itself the most attractive place in that stretch. Words cannot convey the beauty of its situation—a wide sweep of bay with the mountains rising high above. It is a good centre, too, for the friendly little Putnik office runs some interesting excursions—by coach to Dubrovnik, Cetinje (via the

Lovćen pass in one direction) and Ulcinj, and to Miločer, Sv. Stefan and other nearby places by motor-boat. Unfortunately access to Budva is not particularly easy and you have to study time-tables with care. The fast steamers from Rijeka to Dubrovnik continue to Budva only once a week and there are two of the slow boats which also call; there is, too, a service most days of the week between Herçegnovi and Budva, but even Hercegnovi is not the easiest place to reach. There is also a daily bus from Dubrovnik, but here I must issue a warning. It is not difficult to get a seat on the bus from Dubrovnik, because it starts there, but in the reverse direction the bus starts from Ulcinj and it may well be full by the time it reaches Budva.

You can spend a very pleasant holiday at this lovely village. There are some good bathing beaches, delightful walks and small boats for hire. Only one thing really spoils Budva, and that is the "music" which blares forth from loud-speakers in the street. This is not my first protest against something which is so out of harmony with the character of the village that it will spoil it as a tourist resort unless it is stopped. I have told the Putnik manager my views on the matter and I have written to the local authorities in no uncertain terms. Jazz does not blend with a medieval fishing village, and even its most fervent devotee will regret that it comes through the loud-speakers at Budva. I am told that the Yugoslavs do not like it and I am sure that every foreign visitor who has travelled so far must hate it.

The next place on the coast is Miločer, which is a hotel and nothing more. It was built by King Alexander of Yugoslavia (the one who was assassinated at Marseilles) as a summer palace. It stands in a lovely bay.

153

In front of it there is a long terrace and then a beach and the sea. It is in very beautiful grounds, with paths and arbours shaded by flowering shrubs and trees of many varieties. It is a category B hotel and you can reach it by direct bus from Dubrovnik (but remember the warnings I have already given about getting on the bus in the other direction) or by taxi from Budva. It is not a place for the excursionist; for honeymooners I can think of nowhere better in Yugoslavia or, indeed, in all Europe.

From the terrace at Miločer you can see Sveti Stefan, half a mile away, one of the most interesting and unusual villages in Europe. It is not unique, because it is rather like Mont St. Michel off the coast of Brittany, a village crowded on a small promontory connected to the mainland only by a narrow strip of gravel. You will see photographs of Sv. Stefan wherever you go in Yugoslavia, yet it is very seldom visited and you will almost certainly have it to yourself. It once housed several hundred families but it has been neglected for many generations and now there are but five. Fortunately the present government has decreed it to be a national monument and work of reconstruction has begun. It will take many, many years to complete and then Sv. Stefan will be one of the wonders of the world.

The next interesting village on the coast is Petrovac, a little resort with under three hundred inhabitants but yet with two hotels—the Palace and the Sutjeska, both of them category B but very cheap indeed, no doubt because of their remoteness from any form of communication except the daily bus from Dubrovnik and the steamer six days a week from Hercegnovi, both going on to Ulcinj. Even the steamer cannot call in at Petrovac; it stops off-shore and passengers are taken out by rowing-boat. Embarkation is quite exciting if the sea is choppy; if it is rough the people of Petrovac have to wait until the next day. Their village is set amid olive-groves and orchards behind a sandy bay, with two islets off the shore making it even more picturesque.

For ten miles beyond Petrovac the coast is more than usually rugged, with steep cliffs descending to the sea and without even a village. Then comes Sutomore, which I have seen only from the deck of the steamer as it cuts across the bay to Bar. It looks delightful from the distance and I am told there is a pension there and a long sandy beach. A place yet to be explored!

Bar certainly has a beach—a stretch of sand nearly two miles long. It lies in a very large bay, dominated by the mountain of Rumija. The situation is very beautiful but Bar is not a place at which to stay long because the new town, by the shore, is being developed into a large port, and the old town, although very picturesque with old Moslem houses and Turkish forts, is three miles inland. Before many years have passed Bar will be a very important place, the Rijeka of the south. Not only is the excellent harbour to be developed commercially but a new railway is being constructed to link Bar with Belgrade. This is one of the most ambitious engineering undertakings of Yugoslavia. If you look at a map of the country you will see that to the north and north-east of Bar and Titograd there is a large area, which has no railway lines at present. It also has few roads. This region, including almost the whole of Montenegro and a large stretch of Serbia, is to be traversed by the new railway line. There are high mountains right across this part of Yugoslavia and the route will be a very winding one. I have been told that it will include a tunnel several miles long beneath Mt. Durmitor, the highest and wildest mountain in Montenegro.

Finally I bring you to Ulcinj and we have completed our long journey down the coast of Dalmatia. At this last town in Yugoslavia you find a different atmosphere from anywhere further north, for Ulcinj is part of the East as much as the rest of the coast is part of the West. Everywhere we have travelled so far we have been subject to the influences of Venice and Dubrovnik and later of Austria; here at Ulcinj the dominating influence was that of Turkey. It was the port from which the Moslem pirates descended upon the Christian settlements all along the coast and, indeed, much further afield. There is evidence of this in the negroes who still live in the town, descendants of men and women who were seized as slaves when the ships of Ulcinj went plundering the coasts of Africa.

If you have been to other towns which were once Turkish, in Bosnia or Macedonia, you may be disappointed with Ulcinj. If you have not had this experience I can recommend a visit, as you will be able to see costumes and mosques which exist nowhere else on the coast. There is a bathing-beach, which was very crowded when I last saw it, and a few hotels. I have already mentioned the daily bus between here and Dubrovnik.

Ulcinj can be said to be the last place on the coast of Yugoslavia. The remaining ten miles are flat and of no interest and, at the end, there is the marshy island of Vada and the river Bojana—one bank in Yugoslavia and the other in Albania.

(vii) THROUGH MONTENEGRO AND KOSMET TO MACEDONIA

The tourist who leaves the coast and turns inland discovers that as soon as the first ranges of hills have been crossed he is in a very different country. It is not an exaggeration to say that inland he will find a different civilisation. Everyone who can possibly spare the time to do so should divide his holiday between the coast and the other Yugoslavia which lies behind the mountains. In recent years many holiday-makers have returned home, after visits to Rijeka, Split and Dubrovnik and perhaps a few excursions, with the impression that this is a rich and very beautiful land but not so very different from much of Western Europe. Had they travelled inland they would have discovered that half the country is as unlike the West as is Turkey. You must leave the coast in order to find the Yugoslavia of the Balkans.

I have already traced the road from Dubrovnik and Hercegnovi over the Lovćen as far as Njeguši. It goes on to Cetinje, the former capital of Montenegro, and this is the farthest point which is reached by the tourist coaches from the coast. Already, however, you will be conscious of the difference. The people seem poorer and you see many in costume, though not the gay and spotless costume of the Konavli, but something which seems nearer to the soil, coarse and homespun. The air is drier and the roads more dusty, in keeping with the barren rocks and mountains. Even the writing is different, for now we have reached a country in which the Cyrillic characters are used.

Cetinje itself, it is true, is set in a rich, green valley; but it is a small one and is like an oasis amidst the

arid *karst*. It is very drab, too, the houses plain and
without any of the graceful adornments to which we
have become accustomed in Dalmatia. To be frank,
it is a dull town, but its museum is quite interesting.
The large building, stolid as everything else in Cetinje,
was the former royal palace. It was from here that the
Njegoš family organised the defences which kept their
territory inviolate for centuries; it was here that they
held court and received ambassadors from all countries
of the world, right up to the twentieth century. An
exhibit of much interest to me is in a nearby building,
specially constructed to house it. It is an enormous
relief-model of Montenegro which, so I was told, the
last King constructed so that he could at any time survey his territories. At a guess, its area must be about
six or seven hundred square yards. You can walk all
around it (and over it too by a bridge like the one in
the willow-plate pattern) and the wildness of it will
give you an impression of the whole of Montenegro,
from the coast right across to the great mountain of
Durmitor and beyond.

In books published before the war I have read of a
servant of the last King of Montenegro who changed
his rôle to that of a museum attendant. When I was
last at Cetinje he was still there, his military bearing and
his big waxed moustaches a kind of memory from the
days of old when these corridors, now filled with show-
cases and photographs, rustled with the silk of fine
dresses or rang with the bugles of the palace guards.
Today he does not disdain a tip as he bids you good-
bye at the doorway and you descend the steps and go
out into the blazing sunshine.

A night spent at Cetinje does not cost much, for

though the hotel is called the Grand and is graded in category B, it is not at all expensive.

The road to Titograd climbs out of the valley of Cetinje and then runs downhill for ten miles or so, until you reach Rijeka Crnojevića. By now the hills are less barren and there are many trees. Rijeka itself, at the head of the Lake of Scutari, is a charming village; its old houses, tinted with many different pastel shades, have picturesque outside staircases and wooden balconies.

The big lake, which the Yugoslavs call Skadarsko Jezero, is shared with Albania and the frontier between the two countries cuts across the centre of it. (I wonder what has been the fate of any Yugoslav fishermen whom the north-west wind has driven towards the southern end!) There has been talk of draining part of the lake, for it is very shallow and could add a rich tract of land both to Yugoslavia and Albania. Co-operation between the two countries would be essential, however, and unless there is a great change of political outlook it will be a long time before such a scheme could be seriously considered.

The road climbs again after it leaves Rijeka Crnojevića and there are wide views down the lake and across to the four peaks of the Prokletije, the "accursed mountains" of Albania. Then it starts descending and you can see a wide and well-cultivated plain and there, in the distance, is the city of Titograd. It might be more correct to say it *will* be the city of Titograd, for until recently it was quite a small place, a Turkish market town with no political importance. Now it has replaced Cetinje as the capital of Montenegro and an extensive scheme of urban development is afoot. As at so many places in Yugoslavia, unfortunately, they have built splendid government offices and public buildings before flats and houses; but the tourist reaps the benefit because he has the opportunity of staying at one of the most palatial hotels in the country. It had been opened only ten days when I was there in the spring of 1953 and it was not quite in working order, but I could see how magnificent it would be. Yet on looking out of my window I could see below the hotel a battered dwelling, fit only to be demolished, which was still being occupied by a family who were doubtless on the local "housing list". In fairness to official policy I must say, however, that at Titograd as elsewhere the people seem to be very proud of the great public buildings which have been erected and take much delight in pointing them out to the visitor. The name of the hotel is the Crna Gora and it is classified in category B. Crna Gora is the Serbo-Croat word for Montenegro and means the same— Black Mountain.

From Titograd a road and railway lead up the valley of the river Zeta to Nikšić. Some twelve miles short of this town is the shrine of Ostrog, famous for its frescoes and because it is carved out of the solid rock. It is one of the very few monasteries in Montenegro, but we shall see many more soon, in Kosmet and Macedonia. Nikšić is a rapidly developing industrial town and has little to commend it to the tourist. For the adventurous person it can, however, form the starting point for an exciting tour of several days, on foot or mule-back, over Mt. Durmitor and by the Black Lake to Foča, on the River Drina, and Sarajevo. The less hardy tourist can penetrate this region by bus, for a daily service runs from Titograd *via* Nikšić to Žabljak, skirting Durmitor on its way, and from Žabljak it is

CARPET MAKING

Plate 29

In many parts cf Yugoslavia the making of carpets is still a home-craft, usually carried cn by the women. The district around Pirot is especially noted for the beauty of their work.

AT KLADOVO ON THE DANUBE

The Danube is a very varied river, sometimes flowing placidly past green meadows and rich corn-lands, at other times rushing over rocks and through deep gorges. Kladovo, famous for caviare, is in one of the peaceful stretches downstream from the famous Iron Gates.

Plate 30

Plate 31

THE PARLIAMENT HOUSE, BELGRADE

Belgrade is the capital of Serbia and the chief city of the Federal Republic. Apart from its ancient fortress, overlooking the Sava and Danube rivers, it has little of historic interest. There are, however, some imposing public buildings, such as the Parliament House depicted below, and also some outstanding examples of modern architecture.

TREBINJE IN HERCEGOVINA   Plate 32

Many of the smaller inland towns and villages of southern Yugoslavia are
very picturesque and the kind of scene depicted above is by no means uncommon. Gradually, however, modern buildings are replacing the ramshackle
houses of former days.

possible to take other buses to Pljevalja and on to the railway line from Priboj to Sarajevo.

The village of Žabljak is a delightful centre. It is nearly 5,000 feet above sea-level and has a pleasant summer climate. The famous Black Lake is half a mile from the village and a little to the north are the deep canyons of the River Tara. Pine trees give character to the landscape and above them towers Durmitor, with snow on its northern slopes for many months of the year. There is a fine category B hotel here, the Hotel Durmitor, located on a wooded plateau with wide views from its garden and terraces.

Another road from Titograd goes to the north-east and then divides, one fork going to Kolašin and Bijelo Polje, the other to Andrijevica and Peć. It rises from the fertile basin of Titograd and climbs steeply into the mountains, along the gorges of the Morača river and through the impressive defile of Veternik. Then it descends again and reaches Mateševo and there you must choose which way you will go. Kolašin on the Tara river is a quiet, mountain-holiday village, beloved by many Yugoslavs. The woods which surround the town are more varied than in most of the south— beech, maple and ash mingle with the pines and firs, a riot of colour, especially in the autumn. The hotel (category B) of Kolašin is the Bjelasica, named after the nearby mountains. Twelve miles or so from Kolašin is the little Biogradsko Jezero (lake), set in forests which have been declared a Nature Reserve and in which hunting and shooting are forbidden. The Tara itself is a wild yet beautiful river, descending with many waterfalls through very deep gorges.

The other road-fork at Mateševo goes to Andrijevica and on to Peć. The whole route from Titograd to Peć

161

is traversed by a daily bus in each direction but it is a summer service only, for the pass of Trešnjevik is over 5,000 feet high and that of Čakor reaches nearly 5,600 feet, and they are snowbound until late in the spring. They are usually opened to traffic about the beginning of May. Unfortunately this prevents me from describing the route from personal knowledge, for my visits to Titograd have been too early in the year. Friends of mine who have crossed these passes in June have told me that it is one of the most beautiful and exciting roads on which they have travelled, more impressive even than that of Lovćen.

Peć can also be reached from the east, being connected by a comparatively new railway with one of the lines joining Belgrade and Skopje. It has several hotels, including the Metohija (category C) which is cheap, clean and simple. It is one of the principal towns of Kosmet or, to give it its full name, the region of Kosovo and Metohija. This is part of Serbia but, like the Vojvodina region farther to the north, it enjoys a measure of local autonomy.

Kosmet is a land of history. It is full of ancient monasteries, of fortresses whose stones were cemented with lead to defy the centuries, of folk-lore and of costume. In this region, too, is the Field of Kosovo, the great battle of 1389 in which the Serbs were finally defeated, to remain for centuries under the rule of the Turks. The influence of the East is noticeable everywhere in Kosmet and farther on in Macedonia, and the predominating features of every village are the tall, white minarets of the mosques. The call of the muezzin, heard through many centuries, is still heard everywhere today, for the majority of the inhabitants were converted to the faith of Islam. Yet side by side with this religion of Asia is the flowering of the art and culture of the Greek Orthodox Church, seen here as nowhere else in Europe.

Through most of the years of Turkish domination, Peć was the seat of the Orthodox Patriarch of Serbia. It is difficult to think of a parallel in the histories with which more western people are familiar. Suppose that the Moors, having pressed on from Spain, had conquered France and England, but had permitted Canterbury to remain the centre of western Christianity, with its Archbishop continuing to exercise his spiritual jurisdiction over the western world. You can imagine how Canterbury would then have remained a symbol of faith and hope for the nations forced to submit to the yoke of the infidel. So it was with Peć through many centuries. Indeed for one period the national feeling became so strong that the Turks abolished the Patriarchate and it was a Serbian Grand Vizir, a convert to Islam, who later gave his permission for its revival. In later years the Patriarchate actively intrigued with foreign powers and became a focal point for the co-ordination of sporadic rebellions.

Peć today is a colourful town with a very mixed population, many of them in their local costume, ranging from the *zars* or "baggy trousers" of the Turkish women to the black and white garb of the Albanians. The narrow streets are delightful to wander in, with here and there a stately minaret dominating all. The patriarchal church is not so beautiful as many others you can see in the south, but its historical associations make it interesting.

From Peć you should go to Prizren, forty-five miles to the south-east. Soon it will be possible to go by rail, for a new line is being constructed, but the bus journey will still be more attractive. A dozen miles along this road brings you to High Dečani, one of the most famous of all the monasteries of South Serbia. It lies over a mile from the road, on the right-hand side, up an avenue of chestnut trees. (Many of these monasteries, you will discover, are well off the normal routes of communication.) Its architect was from Kotor and he mixed the Romanesque and Byzantine styles in this masterpiece of red and grey marble. The carvings around the doors and windows are of birds and animals, leaves and flowers, and the inside of the church is completely covered with frescoes. The work was commissioned in 1327 by King Stefan Uroš III of Serbia and it was completed eight years later. It can have changed but little during the succeeding six hundred years.

There were many hundreds of such monasteries in the Balkans, most of them built and decorated in the period from the twelfth to the fifteenth centuries. When the Turks extended their power over all these lands a large number of monasteries were damaged and some were left to decay into ruins, while others, as we shall see at Prizren and elsewhere, were turned into mosques. Every visitor to the south of Yugoslavia will inevitably see some of them; the difficulty is not to turn your holiday into a pilgrimage. I shall therefore mention only the outstanding ones, and those which are easiest of access. High Dečani comes into the first class and, because of its richness and the originality of its architecture, deserves the special place it has always enjoyed in the catalogue of monasteries of South Serbia.

The road to Prizren is beautiful enough, but it lacks the impressive character of others we have traversed. Prizren itself is another town of beauty and of history.

It nestles in a curve of the hills and the upper part, of narrow and tortuous streets, is constructed on a natural amphitheatre. Much of the town is extremely primitive. In its market-place, one of the most interesting in Yugoslavia, you can see the peasants selling the products of their home-crafts—silver ornaments, copperware, woven silks and the most delicate, beautiful embroidery. There are mosques, of course, and a church which was used as a mosque for centuries, with its frescoes covered up with plaster. You can stay at the Hotel Šar, a very simple category C.

The mountains to the south of the town are the great range of the Šar Planina and they form an impenetrable barrier except to people on foot or on skis. To reach Skopje one must make a long detour, by bus to Uroševac and then by railway—and having spent most of one night on the platform of Uroševac station I can tell you that the connections are not all good ones.

(viii) MACEDONIA

There can be few names which have survived through the centuries as "Macedonia" has done. We read of it in classical history as one of the districts of northern Greece and again, in later years, as a province of the Roman Empire. Then it lost its political unity, but the name was still used for nearly two thousand years to describe an area which had no precise boundaries. The survival of the name, however, gave rise to intense nationalism when the power of Turkey was on the wane. At first this national feeling tended towards the goal of unity with Bulgaria but later, with the formation of the Internal Macedonian Revolutionary Organisation (I. M. R. O.) in 1893, the aim changed to that of complete independence.

Nearly twenty years of guerilla activity against the Turks came to an end shortly before the first world war, when the Serbs, Greeks and Bulgarians joined in a struggle which resulted in the virtual extinction of Turkey-in-Europe. Then they quarrelled about the spoils, each of them claiming the lion's share of Macedonia. When the Great War came Bulgaria was neutral for more than a year, using her claim to Macedonia as a bargaining factor between the Germans and the Allies. Finally she received a promise from Germany that Macedonia should be hers; but she had backed the losing side and Macedonia became part of Serbia in the new Kingdom of Yugoslavia.

But the people of Macedonian stock stretched well beyond the Yugoslav borders, into Albania and Greece and most of all into Bulgaria, and I. M. R. O., operating from the part of Macedonia which was still within the frontier of Bulgaria, waged an incessant struggle for independence from Serbs and Bulgars alike. The period of terrorism continued until 1933. In the second world war the Yugoslavs obtained the support of Macedonian nationalists by promising them autonomy and cultural freedom, and in 1945 the Republic of Macedonia became a reality.

There are still many Macedonians beyond the borders of Yugoslavia, and on the other hand many of the people in the new Republic belong to minority races—Turks, Vlachs, Gypsies, and especially the Albanians who alone account, according to a 1948 census, for seventeen per cent of the population. It is these varied minority peoples, one in three of the whole population of Macedonia, who add colour and interest to the country today.

However you travel to Macedonia you are almost certain to arrive at Skopje, the capital of the Republic. One ought to speak of Skopje in the plural, for there are certainly two of them. On the north side of the Vardar is the old town, the Turkish Üsküb, with its winding streets and wooden buildings, its many mosques and ancient monastery; on the south side is the new Skopje, mostly built since 1919.

If you travel to Skopje by air or by rail you go straight into the modern town. The palatial new station is at the end of the principal shopping street, the Maršala Tita, and the air-terminal is but a couple of hundred yards away. Here, too, is the Putnik office, with a very helpful staff. The Hotel Skopje (category C) is nearby and at the other end of the Maršala Tita are the Makedonija and Arapska Kuča (both category B). The name of the latter means "Arab House", but its nightmare architecture is seen only in the Arabia of the pantomimes.

You will not be long in Skopje before you walk down the length of the main street and across the stone bridge to the old town. If you carry straight on and then bear to the left you will see the walls of the ancient city fortress, from the battlements of which there is an excellent view over the roof-tops. The dominating features are the minarets—for there are more than thirty mosques in Skopje, one of them claiming to have the tallest minaret in the world. The most beautiful of the mosques, dating from the fifteenth century, is that of Mustapha Pasha.

In great contrast to these Moslem places of worship is the church of Sveti Spas. It is built half underground and when you have passed through its cool and beautiful courtyard you will go down several steps to enter the church itself. It was constructed in this fashion because the Turks decreed that no Christian church should be higher than the roof-tops of their houses. The glory of Sv. Spas is the carved wooden iconostasis, the screen separating the sanctuary from the main part of the church. It was the work of two brothers from the village of Galičnik, near the Albanian frontier, and it depicts many of the stories of the Bible. You can pick out Adam and Eve, Jonah being swallowed by the whale and dozens more; there are scenes from the New Testament, too. Away in a corner is a scene that is not from the Bible; it is a carving of the carvers themselves, seated at a work-bench and creating the beautiful screen which is around them.

Another building of great interest is the Kuršumli Han. A han, or caravanserai, was a place at which the caravans would stop on their journeys and there are many of them in the Balkans. It usually consists of a large courtyard, in which the camels were tethered, with small square rooms all round which were used for sleeping and for business transactions. The Kuršumli Han is of rather a different style, much larger than is customary, and there is a theory that it was built by the Romans. Whether or not there is any truth in this, there is certainly a link with Dubrovnik for this was one of the chief markets of the merchants of that town, who used Skopje as a centre for the collection of goods from all over the East. The Kuršumli Han is now a museum. There is an art museum nearby—in a building that was once a Turkish bath-house!

As you pass through the streets you may see that

even this old town is really two, for there is a Gypsy quarter with even more cramped dwellings than those of the Turkish part. All the time, on this side of the river, you will be fascinated by the many types of costumes worn by the women, and by a few of the men too. Skopje is also a good place for the souvenir hunter. In many of the Turkish shops you can see fine examples of hand-work—leather goods, embroidery, exquisite wood-carving and articles of silver.

There is little of interest in the new Skopje—except the Korzo. It takes place in the Maršala Tita and it seems as if the whole city has turned out for the evening stroll—and Skopje now has a population of more than a hundred thousand! They take up the whole width of the road and both pavements as they go up and down the street, and it is fortunate that cars in Macedonia are so few. The Korzo here is one of the most animated scenes in Yugoslavia and it is colourful too, for there are always many people in costume.

In the Putnik office at Skopje I met a lady who was touring the Balkans with an exhibition of ballet, on behalf of the British Council, and who was negotiating for a taxi to take her to Nerezi, a few miles outside the city. She gladly accepted my offer to share the cost, but the taxi never materialised and, in the end, a British resident of the city kindly offered to lend his. You may not be as lucky as we were, but even if you have to go all the way on foot it is a pilgrimage that is worth while. Indeed, even if you go by car you have to walk the last mile or two, so rough is the only road. Nerezi is a ramshackle yet picturesque little village clinging to the hillside above the Vardar and it has one of the most ancient monasteries in Yugoslavia. It was built in 1164 by the Governor of the district and is a perfect example of Byzantine architecture. The frescoes are among the oldest in the Balkans, and although some were crudely re-painted during the nineteenth century there are many that can be seen today as at any time during the last six or seven hundred years. Even if you know nothing of art and architecture you must still go to Nerezi, to breathe its atmosphere of peace and beauty.

There are other interesting journeys which can be made from Skopje. You can go by bus as far as Strumica in the south-eastern corner of the country or to Kratovo, due east of the city; there is a railway, too, which goes out *via* Titov Veles to Štip and Kočane. All this eastern part of Macedonia is mountainous and very seldom visited, even by the Yugoslavs. Shorter excursions include the famous Markov monastery, the Turkish village of Bardovci and the church of Sv. Andrija at Matka. There are many other places of equal interest, but the difficulty is to find the transport to reach them. This is an undiscovered land from the standpoint of the foreign tourist and even educated Yugoslavs in other parts of the country will ask you to tell them about Macedonia, when they learn that you have been there.

Skopje is on the Simplon-Orient route to Salonica and Athens. The main line crosses the frontier at Gevgeli, passing through the gorge of Demir Kapija, the gateway through which the culture of Greece spread northwards. To the east of Gevgeli is the little lake of Dojran, where fishermen employ the strangest angling method I have ever heard of. They surround part of the water, just off the shore, with a kind of wicker fence, use trained birds to drive the fish into the trap and then close the gates and collect the fish in nets.

In this southern part of Yugoslavia the temperature is very high by the middle of the morning, and the wise tourist will rise at dawn and do his sightseeing during the cooler hours—especially if much walking has to be done. You will welcome the opportunity of catching early-morning trains, too, like the one for Titov Veles and Bitola which leaves Skopje at about 6 a.m. It is a journey of about five and a half hours. From Skopje to Veles you are following in the wake of the old caravans which passed this way to and from the East. Even in Greek and Roman times this was one of the busiest of highways. After the railway line has turned south-west at Veles (a characteristic Turkish town but very, very hot), the country becomes almost desert-like in its barrenness, but it soon crosses a range of hills and begins to descend again to the wide and fertile plain of Prilep.

This is tobacco country. Macedonia produces about sixty per cent of the tobacco of Yugoslavia and a high proportion of it comes from around Prilep, which claims to have the largest curing station in the whole of Europe. A favourite but comparatively expensive brand of cigarette, packed in the American "Chesterfield" fashion, is named after the town; and they are very good indeed. The whole economy of this region is tied to tobacco; one wonders what would happen if the Yugoslavs, who are nowadays heavy smokers, were no longer able to afford so many cigarettes.

Outside modern Prilep, with its factories and packing stations, is a hill made of volcanic rocks piled higgledy-piggledy one upon the other, and on the top are the ruins of a fortress. This was the town of Marko Kraljević, one of the most famous warrior-princes of Macedonian folklore. Here, too, are several churches dating from before the year 1400 and another beautiful monastery, Sv. Arhangel.

The railway line and the road continue along the Prilep basin and the next town reached is Bitola. It was once called Monastir, more recently Bitolj; the reason for the latest change is that many names in this Republic have been altered from their Serbian or Bulgarian spellings and pure Macedonian forms have been adopted. "Skoplje" was changed to "Skopje" for the same reason.

As you approach Bitola you can see the minarets of its many mosques, but your attention is more likely to be fixed on the lofty Mt. Perister which rises high above, its summit and higher slopes covered with snow until late in the spring.

The railway station is some way from the town itself, the approach being through a park which is very gay with flowers in the early summer. There is an ancient bus which carries some of the train's passengers into Bitola; the rest have to walk, but there is no lack of ragged men who beset them with offers to carry their luggage. The best hotel is the Trudbenik (category C) on the left of the road from the station to the main square. In the square itself is a big theatre and, facing it, the Putnik office. This was being reconstructed when I was last at Bitola but the manager found plenty of time to talk to me about his town.

He told me something of its history and of how it was a favourite place with the richer Turks, who built residences here. There is even today a high proportion of Turks and Albanians among the local proportion—and the town has thirty-five mosques but only five churches. My friend of Putnik plans to organise a number of very interesting excursions—by road or

172

railway (not yet re-opened when I was there) across the frontier to Salonika; to Oteševo on Lake Prespa and to Ohrid; and walking and climbing expeditions up Perister (over 8,000 feet high) and the other nearby mountains. You can, if you wish, spend many days climbing here and there are several mountain huts.

At Bitola the railway line goes directly towards Greece and connections with the two lakes on the frontier are by means of a local bus. It starts from Bitola, so you have a good chance of getting a seat, especially with the assistance of the Putnik manager. The road soon begins to climb steeply and winds in zig-zags to the crest of a range of hills, always with Perister and its outliers on view on the left. I remember that when we were just short of the summit we met a team of oxen as we rounded a blind corner; they were running pell-mell downhill, faster than I have ever seen oxen moving before; for a moment it looked as if the oxen and the bus, full of passengers and with its roof piled high with all kinds of luggage—including a perambulator—would be pitched together over the brink of the road, down, down. . . When I opened my eyes and when the dust had subsided there was the driver of the oxen hurling imprecations at the driver of the bus. The latter shrugged his shoulders, everyone laughed and exchanged banter with him, and we drove on. This sort of encounter is quite common on the roads and nobody seems to mind. The bus chauffeurs are excellent drivers, knowing every inch of these dangerous mountain roads, but traffic is so rare that they take chances which sometimes make one's blood run cold. However, the locals do not seem to object, so there cannot be many accidents.

When the crest of the road is reached a new scene

opens before you. Away on the left is a range of high mountains and beneath them is the Prespansko Jezero, a lake that is divided between Yugoslavia, Greece and Albania. It is a very wild landscape, but a lovely one. On a clear day it should be possible to pick out the newly-built holiday centre of Oteševo on the far shore. Here is a collection of half a dozen hotels, run as one unit, and a magnificent beach. It is a kind of holiday village, with its own sports facilities, a collecttion of boats of all kinds from canoes to pleasure-steamers, and with a programme of excursions by coach every week of the season. There is even a special dormitory villa for the younger visitors and a children's restaurant. The lake itself is interesting. It has no outlet except beneath the level of the water, and it is believed that it drains through underground channels into Lake Ohrid, the level of which is about five hundred feet lower.

The road from Bitola to Ohrid passes by the fork to Oteševo and descends sharply to Resen. The bus makes a stop here and you will have time to walk around the town, which is renowned for its beautiful metal work. But for me, Resen means pottery and dancing children. They were dancing in a little square in the main street, railed off as a playground. There were a dozen of them, dressed in the clothes of Alice in Wonderland with "pinnies" and long black stockings, and they danced sometimes in a ring and sometimes one following the other in a chain, stamping their feet as they sang the tune; they kept perfect time, even the tiniest of them who could not have been a day over three. I have not seen the dance anywhere else; it certainly was not one of the usual *kolo* type. Then there are the pots. A long, market-street which is

174

literally full of pottery of all shapes and sizes. It is a very colourful scene.

When I travelled last on the Simplon-Orient Express I met a lady from America who was going back to see her parents at Resen and only a week later, in Belgrade, I met two American boys who were being taken by their father to see his old home, also in this town. I thought it was a coincidence but I heard later that it used to be the common thing for the inhabitants of this remote little place to emigrate to America and to return when they had "made their pile". It was estimated, before the war, that only one in four of the men of the town had not been across the Atlantic!

From Resen to Ohrid the road at first climbs again, then begins to descend through gorges. There are a few picturesque villages here, especially Opejnca, near to which I noticed two women, clad in gay costume, sitting outside their cottage working wih distaffs. A grimmer sight was a party of convicts breaking stones for road-repairs. The Lake of Ohrid, or Ohridsko Jezero, comes into sight quite suddenly and soon you are in the town itself.

Just as we have seen that there are two Skopjes, so there are two Ohrids, one old and one new. The whole of the interest of Ohrid is in the old town, but I shall provide some practical information about the new town first. It has been constructed along the shore of the lake—a string of new buildings, including hotels, behind of tree-shaded promenade. The hotel I can recommend, quite inexpensive, is the Bellevue (or Belvi, to use the local spelling). Most of its rooms overlook the lake, as do many of those in its annexe, the Turist. A larger hotel is the Gorica, but it is rather a long way from the interesting part of the town; it has, however, an excellent situation on the lake-shore. The Workers' Rest Centre, magnificently situated by a lovely beach, is now used as a hotel and is connected to Ohrid itself by motor-boat. All these places have been classified in category C. Also in the new town are a monumental Post Office and a theatre. The Putnik office is at the entrance to the main street of the old town and nearby is the bus station and the harbour from which steamboats operate a service down the lake.

The old part of Ohrid is as difficult to describe as it is to visit. There is so much of it and it is so complicated that one knows not where to begin, and its many beautiful scenes are so distracting that one soon loses one's way. It is built on a hilly promontory, jutting out into the lake. The summit of the hill is crowned by a castle, ruined but still very impressive, which dominates the approaches to the town. Beneath it is a fantastic maze of narrow cobbled streets, climbing one above the other up the hillside, joined by series of steep slopes and steps. Many of the houses are tall, and their upper stories protrude towards each other, so that sometimes it seems as if one is walking beneath archways. Lower still in the town are the smaller houses of the fishermen, huddled together along the lake-shore.

Along the bottom of the hill runs the "High Street" of Ohrid, the shops on either side more modern than most things in the town. Quite a number of them sell tawdry souvenirs, for Ohrid has become a popular holiday centre for the Yugoslavs; but fortunately it has not been spoiled. The twentieth century has not been allowed to penetrate into the parts of Ohrid which date from the eleventh or even before. At the end of this main street (through which, I should mention,

Plate 33

THE OLD BRIDGE AT MOSTAR

The best-known sight in Mostar, the chief town of Hercegovina, is the bridge which spans the river Neretva in one graceful arch. It was constructed in the fifteenth century, and the town itself (Mostar means "old bridge") takes its name from it.

TRAVNIK, BOSNIA   Plate 34

Travnik was the headquarters of the Turkish Governors of Bosnia from the middle of the sixteenth until the nineteenth century. It is a very interesting town, with many fine mosques and old, Turkish houses.

JAJCE, BOSNIA   Plate 35

This ancient town was once the capital of Bosnia and it was here, too, that
the foundations of present-day Yugoslavia were laid at a conference in 1943.
It is in a magnificent situation, overlooking the turbulent river Lašva and a
beautiful waterfall.

Plate 36

SARAJEVO

The present-day capital of Bosnia is known as "The City of a Hundred Mosques". It is set among green hills, from which there are fine views across the dark rooftops, with the graceful white minarets rising everywhere among them.

no traffic is allowed to pass) is an ancient tree beneath which the boot-blacks sit and wait for custom;
then the road divides. The left fork takes you through
a street in which every shop is a smith's or metal-
worker's to the market-place. Market day in Ohrid
is Monday and before dawn the roads from the surrounding villages are alive with the clatter of hoofs as
the peasants drive their mules, laden with produce
into the town. The scene in the market-place is lively
and colourful, but it is here that one can realise just
how poor some of these Macedonians are. One will
have to come many miles to sell no more than a dozen
eggs, another has merely a pound or two of sour-milk
cheese, another a bag or two of onions. There are the
bread-sellers, too, squatting on their haunches with
half-a-dozen dark, round loaves to sell. There are
more unusual things for sale than these, however—
wooden ploughshares, pipes and whistles, rush mats
and even handsome carpets which nobody ever seems
to buy. There are spices, too, piled on the ground in
many-coloured pyramids, and red pepper and corn and
seeds of all kinds. Here in the market-place most of
the women are in the most picturesque of embroidered
costumes, wearing their hair in pigtails with gold and
silver coins fastened to the ends.

These are not the only costumes you will see as you
walk through the streets of Ohrid, for the population is
a very mixed one and each race wears its traditional
dress—the Gypsies, the Albanians, sometimes a
Turkish woman in *zars,* and other types, too. And
rags! Here you do not merely see people whose
clothes are ragged, but some whose clothes are literally *made* of rags, a patchwork of pieces of material of
all shapes and sizes, roughly sewn together to make a

177

N

jacket and a pair of trousers, and whose sandals are
no more than odd pieces of heavy cloth, roughly cut to
shape, tied on to the feet with string. Many, of course,
are barefooted; indeed, this is true of a large number of
the people of southern Yugoslavia. It is, however, here
in Macedonia that it is easiest to realise that the Turks
were in this country until 1912, and to appreciate the
magnitude of the tasks that face the government of today.

We now turn back through the centuries and visit
two of the churches in the town—Sv. Kliment and Sv.
Sofia. Sv. Kliment was built in 1295, and stands on a
hill from which there are magnificent views down the
lake and across to the ruined castle. It is a very beautiful building from the outside, but its chief glories are
the thirteenth- and fourteenth-century frescoes which
have recently been uncovered. For more than six
hundred years soot from the candles, mixed with the
dust, was deposited on the walls until the paintings had
nearly disappeared. In the nineteenth century they
were varnished to make their appearance brighter but
this only made matters worse, for the soot and dust
stuck more easily to the varnish than to the original
paint. They were varnished again and again until
they were almost black—and then in the year 1889
the varnish was whitened and new pictures painted on
it. It is only in recent years that the work of cleaning
has been undertaken. A chemical process is being
used and now the paintings of 1889, the many layers of
varnish and the dust and grease of centuries are being
removed, to reveal the ancient frescoes in all their
glory. Many are in perfect condition; the painting of
Christ before Pilate, for example, looks as fresh in its
new beauty as it did, I am sure, in the year 1300.

More ancient still is the church of Sv. Sofia, at one time the seat of an Archbishop. It dates from the eleventh century, though the foundations are even earlier, and the oldest of its paintings are believed to have been completed about the year 1025. In the fourteenth century the Turks transformed Sv. Sofia into a mosque, added a minaret and covered the frescoes with a thick layer of plaster. After the Turks were driven out of Macedonia the minaret was demolished and in the nineteen-thirties the work of removing the plaster from the walls was commenced. There have been some casualties, for sometimes a large piece of plaster has fallen and brought down the old paintings with it, but numerous frescoes have been successfully revealed for the first time for about six hundred years. It was fascinating to stand beside one of the careful workers as he uncovered a piece of painting with his small knife, and to know that the last person who saw those colours was a plasterer in a Turkish town about the time of the Battle of Crécy.

Of churches and monasteries there are many others in and around Ohrid but I will mention only two more, these for the reason that they have beauty of situation as well as architectural grace and fine paintings. The first is Sv. Jovan Bogoslov, on a rocky promontory overlooking the lake near the fishermen's village of Kaneo; the other is Sv. Naum, situated on the eastern shore of the lake, right on the frontier and with its back door in Albania—or nearly so.

One has to have a permit to go to Sv. Naum and I was duly promised it by Ohrid's Chief of Police, to whom I was introduced one evening on the Korzo. Alas, the next morning he had gone to Skopje on business and nobody else could help me; and my time in the south was up. Of course, I should have boarded one of the little steamers that go near to Sv. Naum, and just walked to the monastery as bold as brass. However, I was not so bold, and I missed Sv. Naum. A party of British people for whom I later planned a tour of Macedonia were more fortunate; they obtained the necessary permits, with the aid of Putnik, and they went to Sv. Naum guarded by two Yugoslav sailors whose only fear was that the British might point their cameras at the Albanians across the frontier and that they would start shooting.

I was fortunate in another respect, however, and that was to have the guidance in some of my walks round Ohrid of Vasil Lahtov, the Director of the interesting town museum. He is an enthusiastic archaeologist, in love with the ancient art and history of his town, and if you have the opportunity of talking to him about Ohrid he will add much interest to your visit.

You will not spend all your time at Ohrid looking at churches or museums or even wandering through the old town, for the call of the lake itself is very strong. You can swim in its waters, the colour of lapis lazuli; you can hire canoes and other kinds of small boats or you can go out with the fishermen in their picturesque boats of unusual shape; you can see the interesting hydrobiological station and the school of wood-carving; and you can find many sandy beaches on which to sleep in the sun and many hills over which to ramble to remote villages. There is a theatre, too, and a cinema, and in summer the town is visited by orchestras, ballet-companies and singers from many parts of the country.

In the journey through Yugoslavia which I have so far described we have come to Ohrid by a very round-about route. In actual fact it is now one of the easiest places to reach during the summer months, for it is then linked by air twice a week with Skopje and Belgrade. On the other hand it is served by the most primitive railway line in the country, the "toy railway" to Gostivar. Until 1952 it went all the way to a station a couple of miles from Skopje, but a new normal-gauge line has been built for the northern section. On the hundred miles or so of narrow-gauge tracks the train climbs the gradients at a snail's pace and tumbles down the other side like a scenic railway—only with far more shaking from side to side. As it averages only six and a half miles an hour there are times, as the train goes uphill, when it is quite possible to walk beside it to stretch your legs! It will probably not be many years before this line is improved, and as a ride on the "Ohrid Express" is an experience of a lifetime I counsel you to seize the first opportunity that comes your way; after all, you need not travel the whole hundred miles!

Fortunately there is a daily bus service between Ohrid and Skopje and that is the way the Yugoslavs generally travel. I caught it early one morning, having been able to buy my ticket the previous day, and found that my travelling-companions were a group of students from Niš. They were a very jolly crowd and sang folk-songs much of the way to Skopje. Not that it is unusual to sing in buses in Yugoslavia; in fact in this one the leading singer was not a student but the bus conductor, who had a fine tenor voice. Music was provided by a guitar belonging to one of the students and a cornet which one of the peasants surprisingly produced from his kit-bag.

Being the only foreigner on the bus I was given a seat of honour at the front and after the inevitable arguments behind me had been satisfactorily settled we drove off through the new part of Ohrid and along the lake shore towards Struga. This was once an important town on the Via Ignatia, the Roman road from Durazzo on the Albanian sea-coast to Salonika, and later it enjoyed prosperity as a halt on the caravan route; now it is in a decayed condition and is of little interest to the visitor. After Struga the scene changes. The broad plain at the head of the lake is left behind and the road climbs up the valley of the Black Drim, sometimes high above the river, roughly following the contours, sometimes through a deep gorge with the river rushing by its side. In places the road is only a few hundred yards from the Albanian frontier, but there is no risk of the bus driver taking the wrong turning as on the whole of the forty mile run from Ohrid to Debar there is no branch road. The road is narrow and winding and on two occasions our driver had to apply his brakes suddenly when a lorry came unexpectedly round a sharp bend. There was then much manoeuvring and gesticulating and it seemed as if our wheels must be dangerously skirting the edge of the deep drop below. Our man was, however, as skilful a driver as any I can remember on a mountain journey, even though he did seem to perform some hair-raising feats at times. The road itself was empty, except for the occasional lorry. Indeed, all the way to Skopje we saw only one Yugoslav car—and the total distance we covered was over 130 miles.

We arrived at Debar which is colourful on market-day and has a beautiful situation but otherwise is rather depressing, having lost all its former prosperity in the same way as Struga. A few miles past Debar there is a small wayside café where the buses make a halt for half an hour. It seemed early for lunch, despite our start at 6 a.m., but I was warned that it would be a long time before the next halt so I fed with my fellow-passengers. As we were eating our meal one of the students from Niš told me about two of the villages nearby.

The first of these is Lazaropole, one of the most successful examples of co-operation in farming. During the war it suffered badly in the course of reprisals taken against the Partisans, but even before that it had been poor enough. At the end of the war, however, the survivors joined together to build up a new and more prosperous Lazaropole and their efforts have been crowned with success. The village now owns many thousand sheep, horses and cattle and has a number of prosperous folk-industries, producing fine carpets, tweeds and other woollen goods. Even though it boasts the most famous of all co-operative farming ventures in Yugoslavia, the life is still very hard for the peasants and their rewards are few, for this is a wild and unfertile district. I have since learned more about this village. Its altitude is nearly 4,000 feet above sea level and some of the surrounding mountains rise nearly twice as high. There is a small hotel there, the Vila Frosa, of category B, and its situation is most delightful. There is good fishing on the River Radika and hunting for wild boar, bears and wolves, as well as foxes. Incidentally, it was from Lazaropole that a folk-dancing team came which won a first prize at a festival in London a year or two ago.

Galičnik, the other village I was told about by my student friend, is even more remote. One has to alight from the bus at the village of Janče and then go on foot or horseback the final three or four miles. It is at a higher altitude than Lazaropole and its surrounding mountains are also loftier, among them being Korab which rises to more than 9,000 feet and is the second highest mountain in the whole of Yugoslavia. Galičnik is another example of successful co-operative farming and is in a strikingly beautiful position.

In the days before the war the men of these villages used to go off to the towns to work and some even emigrated in order to send money home to keep their wives and children alive. The womenfolk had to tend the sheep and do all the hard work of hill-farming, but in July every year the men who were still working in the Balkans or Austria, even though several hundred miles away, would return to see their homes. Their stay would be short, however, for they could not earn money in these mountains, and so the custom grew of having one day for marriages—St. Peter's Day, 12th July. On that day there were great celebrations and many feasts and Galičnik especially is famous for these St. Peter's Day weddings. I asked later in Skopje if the custom still survived and I was told that it does, although to a limited extent. You can go and see for yourself, for Galičnik has a small category B hotel—the Dosta.

We finished the excellent yoghourt with which we ended the meal and then went back to the bus, but we were instructed to walk down the road for half a mile and await it there. We did so, and saw why. A river-bridge, like so many along this road, had been destroyed during the war and now there was merely a crude wooden makeshift, almost level with the water in mid-stream. The driver had emptied the bus in order to lighten the load and I am sure that all the passengers were glad to be out of it when they saw the bridge bend under its weight, the water washing its wheels when it reached the centre. However, we were soon aboard again and on our way.

It was not long before the next stop, this time at the monastery of Sv. Jovan Bigorski. It stands a few hundred feet above the road, on the right hand side as you are going towards Skopje, and is nearly hidden in the trees. I was fortunate to have the students with me for otherwise I should have passed by without noticing it. Their professor had asked the driver to stop and he readily agreed to do so. "Ten minutes", he said, but it took us at least that time just to climb up the steep path to the monastery. The building dates from the eleventh century and has some of the fine frescoes with which you will by now be familiar. Here, however, many of them are painted on the outside of the church, protected only by the shelter of an arcade or loggia and otherwise completely open to the elements. Despite this they are in excellent condition. One of the most interesting of them includes a representation of a tablet on which are painted the characters of the earliest known Serbian alphabet. Inside the church is a magnificently carved wooden iconostasis, the work of the two brothers Filopić who also made the screen in Sv. Spas at Skopje. They came from Galičnik which, with other villages of these parts, has a tradition of intricate craftsmanship in wood dating back for nearly a thousand years.

As we descended from the monastery we could see a village on the far hillside, with the tall white minaret of its mosque looking very attractive amidst the wild mountain scenery. How often through many centuries must the monks of Sv. Jovan Bigorski have looked across the valley and wondered if a Moslem power would always rule in this land?

Fifty minutes had passed, not merely ten, when we reached the road. Our chauffeur seemed not to mind at all. I have found that it is rare for the driver of a bus to keep to the time he has fixed for a halt, but it would be bad advice to suggest that you can always expect to stretch ten minutes to fifty!

After leaving Sv. Jovan Bigorski (and I hope you will be able to persuade *your* driver to stop there) the road continues through a narrow gorge and finally climbs over the watershed near Mavrovi Hanovi. Here you will see one of the most ambitious of the new hydro-electric projects of Yugoslavia. The wide basin below you, with the Mavrovsko lake in its centre, is being dammed so that none of the water can escape towards the south. The valley will thus be flooded when the snows of the surrounding high mountains melt in the spring and the water will be diverted through a tunnel which is being made through the hills which form the eastern side of the valley, to emerge three or four hundred feet below on the left hand side of the road to Gostivar. There will be tremendous power in the fall and the turbines to be constructed will have an output of 200,000 kilowatts. It may be that this scheme will have been completed when you visit Macedonia, and if so you will be able to stay at the mountain holiday village which is to be built on the shore of the new lake.

The road crosses the lip of the Mavrovo basin and then descends many windings into the Vardar valley. As you approach Gostivar you will notice that this district is more fertile than the mountain regions through which you have been passing. There are also more peasants to be seen on the road, riding their donkeys side-saddle as is the custom in the south.

We reached Gostivar, and except for Debar this was the first town we had seen for nearly eighty miles. Even Gostivar is small and uninteresting, though obviously more prosperous than the towns along the frontier. The road changes its direction here and runs north-east to Tetovo, much of it dead straight. This was one of the worst road surfaces I have seen—mile after mile of ruts and pot-holes with our bus often lurching from one to the next. Soon this road will be improved, however, for as we approached Tetovo there was a heap of road-mending material eight miles long, literally continuous save for an occasional gap for the oxen to pass through to the fields. All this had been broken by hand, and at the end of it there were men sitting by the roadside, using hammers to break large rocks into stones of suitable size with which to add a ninth mile to the heap. The lack of machinery for such tasks is one of Yugoslavia's problems. Poor roads mean poor transport; poor transport means few factories; few factories results in insufficient machinery; the lack of machinery in turn means the use of hand labour for work which is done mechanically in Western countries; and so, poor roads. It is a vicious circle which only time can break.

Tetovo is the market town of the Vardar valley. It stands in the centre of what is by Macedonian standards a rich district, but there are too many inhabitants for too few acres of land. Agricultural methods are very primitive, too, and the standard implement is the wooden plough, so one sees much poverty in the streets of Tetovo. The population is predominantly Moslem and there are many mosques and Turkish costumes to be seen. The town itself is not very attractive, though if it is market-day it merits a stop. There is a category B hotel, the Makedonija. I must add that the great range of the Šar Planina dominates the town, with peaks rising to well over 8,000 feet. Six miles by footpath from Tetovo is the winter sports resort of Popova Šapka, with a ski-lift and a wide terrain for ski-touring. Here is the Turistički Dom na Popovoj Šapci, a well equipped mountain hotel. In summer it is possible for experienced mountain walkers to cross the range from Tetovo to Prizren, in Kosmet. It is not an expedition to be lightly undertaken, however, as good maps seem to be unobtainable. Another way of crossing the Šar Planina is to hire horses and guides, which is possible at Tetovo on market-day when so many of the peasants from the mountains come down to the town.

After Tetovo the River Vardar makes a wide sweep to the north but the road cuts across a range of hills more directly to Skopje. It was on this road that we experienced much delay, owing to the poor state of the vehicle. The water-pipe broke between the radiator and the engine and although the driver tried to mend it with rags, cotton-wool, clay from the roadside and sundry other makeshifts, all failed and we were reduced to filling the radiator every couple of miles. If there was no water available, the engine over-heated and we had to stop for a quarter of an hour or so. At this rate of progress we were soon overtaken by darkness and then we had to strain our eyes, looking for water. Suddenly there would be a shout of "vodo" and the brakes would be jammed on and the radiator re-filled and we would be all set for another mile or two. Fortunately there was a full moon and when it rose over the mountains it became easier to spot the streams, but then, alas, we had a puncture. All the men took a hand in the task of changing the wheel; in fact it took three, pulling on a lever, to remove some of the nuts, so long was it since they had been greased. Despite all our delays nobody grumbled; even the driver did not seem much put out, but perhaps he was used to this sort of journey.

We were already six hours late when we reached the outskirts of Skopje! Then the bus stopped and refused to budge. I decided to walk the last mile into the town and it was midnight before I reached the Arapska Kuča. It was a typical Macedonian finish to a typical Macedonian journey. Yours may well be less eventful. If not, you must take the trials and delays in good part and remember that, although great efforts are being made by the authorities to improve conditions, this part of Yugoslavia still suffers from the neglect of hundreds of years of Ottoman rule.

(*ix*) SKOPJE TO BELGRADE VIA KOSOVO POLJE AND RANKOVIĆEVO

There are two railway lines from Skopje to Belgrade —the main Simplon line through Vranje and Niš and the less important route through Kosovo Mitrovica and Raška. I will give some description first of the places of interest on or near the latter of these two lines and deal with the Simplon route and Niš in the next section.

The main road and railway from Skopje crosses the frontier of Macedonia and Serbia (or more correctly

189

the autonomous region of Kosmet) about eighteen miles from the city and pass through the towns of Kaćanik and Uroševac. There are bus services from the latter to Prizren (see section vii). After Uroševac they take different routes—the railway to Kosovo Polje, where there is a connecting line to the town of Priština, and the road direct to Priština itself. (Hotel: Nova Jugoslavija—category C).

Although Priština bears some signs of Turkish influence, including several mosques, it has no special interest for the tourist except as a base from which to visit Gračanica. This is a fourteenth century monastery and one of the most imposing in the country. It stands about seven miles to the south of Priština and can be reached from there by road.

It has a special significance in the history of Serbia, and indeed of all Yugoslavia, for it stands near the battlefield of Kosovo Polje where the Turks conquered the Serbs in 1389 and brought to an end the independence of their country and the dynasty of the Nemanja which had ruled Serbia since the year 1166. The last king, Lazar, slept at Gračanica the night before the battle and rode out to the "Field of the Blackbirds" to perish with all the flower of Serbian chivalry. It was more than a century before the Turks conquered the whole of the north of the country, but to the South Slav peoples the defeat at Kosovo Polje has always signified the end of medieval Serbia. From the fourteenth to the nineteenth century she was an enslaved country. It was not until 1804 that active revolt commenced and the Turkish yoke was not finally thrown off until 1878, when Serbia's independence was recognised by the Great Powers at the Congress of Berlin. Kosovo was a defeat that lasted for five centuries, but throughout those dark ages it was a symbol to the Serbs of the independence that one day must return to the land.

The route continues northwards to Kosovo Mitrovica, an industrial town not far from which are Trepča mines, formerly in British ownership, and then along the beautiful valley of the Ibar to Raška. To the south west of this town is Novi Pazar, at present reached only by bus but soon to be connected with Raška by a new railway line. It is a small, pleasant town with a predominantly Turkish atmosphere, but it does not possess any hotels of a category higher than D. The tourist who wants to see another fine monastery must use Novi Pazar as a base to visit Sopoćani, twelve miles to the west. It was founded in the year 1260, and although half of it was destroyed by the Turks in 1689, the part which is left, including the paintings, is well preserved.

The next place of interest on this route is another monastery, outstandingly beautiful Studenica, which was built in the years following 1180. It is constructed of white marble, and the fabric and the twelfth century frescoes are in an excellent state of preservation. Studenica lies about seven miles by road to the west of Ušće, a small town with a railway station.

The next places of note are Mataruška Banja, a pleasantly situated spa in wooded, hilly country (Hotel Žica, category B) and Rankovićevo, an industrial centre formerly known as Kraljevo, the junction of the narrow-gauge railway line through Čačak to Sarajevo. (Hotels Paris, category B, and Jugoslavija, category C). Between these two towns stands the great red church of Žiča, the seat of St. Sava who was created the first Archbishop of the autonomous Serbian Church.

Our railway and road still run together through two more river valleys, first the Gruža and then the Lepenica, to reach Kragujevac, another large industrial town (Hotels Dubrovnik, category B, and Zelengora, category C). You can continue from here to Belgrade by rail, connecting with the Simplon line at Lapovo, but it is more interesting to travel by bus. There are two or three services each day between Kragujevac and Belgrade, the distance of seventy-five miles being covered in three and a half hours. The route is through the most beautiful part of the Šumadija, a region of rolling hills, woods and vineyards. Some twenty-five miles from Kragujevac the bus passes Topola, the headquarters of the Serbian uprisings between 1804 and 1813. It is now a favourite country holiday-resort for the citizens of Belgrade and has a most attractive new hotel, with a swimming-pool and tennis-court. It is named the Hotel Topola and is a very inexpensive place at which to stay.

The last place of interest to be mentioned in this section is Arandjelovac, another spa. It is surrounded by wooded hills and has a good hotel, the Staro Zdanje, category B. It is connected both by rail and by bus-routes with Belgrade, just over fifty miles away.

(x) SKOPJE TO NIŠ AND PRAHOVO AND THROUGH THE IRON GATES TO BELGRADE

The main Simplon line between Skopje and Belgrade passes through Niš. It is the southern half of this route which is the most interesting; for the northern part I

THE CHURCH OF ST. MARK, ZAGREB   Plate 37

This fine church stands in the old part of Zagreb, on a steep hill which over-looks the modern city. The roof is of brightly coloured tiles, depicting the coats of arms of Croatia, Slavonia, Dalmatia and the City of Zagreb itself.

COSTUMES AT SESTINE

One of several villages on the northern outskirts of Zagreb, accessible by tram or bus from the centre of the city where the peasants go to church every Sunday in traditional dress.

Plate 38

Plate 39

THE PLITVICE LAKES

The district around the beautiful string of lakes at Plitvice has been made a National Park. It is much visited by holiday-makers from all parts of Yugoslavia and from abroad.

USING THE DISTAFF   Plate 40

The distaff, the cleft stick on which wool is wound for spinning by hand, is still seen in many parts of Yugoslavia.

suggest a diversion—between Niš and Prahovo, near the Rumanian frontier, by rail and then along the Danube to Belgrade by steamer.

Near Preševo, thirty-five miles from Skopje, the railway-line crosses from Macedonia into Serbia, but it is not until Ristovac that it reaches the 1912 frontier of Turkey. A road to the south-east from here leads across a fertile plain to Klenike, from which one may walk to the monastery of Sv. Prohor Pčinski. This is a modern building (though the foundation is an old one) and its attraction lies in its setting. Further along the line to Niš you reach Vranje, an unattractive town, but above it, approached by a road over which there are regular bus services, is Vranjska Banja, a spa with many hotels of all categories. Another road from Vranje leads across the rolling hills of Besna Kobila to Bosiljgrad. This is very delightful country for walking holidays in the late spring and also for winter sports, and can be reached by bus most days of the week.

Fifteen miles past Vranje along the route to Niš we reach Vladičin Han, whose name reveals the fact that it was once a caravanserai, and from here a road goes to the Vlasinsko Jezero. This mountain lake is peaceful rather than magnificent and, indeed, this is true of much of this south-eastern corner of Serbia. Leskovac, the next town to the north, is an important industrial centre, as also is Niš, which is reached in four and a half hours from Skopje by the one fast train of the day.

Niš is of little interest in itself, therefore, but its surroundings are attractive. To the east lies the Nišava valley, through which the river passes to the high watershed of the Stara Planina, which forms the frontier of Yugoslavia and Bulgaria. There are impressive gorges between Niš and Dolac, with the Sićevačka Klisura (dam) a focal point of interest. Farther up the valley is Pirot, the centre of a great sheep-grazing region and renowned throughout Yugoslavia for the beauty of its carpet-weaving. This craft is still carried on in the cottages of the peasants, but only by the women, and its antiquity is evidenced by the Greek and Turkish names which are used for the colours, the carpet-sizes and the intricate patterns. In the days of the Ottoman Empire the looms of Pirot and its surroundings produced carpets for the *élite* of society in Constantinople; today they use the same age-old methods and designs, but there are few people in their country who can afford to buy their products.

Not far from Niš is Niška Banja, magnificently situated as are all the spas of Yugoslavia. It lies on a plateau under the slopes of Mount Koritnjak and from the hills above there are wonderful views across the Nišava River. (Hotels: Ozren, category B, and Zelengora, category C). In Niš itself the most convenient hotel is the Gradski, of category B. The most famous sight of Niš used to be the Čele Kula, the "Tower of Skulls". The story of this is interesting but grim. In the year 1809 the Serbs, in rebellion against the Turks, were surrounded at Niš by overwhelming odds but, rather than surrender, they waited until the enemy had closed with them and then they blow up their powder-magazine, destroying not only the Turks but themselves as well. As a revenge for this deed the Turks built the Čele Kula, embedding in the mortar the skulls of nine hundred Serbs. These remained in position for many decades, but were removed when Serbia finally achieved liberation—save two only, which remain today as a reminder of this gruesome piece of architectural embellishment.

The railway-line from Niš to Prahovo follows the Timok river to Zaječar and Negotin, most of the route being only a few miles from the Bulgarian frontier. At Zaječar a narrow-gauge line branches off to Bor, a copper-mining town, from which the line is being extended further to the north-west. Above Bor there are rolling uplands, rising to 4,000 feet above sea-level, and an excellent walking tour can be made across the Crni Vrh and Beljanica to Despotovac, which has rail connection with the main Simplon line. There are two or three mountain huts on this walking-route.

At Prahovo you reach the terminus of the railway-line from Niš. The train takes you directly to the landing-stage for the river-boats and you look across the Danube to Rumania. From here begins one of the most famous and impressive of all river-journeys—through the Iron Gates and the Djerdap gorges and on to Smederevo and Belgrade.

First I will give some practical advice. The steamers are small, but quite comfortable, and accommodation is available in two classes—first and second. There are berths in both classes and a few *de-luxe* cabins as well. There is very little difference between the first and second class fares and this is a case where economy is not really worth while. The whole journey from Prahovo to Belgrade costs about £2 or $6, including a first-class berth, and a *de-luxe* berth costs very little more. A modest charge is made for the use of a bathroom. Deck chairs are available for hire and, of course, there is a dining saloon. The whole journey takes twenty-two hours of actual sailing time, plus a stop during the night of about six hours, and the distance is nearly two hundred miles. It is thus quite a travel bargain—and I must add that holders of tourist visas secure a reduction from the fare. The steamer leaves Prahovo for Belgrade at about 4 p.m. and there is an early-morning train from Niš which makes the connection. There are only two steamers in each direction per week and winter services, from October to March, are occasional only. Tickets for the journey and for berths and meals can be obtained from a travel agent before you leave home.

The evening run to Kladovo is through lush green meadows, giving little promise of the grandeur to come. One sight of interest along this stretch is the anchored boat-mills—flat vessels with great wheels on either side —which are turned by the Danube to grind the corn of this rich district. Kladovo itself has little to commend it, except the caviar for which it is famous, but Turn Severin, the town which faces it on the Rumanian shore, has a history dating back to the days of Trajan.

Next morning the engines start turning before dawn and soon everyone is astir as the boat casts off from the jetty and steams upstream into the gorges—the Iron Gates through the Carpathians. It is danger rather than beauty which has made them so famous for, as we shall see, the later gorges of Djerdap are more magnificent. As one sees the jagged rocks in mid-stream and the foaming whirlpools and sandbanks, and hears the roar of the water, one can imagine how terrifying it must have been in former days for the travellers who had to pass this way, their small craft entrusted to the skill of the local pilots. Today you travel in a powerful steamer, but the passage of the rapids themselves is

196

avoided by a canal which has been constructed along the Serbian shore.

Beyond the Iron Gates is the island of Ada Kale (or Kaleh). It was still an Ottoman outpost as late as the year 1913 for it was forgotten by the powers at the Congress of Berlin in 1878 and remained a Turkish *enclave* for thirty-five years. Today it belongs to Rumania. Next we pass Orsova on the Rumanian shore and then a brief call is made at Tekija.

The gorge now becomes wilder and the sides more precipitous; indeed the whole of the sixty miles from Tekija to the fortress of Golubac is a river-journey which it is difficult to equal. On the Yugoslav side, especially, are sheer precipices rising two thousand feet above the Danube.

Two roads have penetrated these gorges. One, on the Rumanian side, can be clearly seen today. It is the Szechenyi road, made by the Hungarian government in 1834-37. The other road was on the right bank and was an even more outstanding piece of engineering, for it was constructed by the Roman Emperor Trajan in the year A.D.103. At several points, where the rock wall is perpendicular, it was carried on a kind of gallery built out over the water and you can see to this day, just above the high-water mark, some of the holes into which the massive supporting beams were inserted. At the narrowest point, where the river is little more than a hundred yards across, is the celebrated Tabula Trajana, an inscription carved by order of Trajan to commemorate the construction of the road.

This narrow part of the river, which continues for many miles, is known as Kazan—the Cauldron. Then the gorge widens and the steamer enters a lake-like stretch and calls at the town of Donji Milanovac. After this it plunges again into narrow gorges, called the Mali (or Lesser) Djerdap, impressive enough but not so awe-inspiring as the part already traversed. The next short call is at Dobra and later the ruins of the medieval fortress of Golubac can be seen ahead, guarding the entrance to the gorges. Once we have passed Golubac the interest of the scene wanes—and it is just as well, for we have been on deck since dawn and it is time for lunch in the saloon below!

Later in the afternoon, after we have left the Rumanian frontier, we shall see the town of Smederevo. This ancient stronghold deserves more than the quarter-of-an-hour which is all the steamer's halt gives to it and my advice is to disembark here, stay the night and catch a bus to Belgrade early next morning. The Hotel Smederevo, category B, is about five hundred yards from the quay and I can recommend it. The old citadel was built in the shape of a triangle, with twenty-four towers along the ramparts, and it is still an unusual and imposing sight. For one brief but glorious period, in the fourteenth century, it was the capital of Serbia but it fell to the Turks in the year 1459 and, like Kosovo, represented a substantial advance for the Ottoman Empire in its drive northwards.

It took the Turks a further sixty-two years to conquer Belgrade, however, though from Smederevo to the capital is a distance of only thirty miles.

(xi) BELGRADE

The capital city of Yugoslavia has a population of about 400,000 and it stands on the banks of the rivers Danube and Sava. On one side of it lies the flat, fertile region of Vojvodina, on the other side the hilly country of the Šumadija. It has always stood at the crossroads of communications between the eastern and western worlds and its dominating position has made it an important strategic centre and the subject of many struggles through the centuries.

It was fortified by the Celts and later became a Roman city; then it passed in turn through many hands —those of the Huns, Goths, Avars and others. During the seventh century it was settled by Slavs and later it became the chief city of the state of Serbia, to be captured by the Turks in the year 1521 after many centuries of independence. During the wars between Turkey and Austria during the seventeenth and eighteenth centuries, Belgrade was occupied by the Austrians for several short periods and during the longest of these, from 1718 to 1739, they fortified the citadel and gave it the appearance which can be seen today. The Serbs themselves seized control of Belgrade in 1806, but seven years later the Turks fought their way back and it was not until 1867 that the last Turkish garrison departed.

Belgrade suffered bombardment from the Austrian forces in the first world war, and the bombing of the city by Hitler's Stukas in April 1941 brought Yugoslavia into the war by the side of Britain, at that time facing the Germans alone. Finally, in 1944, the city was liberated by the Partisan forces and those of Russia.

Much of present-day Belgrade has been built during the twentieth century and a good deal of it in the years of reconstruction since 1945. It has a few ancient monuments but they are of more interest to the Yugoslavs, steeped as they are in their nation's history and tradition, than to the ordinary foreign visitor. One cannot, therefore, enthuse about the ancient beauty of this city as one would of, say, Vienna or Rome or London. The following are the most interesting things to do and see and a few practical notes.

Terazije: This wide tree-lined street or square (it is difficult to know how to describe it) is the focal point of Belgrade. Here are many of the hotels, the best shops and innumerable restaurants and cafés, with their tables out on the pavement. In the early evening it is the site of a big Korzo. A short walk from the end of Terazije brings you to the park of Kalemegdan.

Kalemegdan: This was originally the waste land outside the citadel but it has now been transformed into a very beautiful park. On one side of it is a terrace, overlooking the river Sava, and from here there are wide views of the city. At the end of this terrace is the entrance to the Upper Fortress, built early in the eighteenth century. There are several fine gateways around this fortress and through one of them (Diz-dareva Kapija, on the left) you reach the Lower Fortress. Bearing downhill steeply to the left again you come to the ramparts overlooking the rivers and you can walk right round these, entering the Lower Fortress again by the Vidin Kapija (gate). You can go on to the Kapija Princa Evgena (Prince Eugen's Gate) and climb back from here to the ramparts again, finishing the walk at the Kalemegdan restaurant, with its beautiful terrace.

It is not easy to find your way around the citadel and the above description is intended to be a rough outline of one of the best routes and not a complete guide. You will find it best, perhaps, to go on one of Putnik's conducted tours of this most ancient part of Belgrade, returning at your leisure when you have discovered how not to lose yourself!

Along Bulevar Revolucije: From Terazije turn left at the Putnik foreign reception office. Soon on the left you will see the headquarters of the Communist Party and a little further on, on the opposite side, some gardens behind which lies the President's building. On the left are the Parliament House and the new central Post Office. Past the air terminal is a new park, the Tašmajdan. Farther on the University buildings are reached.

Avala: This is a conical, forested hill 1,700 feet above sea-level, easily accessible by public bus (service No. 30). Avala is a favourite place for picnics with the people of Belgrade. On the summit is the great grave of the Unknown Warrior, designed by Meštrović and built in the year 1934.

Topčider: A large park to the south-west of the city reached by bus service No. 3. It contains the mansion of Prince Miloš, built in Turkish style, and the present residence of Marshal Tito.

Public Transport: Belgrade has trams, buses and trolley-buses, the services of all of them starting before 5 a.m., when most of the city's population is already astir, and terminating at various times between 9 p.m. and midnight. One of them, tram No. 2, makes a circular route of Belgrade railway station, Trg Dimitrija Tucovića, Bulevar Revolucije, near Tašmajdan park, Kalemegdan, thence back to the railway station.

Hotels and Restaurants: The hotels in Belgrade are the most expensive in the country, the best being the the Majestic (which is mostly reserved for foreign visitors), the Excelsior and the Moskva, the latter overlooking Terazije. In the next price range are the Balkan and the Kasina, also on Terazije, but these, too, are by no means cheap. Less pretentious places, in category C, are the Palas, Pošta and Union.

The visitor has a wide choice of restaurants, ranging from smart places like the "Atina" to the self-service "Kasina", both on Terazije. I have made it my policy when in Belgrade, to eat at the Kasina when I am in a hurry, and to patronise the Atina when I want a really well-cooked and well-served meal and I can afford both the time and the cost.

Theatres: The National Theatre in Trg Republike is the most popular one with foreign visitors for it stages opera and ballet as well as plays. The Puppet Theatre in Topličin Venac is interesting, even to people who have left their childhood far behind them. The Open Air Theatre in Kalemegdan, with films and musical recitals as well as plays, is in a delightful setting.

Museums: The National Museum, Ethnographic Museum, and City Museum are the most outstanding, but the most unusual is the Museum of the Illegal Party Printing Works. This is in a house of which the basement was used during the war to produce illegal documents even whilst Gestapo officers were quartered above. Not merely pamphlets but whole books were printed here, and the machinery was never discovered by the Germans.

* * *

Before leaving Belgrade I will note a few of the things I always remember most clearly about it:

—The many kinds of costumes seen in its streets, a remarkable sight in a European capital.

—The panorama of Belgrade from the road bridge across the Sava; but how much finer it could have been had this magnificent site been intelligently town planned!

—The many tablets which can be seen, commemorating the underground work which was carried on beneath the very noses of the Germans.

—The quietness of the streets, owing to the lack of motor traffic. This is especially noticeable in the early evening, at the hour of the Korzo.

—The Café Question Mark, an exquisite little building.

—The huge steel skeletons below Belgrade on the road to Zemun. In the days following the war they were being constructed as government offices; but the money ran out, and then it was found that the foundations were on silt. The Belgrade people call them the "Temples of Bureaucracy".

—The helpfulness of the citizens when they discover that one is a foreigner and may therefore be in need of guidance and advice in a strange country.

(xii) BOSNIA AND HERCEGOVINA

The twin provinces of Bosnia and Hercegovina have been linked together through much of their history and now form one of the republics of federal Yugoslavia. They are mountainous regions, but there is a great deal of difference between Bosnia, in the north, and Hercegovina, the southern point of the republic. Although Bosnia has its mountains and rough moorlands, most of the land is green and wooded, with many stretches of fertile soil and countless orchards. Hercegovina, on the other hand, is mostly a region of *karst*—barren limestone, wild and rugged, and almost wholly unfertile except in the valleys known as *poljes*. These *poljes* are one of the strange features of the *karst* landscape; in spring they are shallow lakes, whereas in summer the water has disappeared completely, leaving a deposit of good red earth. Sometimes, therefore, as one travels through Hercegovina in springtime one comes across a lake which does not appear on the map and, on the contrary, in summer one will see no trace of a river where the map indicates one should exist. It is not the sun which has dried up the waters, nor have the rivers drained away to the sea in any normal fashion; the outlet of such rivers is usually a hole in the ground or a cleft in the hillside, through which the stream disappears into immense and unexplored limestone caverns.

These provinces, together with Macedonia, have the most eastern character of all the districts of Yugoslavia. By far the greatest concentration of Moslems in the country is in Bosnia, and this is due to a very strange circumstance of history. Before the Turks came a heresy known as Bogomilism had spread to this region from Bulgaria. Although in Bulgaria itself and in Macedonia, through which it passed, it did not find any secure foothold, in Bosnia it took on the character of a national religion. The Bogomil teachings, including a defiance of all forms of priestly authority, were viewed with concern by Rome and by the Eastern Church alike. The Pope even went so far as to send a crusade against the Bosnians.

When the Turks came, therefore, they found a Christian religion which had no contact with either the east or the west. They were more tolerant of the Bogomil religion than the Bosnian's fellow-Christians had been, and as a result they succeeded in obtaining the allegiance of the majority of the people in a manner which had not been possible in their other Balkan provinces. In time the chief Bosnians obtained leading positions in the administration of their own country and this close co-operation with the Turks eventually led to the conversion of very large numbers of Bosnians to the faith of Islam. The effects of this can be seen today in the eastern characteristics of the whole of this region.

Bosnia and Hercegovina are ill-served with communications, a heritage of Ottoman rule. It is only in comparatively recent years that Sarajevo has been connected by rail with Belgrade; Banja Luka, one of the most important Bosnian towns, had no direct railway connection with the rest of the province until after the end of the last war; and these two new lines are still the only normal gauge routes in Bosnia and Hercegovina. The rest of the railways have narrow tracks, generally with slow and infrequent services.

It is one of these lines which takes the traveller from Dubrovnik on the coast to Mostar and on to Sarajevo; but on this line there are a number of comparatively fast trains, including an occasional service of diesel cars (motorni voz). In any event, however slow this journey is it is well worth taking for the magificence of its scenery. Soon after leaving Dubrovnik the line climbs steeply over the *karst* and then descends again to the rich Popovo Polje—one of the valleys which is lake, river or rich fields of maize and tobacco, according to the season. The line continues along one side of the long valley and passes near to the place where the river in spring disappears into the hillside; then soon there is a descent to the river Neretva, which is followed all the way to Mostar.

This is the chief town of Hercegovina, and it shows the influence both of Venice and of Turkey. The streets are paved like those of Dubrovnik and the houses are of stone, yet there are many mosques and narrow streets of Turkish-style shops with their fronts open wide to the gaze of passers-by. The most famous sight of Mostar is the fifteenth century bridge which spans the river in a single arch, and which gives the town its name. (Most = bridge; star = old.)

Most people will do no more than break at Mostar, perhaps for a day, their journey between Dubrovnik and Sarajevo; but those who decide to stay longer will be able to make several interesting excursions, including a visit to the source of the river Buna, which emerges from the mountain side, about eight miles from Mostar, through a grotto which contains many stalactites. There are two hotels in Mostar, both of them near the railway station. They are the Hotel Neretva (category B) overlooking the river, and the smaller and less expensive Hotel Mostar (category C).

It is after leaving Mostar that the scenery of the Neretva valley is most impressive. The line runs for many miles through a wild, narrow gorge, with the limestone rocks carved into fantastic shapes. At Jablanica has been erected in recent years a great power-station which is providing electricity to large areas of the country. Jablanica itself is an excellent base for climbs in the neighbouring mountain ranges and especially on the Prenj Planina. Beyond Jablanica we still continue to climb through the Neretva valley and soon the line is near to the ridge of Ivan Planina, which is the boundary between the *karst* of Hercegovina and the more fertile districts of Bosnia, and which forms the watershed between the Black Sea and the Adriatic. The railway line does not climb over the summit of the ridge but cuts through it by means of several tunnels. It is then a fairly speedy descent to Sarajevo.

Whatever other claims to fame Sarajevo may have, it will always go down in history as the place where the shots were fired which precipitated the war of 1914-1918. Austria had shortly before unilaterally annexed Bosnia and Hercegovina, Turkish provinces which she had been allowed to administer since 1878 under a mandate granted by the great powers at the Congress of Berlin. An official visit to Sarajevo of the Archduke Franz Ferdinand was regarded by the Bosnian patriots, who hated the domination of the Austrians no less than that of the Turks, as an outward symbol of the foreign oppression against which they had pledged themselves to struggle. One of their number, a student called Gavrilo Princip, stationed himself at the end of the bridge which now bears his name, and assassinated the Archduke and his morganatic wife as they passed by. Today he is regarded as a national hero; not only does a plaque tell of his deed, but engraved into the pavement in the place where he stood to fire the fatal shots is a representation of his footprints.

For Sarajevo, however, this is very recent history, for the growth of the town as a place of importance dates from the beginning of Turkish rule. Its most interesting buildings are the mosques, and the eastern atmosphere of the old town is its main attraction to the tourist.

Whether you are travelling to Sarajevo from Belgrade or Zagreb, or from Dubrovnik, you will enter at the western end of the city. The railway stations lie well away from the centre and are connected with it by two tram routes. One of these runs along the Maršala Tita Ulica and the other along the north bank of the river Miljacka, both of them finishing near the eastern end of Sarajevo, close to the old Turkish quarters. Between these two routes and parallel with them runs the main thoroughfare, called the Jugoslavenske Narodni Armije. The principal hotels are the Europa (category B), which is situated in this main street, and the Beograd (category C) in a smaller street connecting it with the Maršala Tita Ulica. Most foreign tourists stay at the Europa, which is well known for its excellent cuisine and has a very pleasant courtyard with an open-air café around two sides of it. This hotel is a very good base for exploring Sarajevo, as it is near to most of the buildings of interest. Chief among these without doubt is the Begova Džamija, or Mosque of the Beg. It was built in the sixteenth century by a Turkish General, Ghazi Husrav Beg, and it is said to be one of the finest in the whole of the Moslem world. Visitors who look into the interior of the mosque will see that the floor is covered with large and beautiful carpets; but the main treasures of this mosque are an ancient copy of the Koran and a coffer which contains a hair of the Prophet. You will also notice the lime-shaded forecourt with a large fountain which is still used for solemn ablutions on Moslem holy occasions, the magnificent loggia—and as you go through one of the gateways you will not miss, I hope, the quaint

IN THE TRENTA VALLEY

Plate 41

Yugoslavia's highest mountains are found in the Julian Alps, in Slovenia, the northernmost of the six republics. One of the most beautiful parts of this district is the Trenta Valley.

MAIZE DRYING AT NOMENJ

A colourful sight in Slovene villages in the autumn is the masses of golden maize hanging to dry in the sun on the walls of the barns and farmhouses.

Plate 42

In the north-east corner of Slovenia, not far from Maribor and the Pohorje hills, is the town of Ptuj. It was a place of importance in Roman times and to-day is the centre of a region famous for excellent wines.

SVETI DUH, BOHINJ   Plate 44

This charming little church stands beside the Lake of Bohinj, one of the loveliest stretches of water in the Alps. The district has been made a National Park, and so that its beauty may be preserved, no building is now permitted near the lake-shores.

notice which prohibits entry into the courtyard during times of prayer. The other principal mosques are that of Ali Pasha, a fine sixteenth century building in the centre of the city, surrounded by a park, and the Careva Džamija, which dates from the fifteenth century. Near to the Begova Džamija is a tall tower with a clock which is, I think, unique in Europe; it still tells the time in old Turkish characters. Another nearby building in a very strange architectural style is the Kuršumli Medresa, or Moslem Theological College.

The Moslem buildings which I have briefly mentioned are just a few among scores in Sarajevo. The Yugoslavs still call it the "City of a Hundred Mosques". Although this description is a slight exaggeration, one can believe its accuracy when one looks over the town from the hills which rise above it and sees the dozens of graceful white minarets towering everywhere above the dark rooftops. One believes it also when the time of prayer is approaching and the call of the *Muezzin* is heard in all parts of the city.

In former times one of the outstanding interests of Sarajevo was the Baš-Čaršija, the ancient eastern market. It had the same kind of character that one finds in the market-places of Moslem peoples everywhere, from the *Souks* of north-west Africa or of Cairo to the bazaars in Istanbul. Much of the *čaršija* has been destroyed in recent years but the part that remains is still picturesque. In the front of their open wooden booths one can see silversmiths making fine filigree jewellery, shoemakers fashioning slippers of red and yellow leather, men hammering out copper plates and coffee-pots, or carrying on many another ancient craft. Every now and then one passes a coffee-shop, invariably full of men whom the delicious aroma has enticed away from their work. Although the passers-by look more western than they did before the war they are still Turkish enough in appearance and dress to make one realise that the *čaršija,* and indeed much of Sarajevo, still belongs to the east as much as to the west. The women no longer wear the veil, for it is now forbidden in Yugoslavia, but young and old go about in the voluminous baggy trousers known as *zars*; and if they see a man looking attentively at them will still draw their scarves about their faces. It takes more than the decree of a government to uproot a habit which is so instinctive to a Moslem woman.

Not all of Sarajevo is Moslem, however, and one of its most interesting buildings is the old Orthodox church. The Turks permitted its construction on the express condition that it was to be concealed from the eyes of the Faithful, and in order not to offend them it was surrounded by a high wall, one side of which still stands today. A visit should also be made to the National Museum, which has a very fine collection of peasant costumes and embroideries.

Sarajevo is surrounded on all sides by hills, and except in the months of high summer the views extend to snow-capped mountains. A number of interesting excursions can be made into the countryside and for those whose tastes lead them farther afield there is excellent walking and mountaineering. The nearest resort is the spa of Ilidža, whose hot sulphur springs were known to the Romans. Today it is the favourite picnic-place of the people of the city and it can be reached by train or bus in about twenty minutes. Kiseljak and Fojnica are two other spas, both in beautiful surroundings; the bus journey to them takes two hours from Sarajevo. The finest mountain regions lie to the south and rise to the watershed along the border of Bosnia and Hercegovina. Near to Sarajevo itself is Trebević (5,343 feet), the summit of which can be reached on foot in under two hours from the centre of the city, and further away are the wild ranges of Romanija, Jahorina, Bjelašnica and Treskavica—a paradise for the mountain walker, rock-climber and camper. In winter, too, these are magnificent ski-ing terrains. There are many mountain huts, and a number of small hotels and pensions in the valleys. This is a rich region for the huntsman, too, as the hills and forests abound in deer, wild boar, fox and chamois. This is also a district in which wolves still range; indeed, their numbers have increased in recent years because they were not hunted systematically during the years that Bosnia was occupied by the Germans. They have become a source of much danger to the mountain flocks and a premium is now offered for every wolf-skin brought back by the huntsmen.

The main railway line from Sarajevo to Zagreb and Belgrade runs through a region of fertile fields and forests past Lašva, the junction for Travnik and Jajce, then past Zenica, a great and still developing steel-city, and through Doboj Novi, whence the newly-constructed branch line runs to Banja Luka. Everyone bound farther west has to change at Lašva on to a narrow-gauge train which puffs slowly over the mountains. Travnik, about thirty miles from Lašva, has a history which has left its imprint on the town of today, for most of the three centuries following the year 1555 it was the headquarters of the Turkish Governors of Bosnia and it was in effect the capital of the province. It has several fine mosques and many picturesque Turkish houses and narrow winding alleys. Its position is magnificent, overlooking the wild river Lašva. Its small hotel, the Vlašić (category C) is named after one of the many high mountains in the ranges which surround it.

On leaving Travnik the railway climbs over a watershed and then descends into the valley of the river Vrbas, which it follows to Jajce. This ancient town, the one-time capital of the Kings of Bosnia, is one of the beauty-spots of Yugoslavia. It stands on a hill amid thickly-wooded mountains and its walls climb up to the ruined castle of Hrvoje Vukčić. Around Jajce flows the river Pliva and just below the town there is a magnificent waterfall, over which the river drops a hundred feet or more. Inside the walls of Jajce is a picturesque medley of steep narrow streets, with many beautifully designed stone houses standing beside incredibly tumble-down wooden dwellings. It is another town of mosques and minarets, but among them stands an extraordinarily beautiful campanile in the Venetian style. The town's best hotel is the Pliva (category C), which is near the railway station.

Jajce has recently acquired a new significance in the history of the Balkans, for in 1943 there was held here the second session of the Anti-Fascist Council of the National Liberation of Yugoslavia. The decisions taken on that occasion are regarded by the Yugoslavs as having laid the foundations of the federal state of today.

The railway journey from Jajce to Banja Luka is a very picturesque one but unfortunately it is also very slow and tiring, involving two changes, usually without adequate connections. Most people, therefore, will travel between the two towns by one of the occasional public buses. This, too, is an attractive journey. If you have any choice it is best to take the route which passes by the lake formed by the river Pliva but in any event much of your journey will be along the banks of the Vrbas, and extremely picturesque it is with the river flowing through deep gorges.

Banja Luka lies by the side of this river and is another town of oriental houses and narrow winding streets. It was known as a watering place even to the Romans. A person who has seen Jajce or Travnik will probably find Banja Luka rather less interesting. It should not, however, be missed by the tourist who is not planning to go far beyond Zagreb but who would like to spend a day or two in a part of Yugoslavia which was Turkish and is therefore very different from Croatia and the north. There is a regular service of express buses connecting Zagreb and Banja Luka, the journey taking only about three and a half hours. The two hotels of Banja Luka, both of them of category B and near to the railway station, are the Bosna and the Palace.

(xiii) ZAGREB AND INLAND CROATIA

Zagreb is the capital of Croatia and the second largest city of Yugoslavia. Through many centuries it has been a place of importance, due to its strategic position between the range of hills known as Zagreb Mountain and the river Sava. In former times there were two distinct units of Zagreb—a secular town on the hillside, dominating the river valley, and an ecclesiastical city just beneath it to the east. Each of these settlements maintained its separate individuality up to the nineteenth century; the upper town, known as Gradec, was administered by a council elected from among the townsfolk, mostly small traders and craftsmen, whilst the Kaptol surrounding the Gothic cathedral and bishop's palace was ruled by the bishops and canons.

Zagreb suffered great damage during an invasion of the Tartars during the year 1241 and it was following this that the walls of Gradec were constructed and many special trading privileges were given to the town. As a result of this many enterprising foreign merchants and tradesmen began to settle there and to take part in the development of Zagreb's commerce.

The Kaptol was not fortified until much later, when the Turks were threatening Zagreb. Much of inland Croatia was conquered by the Turks, but though on many occasions their cavalry raided the outskirts of the city neither the secular nor the ecclesiastical part ever fell into their hands. Up to the seventeenth century the houses had been mostly constructed of timber, with thatched or shingled roofs, but from then on a great change took place and the original parts of Zagreb were given the character which remains today. New buildings began to be constructed of stone and with red, tiled roofs, in the baroque and classical styles of architecture, and it is these which now give such grace to the older sectors of the city. Meanwhile, of course, Zagreb has spread far beyond the boundaries of the two original settlements, and the modern city stretches in all directions, filling the plain between the hills and the river, extending east and west and also climbing up the lower slopes of Zagreb Mountain.

As you emerge from the Central Station, or Glavni Kolodvor, everything of interest in Zagreb lies in front of you or towards your left. Immediately ahead is a green square, the Starčevićev Trg, with the monumental Hotel Esplanade (category B) on your left, the Putnik office on a corner facing the station exit and the Hotel Central (category C) and one of the main post offices away to your right. Behind the square is the park of Zrinjevac, a wide strip of formal gardens which stretches deep into the heart of the city. To reach the older parts of Zagreb you can take a No. 2 tram from the station to the Trg Republike. As you cross over to the tram-stop you will see a sight which is a common one everywhere in the country—a line of bootblacks. Here a dozen or more of them have their pitches along a tree-shaded island in the middle of the road, spaced out neatly as if to form part of the symmetry of the square and gardens. The dusty condition of Yugoslav roads means that here, as elsewhere, they have no lack of customers.

Your ten-dinar ride takes you along one side of the gardens, passing on your left the children's Puppet Theatre, the Hotel Palas (category A), the Modern Art Gallery, with works by Degas, Renoir and other foreign painters as well as modern Yugoslavs, and the Archaeological Museum. On the right-hand side, in the gardens, are an exhibition gallery and the Yugoslav Academy, with a fine collection of old masters of all schools from the early Italian Renaissance to the French of the nineteenth century. Away to the right, across the gardens, is the Hotel Beograd (category B).

After passing the end of this green stretch the tram turns into the busy Trg Republike, the Square of the Republic. This is the hub of modern Zagreb, and from it runs towards the west the main shopping-street of the city, known as Ilica. In the square itself are the

215

Hotel Dubrovnik (category B) and many cafés and restaurants.

From Trg Republike there are three ways of reaching the old district of Gradec, now known to the people of Zagreb as the Gornji Grad, or Upper Town. You can walk up the street called Radićeva (signposted "Gornji Grad") which runs from the north-western corner of the square and, turning along the first alley on the left-hand side, climb up two flights of steps to the Strossmayer Promenade, overlooking the modern city; or you can continue farther up Radićeva and enter Gornji Grad through the Kamenita Vrata, or Stone Gate. If you are less energetic you can walk a short distance along Ilica and then ascend to the old town by the funicular railway for a fare of five dinars.

At the top of the funicular is the Dverce tower, once the southern entrance to Gradec. Even today a bell is rung each evening from the tower, a reminder of the times when the curfew was sounded and the town securely closed for the night. The ancient walls can be seen here and below them is the Strosmajerovo Šetalište, a shady promenade with an extensive panorama to the south and, from the eastern end, at the top of the steps I have mentioned, a superb view of the cathedral over the red rooftops of Kaptol. Pass through the Dverce tower and you will see the Church of St. Catherine in a square on your right and St. Mark's in the Radićev Trg straight ahead. These two churches are very different in their styles of architecture and decoration. St. Catherine's was once the church of a Jesuit monastery and it dates from the seventeenth and eighteenth centuries. Its extravagantly decorated interior is a fine example of the baroque. St. Mark's is one of the most interesting buildings I know, and no visitor to Zagreb should fail to see it.

The square in which it stands used to be the centre of the life and activity of the old town. Here was the market (now removed to the newer part of Zagreb), and the fairs which were held in the Radićev Trg were as important to the commerce of the middle ages as the great Industrial Fair, which is held each autumn in specially built pavilions near the Central Station, is today. In the centre of the square stands St. Mark's. Its main structure dates from the fourteenth and fifteenth centuries, but its outstanding glories are of much more recent dates. In the second half of the nineteenth century the church was completely restored and it was then that it acquired the brightly-coloured tiled roof with the coats of arms of Croatia, Slavonia (one of the provinces of Croatia and not to be confused with Slovenia), Dalmatia and the city of Zagreb itself. Some architectural experts have been critical of this roof, but to my mind the bold decorations blend strangely but well with the older and more formal buildings in the square.

At the same time that this exuberant roof was made the interior of the church was refurbished, but this, so I have been told, was carried out in the crude and unsympathetic manner so common to mid-nineteenth century restoration everywhere. Under an enlightened bishop a new restoration was carried out in 1937 and the work was entrusted to two modern Croatian artists, the painter Joza Kljaković and the famous sculptor Ivan Meštrović. This work is very far from being traditional in style, yet it blends successfully with the Gothic architecture. It includes a superb wooden crucifix and a beautiful and impressive relief of St. Mark, both by

Meštrović, and some interesting frescoes by his friend and colleague. In these paintings Kljaković has used typical Croat peasant types and costumes in his portrayal of the Christ-story, thus following the Slav fresco-painters of medieval times who always used the people of their own day and countries to illustrate the stories of the Bible. Today as you watch the village women selling their lace or their vegetables in the market place above Trg Republike or as you see the peasants kneeling at the shrine inside the Stone Gate, you will observe the same quiet countenances, the sad but peaceful features that we have come to associate with Mary and with Joseph. It is these that Kljaković has used in his frescoes in St. Mark's.

I need not describe any other of the buildings in the Gornji Grad. It is the quiet atmosphere of the streets the dignity of the façades and of the courtyards, the feeling that this is something from another age, that give to this old town a character and a beauty which are more important than the detail of any one building.

As you descend from the Radićev Trg you pass through the Kamenita Vrata, or Stone Gate, which I have mentioned. Inside the gate is something which, to my mind, is one of the great witnesses to the importance of religion in the life of the Croats. It is a shrine in which the candles are always burning and which is never without devout people kneeling at prayer. Even the men who hurry through raise their hats as they pass. Here, if anywhere in Yugoslavia, is an example of the fact that religion is as free and as open for the common people today as in former ages.

By comparison with Gornji Grad the buildings of the Kaptol are not particularly outstanding. The cathedral has an imposing exterior, with graceful twin spires, but it suffered badly last century owing to enthusiastic but uninspired restoration, and the interior is now of little interest. The bishops' palace beside it was constructed at the same period and in the same baroque and classical styles as most of the buildings in Gornji Grad. Near the cathedral is the market place, which can also be reached by a flight of steps leading up from Trg Republike. Here, every day of the week, you can see the peasant women, gay in their colourful costumes, who have come in from the nearby villages to sell their fruit and vegetables and dairy produce. Some, too, display beautiful lace and other hand-made craft-work. It is a very gay scene and it offers countless excellent opportunities to the photographer.

Some way to the west of the stretch of gardens between the station and the city centre, and parallel with it, is another green strip. Here are the National Theatre and Opera House, where the productions are of a high standard, the Ethnographical Museum with a rich collection of national costumes and handicrafts and some interesting reconstructions of interiors of Croatian peasant houses, the Museum of Arts and Crafts, the University Library, which is the largest in the Balkans, and the Botanical Gardens. Apart from the hotels already mentioned there are the Imperial, in the street called Frankopanska, near the National Theatre, and the Jadran, which is in Vlaška, not far from the cathedral. Both these are included in category B. The main post office of the city is in Jurišićeva, the street which is a continuation of Ilica on the eastern side of Trg Republike.

The trams of Zagreb go well out into the country and, provided that you name your destination on boarding the first one and ask for an exchange ticket, you can change to a tram of another number, still continuing in the same general onward direction, without paying a second ten-dinar fare. For example, if you board a No. 14 tram at Trg Republike and ask for a "prelazna karta" to Gračani, you change at Mihaljevac, the No. 14 terminus, on to a No. 21 all the way to the country village of Gračani.

The whole of the No. 21 tram route has been constructed by voluntary working-parties and, as it climbs steeply along one side of a deep, wooded valley, it was quite a skilful piece of engineering and involved a great deal of manual labour. A start was made on a more ambitious project, an extension of the tram-route from Gračani through a tunnel under mount Sljeme to Stubičke Toplice, a beautiful spa much visited by the Zagreb people. Unfortunately, this project has had to be abandoned due to lack of money, but I hope that it will be possible for the work to be taken up again before very long.

You should visit Gračani on Sunday, when the village women go to mass in their beautiful costumes. Another "costume village" is Šestine, which can be reached by a short bus ride from the No. 14 tram-route terminus at Mihaljevac. Above these northern outliers of Zagreb rises the range of hills called the Zagrebačka Gora, or Zagreb Mountain, rising to their highest point at Sljeme, 3,000 feet over the city and 3,400 feet above sea-level. The citizens are indeed fortunate in having so much wild and beautiful country almost on their doorsteps and they make much use of their opportunities; at week-ends and holiday times thousands of them go rambling among these hills, and there are several mountain huts. Near the summit of Sljeme is a hotel of category B, owned by the Mountaineering Association of Croatia, which commands a wonderful view across the plain of the Sava—and which can also be reached by road.

Away to the north of Sljeme are the rolling hills of the Zagorje, a beautiful district rich in folk-lore and costumes as well as in forests and vineyards. Through the Zagorje the river Sutla runs in a very pretty valley and near to the border of Slovenia is Kumrovec, the simple little village where Marshal Tito was born. Set in a picturesque landscape, Kumrovec has become a place of national pilgrimage. Tito's birthplace has now been made into a museum and the village has a small hotel, the Kumrovec (category B). Another attractive region is around Zlatar, due north of Zagreb.

The Zagorje is a land of medieval castles. The fortress of Trakošćan, the best preserved and one of the most impressive, stands in a dominating position overlooking a charming lake. Inside this castle is now an interesting museum. Another splendid castle is at Veliki Tabor, dating from the fifteenth century and used today as a students' holiday-home. The Zagorje also has several spas, the best known being Stubičke Toplice, near Zagreb, and Varaždinske Toplice, which is farther to the north. Not far from the latter is the old town of Varaždin, with many ancient buildings and palaces in the baroque style. Excursions to Kumrovec, Trakošćan and others of the places I have mentioned are arranged by the Putnik office in Zagreb; but the Zagorje is, above all, an excellent region for walking tours.

A journey which I strongly recommend is the one from Zagreb to Split, with a break at the National Park and the famous lakes of Plitvice. At first the railway crosses a fertile plain but beyond Karlovac it commences to climb into the hills, and then, until the coast is in sight, a distance of well over two hundred miles, it is mountains, mountains all the way. At first they are green and forested but gradually they become more barren until, beyond Oštarije, the typical dry *karst* is reached. The railway climbs more steeply and then for mile after mile it contours around some of the wildest and most sterile mountains of Europe. It is a landscape of stones and of relentless rock, almost completely devoid of villages and inhabitants.

The tourist who is not going beyond the Plitvice lakes will alight at the station of Vrhovine-Plitvička Jezera. There the train is met by a local bus, which takes him the last ten miles to Plitvice. The lakes, sixteen in number, form a chain nearly eight miles in length and they follow one beneath the other on a series of terraces, connected by cascades and waterfalls. The upper lakes lie amid wooded hills which slope gently down towards them, the colours reflecting on their quiet surfaces. The lower lakes are wild and impressive, turbulent water in deep gorges, with rushing falls joining one lake to the other. The climax comes in the lowest of them, where a river plunges over one of the walls of the gorge, to fall a sheer 250 feet into the lake below.

The Plitvička Jezera are surrounded by the woods and mountains of the National Park, an area which will delight every lover of natural beauty. For the person who likes quiet country rambling and for the fisherman, too, it would be difficult to recommend a more pleasant place than Plitvice. There are several hotels, especially by Lake Kozjak in the centre of the chain, the Vile Na Plitvičkim Jezerima (category B) being the most convenient.

(xiv) SLOVENIA

Slovenia is the northernmost of the Yugoslav republics and is bordered by Italy along the western frontier and by Austria in the north. Although the Slovenes are a Slav people, their history and their language have given them characteristics which are different from most of the other peoples of the country. Their forefathers settled among the mountains about the sixth century after Christ and they were later incorporated in the Empire of Charlemagne. Eventually Slovenia became part of Austria, and remained so until the formation of Yugoslavia after the first world war.

The towns of Slovenia today are in many ways hardly distinguishable from those of Carinthia or Styria. There is the same style of architecture, the formal gardens have changed little since they were laid out in Austrian days and the cafés and restaurants have a character similar to that one finds across the frontier. The nationalist spirit in Slovenia belonged essentially to the common people, its strength being found in the rural districts, farther away from Austrian influences. In these remoter parts the peasants retained their Slav language and their Slav traditions and it was among the fields and forests and the mountain villages that the longing for independence persisted for more than a thousand years. It became woven into the folk-lore and legends of the people and its theme was taken up by poets and writers in the nineteenth century. It was fostered by some of the village priests and even by Slovene Bishops of the Roman Church. Eventually it spread to all of the people and culminated in a common front of independence which was established by the Slovenes and Croats together.

The centuries of Austrian occupation have left their mark on the character of the Slovenes. They are more business-like and efficient, have a greater cultural heritage, are smarter and "more western" than the Serbs; their towns look, and indeed are, busier and more prosperous; their roads are well-surfaced and carry far more cars and other vehicles than those of the districts farther south. It is rare to find a person who does not know some German and a high proportion of the inhabitants speak it with fluency. Yet German is not used except to talk to foreigners; if there are any parts of Slovenia where it is still the everyday language of the people I have yet to discover them.

Slovene is a language in its own right and not, as is sometimes supposed, a dialect of the Serbo-Croat which is spoken in most of the rest of Yugoslavia. A large number of words are common, although often with slight changes, to both languages and there are many similarities between the two grammars. So it is that one language is comprehensible to the people who speak the other, and the tourist who masters a few words and phrases in Serbo-Croat will find them of use in Slovenia, and vice-versa. If you make any attempt to study the Yugoslav languages you should start with Serbo-Croat, for not only is it generally more useful but its grammar is much less complicated and archaic than Slovenian.

Most of Slovenia is mountainous and wooded. In the north are the great ranges of the Julian Alps, the

Plate 45

DOM NA POKLJUKA

In winter there is excellent ski-ing in the Slovenian Alps. The Sport-Hotel of Pokljuka, not far from the popular tourist resort of **Bled**, is an excellent centre for the winter-sports enthusiast.

CHESS PLAYERS   Plate 46

Wherever one travels in Yugoslavia one sees people playing chess. Most Slav
peoples excel at the game; the Yugoslavs are no exception to this and they
have produced some outstanding international players.

YUGOSLAV BAGPIPES   Plate 47

The clansmen of the southern mountains of Yugoslavia are in many ways like
the Highlanders of Scotland. The bagpipes are often heard when there is
folk-dancing in progress.

YUGOSLAV FOLK-DANCING

Every district has its traditional folk-dances and the teams of dancers who have travelled through Europe have gained an international reputation. The men's dances are often vigorous, needing much strength and agility, whereas those of the women are usually lyrical and graceful.

Plate 48

Karavanken and the Kamnik or Savinjske Alps. To the north-east, near Maribor, lie the beautiful, rolling hills of the Pohorje. These are the main groups, but everywhere else is hilly also—the Zasavje and Dolenjska groups, on either side of the River Sava to the east of Ljubljana; the Polhograjski Dolomites west of that city; the mountains of Bloke and the Karst hills (known in Slovenia as *kras*) through which the Simplon line passes between Trieste and Rijeka—these are but a few of the ranges in a republic which for the beauty of its inland scenery is unsurpassed in Yugoslavia and which will bear comparison with any part of Europe.

Yet Slovenia is rich not merely in scenery. The forests which cover the lower slopes of the mountains form a reservoir of wealth for the republic, and many industries have arisen as a direct result. You will see furniture from Slovenia everywhere in Yugoslavia and it has long been an important export to Central Europe —and very good furniture it is, too. Between the mountain ranges and in the river valleys, and also among the lower hills, there are fertile agricultural areas, with maize and other cereals and dairy-farming. Slovenia is also an important wine-producing region, the district around Maribor being the best known in this respect.

The capital of Slovenia is Ljubljana and it is the place where a large proportion of visitors spend their first day or two in Yugoslavia. It stands at the cross-roads of three important routes—Vienna to Trieste, a vital line of communication to the old Austrian Empire, and the Simplon-Orient and Tauern Express routes of today. It is a city which is well worth a brief visit, but it regards itself essentially as a transit place from the point of view of the tourist.

The railway station is quite near to the centre of the city. As you emerge you will see tram-lines in front of you and if you take any tram going in the right-hand direction you will reach the post office (pošta) in a few minutes. A stone's throw from the post office are the Putnik office, which is a very efficient one, and the Hotel Slon, category A. This is one of the best hotels in Yugoslavia and it has many rooms with private bathrooms—though most of them overlook one of Ljubljana's main thoroughfares, and if you are a light sleeper you may be disturbed very early in the morning when the noisy trams start to rumble round the corner. The restaurant at the Slon is expensive, and I usually eat at the cheap and characterful No. 6 Restaurant, or Šestica, a little way along the same street. Almost facing this is Ljubljana's skyscraper, with the Café Nebotičnik on the top floor commanding a wonderful view of the city and the surrounding hills and mountains. This is an excellent place to go for your morning coffee or for your šljivovica.

At the end of the street behind the skyscraper is the National Gallery, and nearby are the Opera House, the National Museum and the Gallery of Modern Art. All these buildings stand in wide squares, surrounded by lawns and flower-beds, and beyond them stretches the Tivoli Park and some pleasant wooded hills, on the slopes of which is another hotel, the Bellevue (category B). If you are spending a night at Ljubljana you should make a point of going to the opera. There are nightly performances throughout much of the year and the productions are of a high standard. Charges for admission are very low indeed and the Putnik office will book your seat for you.

The hotel most used by foreign holiday visitors is

the Union (category B), in the street named Miklošičeva. It is about ten minutes walk from the station
and five minutes from the Pošta tram-stop. A new
hotel of the same category, the Turist, which has
recently been opened, is nearby. Almost facing the
station itself is the Dom Jla, an inexpensive category
C hotel.

At the far end of Miklošičeva you will see a fine
statue of Prešeren, one of Slovenia's greatest national
poets, and beyond is the attractive little river
Ljubljanica, here crossed by three graceful bridges and
with a fine loggia along the top of one of its high
embankments. Beyond the river lies the old part of
Ljubljana, with its red-roofed houses of the seventeenth
century, above which rises the great hill on which
stands the castle, dominating the city. It is reached by
a footpath which winds steeply from the old town, and
no visitor should fail to go up to it. It is now surrounded by a wide terrace with extensive views on
every side, but a better view still can be obtained by
going through the gate of the castle and across the
inner courtyard to the tower, from the top of which one
surveys the country for many miles around. There are
two pointers indicating the names of the various mountains on the skyline, and the view extends as far as the
Julian Alps, including the summits of Triglav, the
highest mountain in Yugoslavia.

One of the best-known places in Slovenia, and indeed
in all Yugoslavia, is Bled. Its beauty lies in its mountain lake with an islet, crowned by a white-towered
church, in the centre. A fourteenth-century castle
stands on a bluff overlooking the lake, which is encircled by dark forests of pine and spruce, with the
peaks of the Karavanken and Julian Alps, snow-

capped until early summer, forming an impressive background.

Most of the hotels are found in the town of Bled itself, at the eastern end of the lake. It is most conveniently reached by local bus from Lesce-Bled, on the main Tauern Express railway line from Jesenice, the frontier station, to Ljubljana. Bled is also connected with Ljubljana by a regular direct bus-service. The hotels are very numerous, ranging from the palatial Toplice (category A) with its own natural warm-spring swimming-pool to several in category C, such as the Union and the Lovec, the latter being especially recommended. In between these extremes are the category B hotels—the Park, nearly as expensive as the Toplice, and the Jelovica. At the eastern end of the lake is the railway station of Bled Jezero, on a branch line from Jesenice. This is a much less sophisticated part of the Bled valley, but people who want to go on excursions organised by the Putnik office may feel that it is rather too remote. The hotels are the Zaka and the Triglav, both category C, situated nearly five miles from the village of Bled itself. It is near here that the Yugoslav Government has a large and beautiful villa, sometimes used by Marshal Tito as a summer residence and for the reception of foreign visitors. It stands on the site of a villa which belonged to the former royal family and which was destroyed by fire during the war.

There are many delightful walks around Bled. You can climb up to the old castle in about twenty minutes, and from its courtyard you have some fine views of the lake and mountains. The castle itself is interesting; it dates from the year 1004 and its medieval character has been faithfully preserved. There are several other view-points on the hills around the lake, all providing pleasant walks of an hour or so, and a leaflet describing the routes, which are along marked paths, can be obtained from the Putnik office. (This will be found in the terrace of shops beneath the Park Hotel.) Longer walks, taking half a day, can be made to the waterfalls and gorge of Vintgar, to the crag called Babji Zob (or "Granny's Tooth") and an interesting cave nearby, and to the natural gardens of Pokljuški Vrtci. For trips such as these it is advisable to have boots or very stout shoes.

The Putnik office organises many excursions to places more distant. A pleasant trip is to the plateau of Pokljuka, eleven miles from Bled. Here is a very fine mountain hotel, the Dom na Pokljuka, category B, which is an attractive place at which to stay for a few days. Its height above sea-level is 4,600 feet and it is a good centre for short mountain walks. It is also an excellent and very well-known ski-ing resort. The lake of Bohinj, to the south-west of Bled, is visited on another beautiful half-day excursion which is regularly organised by Putnik. They also run coaches to Kranjska Gora, near the point where Yugoslavia, Austria and Italy all meet; to the Trenta Valley, near the Italian frontier to the west of Bled; and even as far as the grottoes of Postojna. Ljubljana can, of course, be visited by the regular bus services, or by rail.

One short trip which I made from Bled and which I found very interesting indeed was to the village of Kropa, which lies to the west of the road and railway from Bled to Ljubljana, not far from the industrial town of Kranj. This is the village in which is made most of the black, wrought-iron work—lamps, candle-sticks, ash-trays, chandeliers, door-knockers, gateways and window-grills—which is seen all over Slovenia.

Most of the men of this village are blacksmiths and their families have been engaged in this craft since the sixteenth century. The mountain streams have been diverted through culverts to provide the motive power for their bellows and hammers and the work is carried on as for many generations past, the secrets of the craft being passed from father to son. If you visit Kropa you will admire not only the beauty of their creations, many of which adorn their own houses, but the patience and precision with which they work.

Bohinj is a strong rival to Bled as a place at which to spend a holiday, and in my own opinion it is more beautiful. Its lake is much larger, its surroundings grander and more rugged, its atmosphere far less sophisticated. The mountains of the Julian Alps enclose it on three sides, on the north shore falling nearly sheer to the water's edge. Around the lake there is an almost complete absence of buildings, and the fact that the district is now a national park means that further building is prohibited. The former Yugoslav royal family owned a villa at the eastern end of the lake and it was from here that was announced the engagement of the late Duke of Kent and Princess Marina of Greece.

The beautiful little church stands at this end of the lake, where there is a comparatively level river valley stretching down to the village of Bohinjska Bistrica. Here is the railway station, on a branch line from Jesenice. Buses meet some of the trains and take passengers to the lake and the few hotels always arrange taxis to meet their clients. For those who walk it is nearly four miles to Sv. Janez, the village at the eastern end, and a further three miles to the Hotel Zlatarog at the western end. At Sv. Janez are the Hotels Bellevue and Jezero. They are both in category B, but the latter also has an annexe, called the Vila na Koku, which is in category C. The Zlatarog is in category B also, but it maintains an alpine-hut style annexe, with dormitory accommodation. Half-way along the lake, on the southern shore, is the magnificently situated Hotel pod Voglom (category C), near the charming little church of Sv. Duh. The unspoilt and natural character of Bohinj can be emphasized by saying that when one has named these hotels, one has mentioned almost all the buildings by the lake-shore. Of course, Bohinj is no place for the tourist who is anxious to see a lot of Yugoslavia. Once you are at Bohinj it takes a lot of effort to leave; it must be visited for itself and not for places to be reached from it.

The walker can make Bohinj a base from which to start off for a tramp through the Julian Alps, for the valley is one of the natural gateways into these magnificent mountains, which are among the most beautiful ranges of Europe. Although they are all of limestone, the variety of the scenery is amazing. There are deep, wooded valleys, great pinnacles of rock and peaks as pointed as the Matterhorn, roaring waterfalls and many lakes. The great triple-peak of Triglav dominates the range from its central position, but there are countless others which are as fine to climb, among them Razor, Prisojnik and Mojstrovka; Mangart and Jalovec; and Škrlatica, the Scarlet One, so named because of its red hues at sunset.

It is an area which even the man or woman who is practised in mountain walking or climbing will find can offer some exciting moments, but there are many fixed ropes in dangerous places and nearly all the main peaks can be climbed by routes which do not involve rock-climbing proper. There are, too, routes which avoid the more precipitous ascents, yet pass through some of the most attractive scenery. There are numerous mountain huts and of these I have already said something on page 40. They are well used by Slovene mountaineers and they and the hut-keepers will always be prepared to give you helpful advice, but it is essential for people who plan to go to the Julian Alps to have had some experience of strenuous mountain walking elsewhere. This part of Slovenia is no place to make your first essay among the high peaks unless, of course, you are with more experienced companions.

Those who do not feel that they can tackle the really big summits can get near to them, however, in a pleasant walk of a few days from Bohinj. They should start by taking the path from the Hotel Zlatarog and go on to the Savica waterfall. Here the Sava gushes, a full-grown river, from a limestone cliff in the face of the rock and falls nearly 200 feet. It is an impressive sight. Three hours' walk beyond the fall brings you to the Koča pri Triglavskih Jezerih, the Triglav Lakes mountain hut. Next day you can follow the Valley of the Seven Lakes (though there are really more than seven of them) to the Koča na Doliču. A good walker will reach this hut in three hours or less. This short and easy excursion from Bohinj will whet your appetite for more strenuous days, but it will at least give the complete beginner an introduction to the Julian Alps and will take him through a lovely area of woods and lakes, with the valley-floor carpeted with alpine flowers, to the threshold of the world of the high mountains.

The frontier town of Jesenice, on the direct line from Salzburg to Ljubljana and the south, is also the junction for the railway which runs through the upper valley of the River Sava to Planica, on the Italian border. This is the valley which divides the Julian Alps from the Karavanken range. Along it is a succession of mountain villages, each of them a delightful summer resort. The valley is, however, more famous as a winter-sports region—indeed it is the best-known and most-visited ski-ing district in Yugoslavia.

The first settlement up the valley is Mojstrana, and despite its well-deserved popularity as a holiday resort it still retains much of the simple, unspoilt character of a typical Slovene mountain village. It stands at the entrance of the alpine valley of Vrata, which leads up to the Aljažev mountain hut and to the northern wall of Triglav. The hotel of Mojstrana is named after the latter, and is in C category. The next place is Gozd-Martuljek, an exceedingly pretty village. It lies below a crescent of unbelievably rugged peaks, named the Martuljek Group, whose dozen chief summits rise to altitudes of over 8,000 feet. Most of these climbs are difficult ones, only to be attempted by first-class rock-climbers unless a local guide is employed, but there are many delightful walks from Gozd which do not take the rambler into wild and dangerous places. The village possesses a large trade-union hotel (the Sindikalni Počitniški Dom, category B) and one or two smaller and simpler pensions.

Two miles from Gozd is Kranjska Gora, the largest village in the valley. It is an ideal alpine resort in summer, and the fact that it has a ski-lift, a rarity as yet in Yugoslavia, makes it a popular winter sports centre. Many hotels and villas have sprung up, but the old village atmosphere remains. The best-known hotel, and the most convenient for the ski-lift, is the Erika,

233

S

category B. The Razor and the Slavec, both category C, are others which are recommended.

At Podkoren, two more miles up the valley, the road branches off to the Koren Pass towards Villach in Austria. For the motorist this is one of the most dramatic points of entry into Yugoslavia. The road is usually open from April till the end of November. During the remaining months of the year cars are carried by rail between Rosenbach and Jesenice, through the long tunnel under the Karavanken.

The last Yugoslav village on the upper Sava is Rateče, picturesque and unspoilt, and a good base for some pleasant walks and for mountain climbs of all grades. Unfortunately its position near the boundaries of three countries tends to restrict the visitor, as these frontiers are strictly closed and are patrolled by soldiers. Rateče comes into its own in March each year, when the mammoth ski-jump in the Planica valley, which leads to the south from the village, is the scene of international contests. The hotel of the village is the Dom v Planici, category B, but it has several annexes of both B and C categories.

Let us now return to Kranjska Gora and take the road which runs from it towards the south. This is the road which leads over the Vršič Pass to the Trenta Valley and then along the Italian frontier to Bovec, Tolmin and Nova Gorica. It is one of the most attractive roads in northern Yugoslavia and no motorist should omit it from his itinerary. It is also a favourite route for excursions organised by various Putnik offices in Slovenia, such as the ones at Bled and Ljubljana. Along this road there are several mountain huts—Erjavčeva and Tičarjev near the summit of Vršič and Zlatarog farther south command the finest positions—

and hotels of C category at some of the villages, especially at Soča and Bovec.

Before leaving the western part of Slovenia we must have a look at the Grottoes of Postojna. These are the most famous of the many underground caverns found in the *karst* region between Ljubljana and Trieste. The subterranean waters have, through the ages, deposited tiny particles of limestone and they have grown into great pillars and needles, curtains of shining stone, and countless fantastic shapes, some of them of the greatest beauty, others weird or grotesque. The caves are visited by thousands of people every summer and they are certainly one of the natural wonders of Yugoslavia. They stretch for several miles, but you do not have to walk—the visit is made by a little electric railway! Many people will feel that the commercial atmosphere of Postojna—the railway, the pathways and railings, the crowds of people—introduce a discordant note into a place of such great beauty. To them I recommend a visit to Škocjan caves, near Divača. These are smaller than those of Postojna but are just as beautiful, and they have a wild and romantic character which Postojna has now lost.

Both Postojna and Divača are within a few miles of each other on the main Simplon railway line between Ljubljana and Trieste. Postojna has a category C hotel, the Javornik, and there is also a large restaurant at the grottoes themselves. If you stay at Postojna and can hire a car (or, of course, if you have your own) I strongly recommend a visit to Predjama, about five miles to the north-west. A ridge of rock rises steeply above the surrounding countryside and a beautiful castle is dramatically perched on its flank, partly built into the entrance of an enormous cave in the hillside.

Within the cave there continues for several miles a labyrinth of underground passages. The castle itself now contains a most interesting archaeological collection.

Away to the east of Slovenia is the town of Maribor. It stands on the Vienna-Ljubljana railway, not far from the Austrian frontier, and it has always been a place of importance. Today it is the second largest city of Slovenia, but it has a more provincial and less hurried atmosphere than Ljubljana. It possesses one of the best-arranged museums that I have visited in Yugoslavia, with a most friendly and enthusiastic curator. I spent a whole day in his company whilst on a visit to Maribor and it was from him that I learnt a great deal about the town and the surrounding district. The museum is in the centre of the town and is housed in the castle, an imposing building of the fifteenth century. The Putnik office and the Hotel Orel, category B, are both nearby.

The chief delights of Maribor, however, are not in the town itself but in its surroundings and particularly in the Pohorje, a long range of mountains lying to the west. Here are no craggy summits and rock-pinnacles, glaciers and precipitous ridges, but rolling hills, deep combes and magnificent forests. It is a region which much resembles the Cairngorms in Scotland and it covers about the same area. The Pohorje is ideal for walking holidays, and a number of mountain huts and marked footpaths have been established by the Mountain Club of Maribor. A very pleasant week can be spent walking from one to the other, and if this is done from east to west, starting from the town, one can continue in the same direction to the higher mountains of the Savinjske Alps. Pohorje is also a pleasant region in which to spend a quiet country holiday. The hills rise to well over 3,000 feet within a few miles of Maribor and here will be found the comfortable Poštarski Dom, Planinka and Železničarski Dom, holiday centres for the various industrial enterprises of the town. They are all graded as category B hotels, but the charges are very low indeed. In winter the Pohorje is a ski-ing district; a ski-lift two miles in length gives the opportunity for fine downhill runs.

A few miles to the south-east of Maribor is the medieval town of Ptuj. It is off the usual track of tourists, but it is very well worth a visit. You can stay at the Beli Križ pension (category C). The great castle is a joy to behold, whether from afar, whence it will be seen on its hilltop, dominating the town and the surrounding countryside, or from its delightful triangular courtyard, above which rise its graceful three storeys, one sweeping loggia above the other, covered by a roof of red tiles of a most lovely hue. Inside the castle is a museum and there is another in the old Dominican monastery; but it is the peaceful atmosphere and the grace and beauty of Ptuj which appeal to me most of all.

Ptuj has also a most interesting Mithraic temple. The cult of Mithras, the sun-god, was Persian in origin but it spread to the Western world; and the Mithraeum at Ptuj owes its existence to the fact that the town, then called Poetovium, was a place of importance to the Romans and the headquarters of the VIIIth Legion. Much of the Mithraic ritual was adopted by the early Christians and has survived to this day. The shape of the church, with the central nave and two side aisles; the position of the altar; the holy symbolism of bread and wine, and of baptism; the observance of 25th

December as a holy day—all these have been identified as being as much part of Mithraism as of Christianity.

Above Ptuj rise the hills of Ptujska Gora and here is a magnificent fourteenth-century Gothic church. Most of the churches of Slovenia were extensively restored during the period of baroque architecture and decoration and lost their former grace and simple beauty. This church was left almost untouched at that period. It is certainly one of the finest Gothic churches in eastern Europe and it is now in the care of the government and carefully preserved as a national possession. Behind the altar is a wonderful piece of carving, which was originally outside, above the entrance-doorway. It depicts Mary shielding with her cloak, which is held open by angels, a hundred or more figures, many of them being famous personages of the time and including the Kings of Bosnia and Hungary.

Also near Ptuj are two castles which are now used as hotels—and graded in category C. The first of these is Borl, dating from the thirteenth century but with most of its decoration being of the seventeenth. It stands on a hill overlooking the River Drava and a landscape of green hills, meadows and vineyards. A few miles further to the west is Štatenberg, a building which reminded me of some of the smaller chateaux of France. It, too, is built on a hill and dominates a rolling landscape of woods and meadowlands which were once the extensive domains of its owner. Although these two castles have been converted to modern use, in neither case have their fine apartments been shorn of their dignity. The guest of today can sleep in a suite beneath beautiful stucco ceilings and surrounded by furniture and decorations of great artistic and intrinsic value.

(xv) TRIESTE AND ISTRIA

The problem of the disputed city of Trieste is always very much in the minds of Yugoslavs and the intelligent visitor to their country will be expected to know something about it when the subject comes up in conversation. Modern Trieste was constructed by the Austrians during the nineteenth century and was the most important port in their empire; railway lines were built to connect it with Vienna, Prague and Budapest and it became a very prosperous and vital centre for the commerce of the countries of Eastern Europe. The population of the city became very mixed indeed—Germans, Austrians, Italians and people of the Slav races—but the rural hinterland, with its Slovene inhabitants, remained unchanged.

The Istrian peninsula, the port of Trieste and northern Dalmatia were among the baits offered to Italy to enter the war of 1914-18 on the side of the Allies. At the end of the war, however, the peacemakers were faced with claims from Yugoslavia for these same territories, in which the Slovenes and Croats far out-numbered the Italians. President Wilson was anxious that such problems should be solved on an ethnographical basis, but a compromise had to be reached. A large area of predominantly Slav population, including Trieste itself and the whole of the peninsula, were awarded to Italy and the port of Fiume (now called Rijeka) became a free city. On the other hand, Dalmatia was incorporated in the new state of Yugoslavia, except for the town of Zadar and a few of the islands which also became Italian.

Hundreds of thousands of Slavs who had been fighting for independence from Austria thus found themselves under Italian rule, and Yugoslavia was very far from satisfied with this arrangement. Their resentment was intensified when the Italians seized Fiume, and they became embittered when they saw how their brothers across the frontier were being treated. The Italians suppressed all Slav schools and cultural institutions, family names had to be Italianized, the use of the Slovene language was proscribed. In fact there was a vigorous and ruthless attempt to destroy the national characteristics of the Slavs in as short a time as possible.

This uneasy situation continued until 1941 when, on the collapse of the Yugoslav forces, the remainder of Slovenia was partitioned between Italy and Germany and the Dalmatian coast as far as Split was annexed to the Italian crown. There followed a period of repression of the Slovenes and Croats and of savage cruelties which are remembered with bitterness by the people today.

By the end of the war the Yugoslav partisans had gained control of all the areas awarded to Italy by Versailles, but they withdrew from the port of Trieste under pressure from the Allied powers. Another compromise was eventually arranged. A free territory of Trieste was to be established, with a neutral governor appointed by the powers which signed the Peace Treaty. Unfortunately the Great Powers failed to agree upon a suitable appointment as, in effect, Russia and the other eastern states would not accept anyone who was not a Communist. Meanwhile the area had been divided into two zones—Zone A, consisting of the port with its now mainly Italian population and a stretch of hinterland almost entirely Slovene, continued to be occupied by British and American troops; Zone

B, adjoining it to the south, predominantly Slav but with a few centres of Italian population along the coast, was occupied by the Yugoslavs. The British and Americans had no desire to remain in Trieste (which cost British taxpayers alone more than £2,000,000 a year) and in 1948 they proposed that the whole area should revert to Italy. At that time, of course, Yugoslavia was still linked with Russia and the Allied move was interpreted as a bribe to the Italian people, made at a time when the Communist Party in Italy was gaining strength.

However, no action was taken to follow up the proposal and the situation remained unchanged until 1953, when on October 8th the British and Americans suddenly declared that they intended to withdraw their forces from Zone A and hand it to the Italians to administer. Nothing was said about Zone B but, remembering the statements made in 1948, the Yugoslavs felt that it would be merely a matter of time before this, too, was awarded to the Italians. Immediately there was a great uprising of national feeling. I was in Yugoslavia at the time and I was impressed by the sincerity with which all the people, ardent supporters of Tito and the strongest critics of the *régime* alike, declared that their "Slovene brothers must not be handed over to Italian slavery". Owing to the experiences of the years between the wars and those of the war itself, that is the natural reaction of all Yugoslavs to the suggestion that any of the districts with a predominantly Slovene population should be administered by Italy. Britain and America were bitterly criticised, too, because their decision had been taken without prior consultation with Belgrade. The people felt that they were being made pawns in the game of international politics and were united in their view that the Slovenes must not be subjected to a further process of Italianization.

So much for the politics of Trieste. Now let us briefly look at the towns and countryside. Within Zone B is the seaside resort of Portorož. It is a fashionable place, rather like Opatija, and has many hotels, ranging from the Palace, category A and with 300 beds, to small category C establishments like the Helios and the Bristol. Nearby is Piran, an ancient seaport which is very picturesque, more like those to be found further south in Dalmatia, with the towers and pinnacles of an old fortress stretching skywards among olive-groves. Other attractive places along the coast are Koper, Ižola and Umag, all easily reached from Portorož.

Apart from Zone B, the Istrian Peninsula belongs to the republic of Croatia. The first town across the zonal boundary is Poreč. It was a Venetian settlement, and there are many very lovely buildings in its streets, and a fine sixth century basilica. The main hotel is the Istra, category B. A few miles farther along the coast is Rovinj, another place of charm and character, famous for its excellent wines (Hotel Jadran, category B), and at the extreme south of the peninsula lies Pula. This has been an important port for more than two thousand years and under the Romans it became a naval base and a flourishing trade centre. During the rule of Augustus and his successors many magnificent monuments were constructed, the largest being the great amphitheatre. Though not as large as the Colosseum in Rome, it is worthy of comparison with it. It was built to hold 23,000 spectators, and where the gladiators used to fight with wild animals the municipal authorities today stage operatic performances and concerts. Pula has many other Roman remains, including the Temple of Augustus, two beautiful triumphal arches, a thirteenth-century town hall and a citadel which was built by the Venetians. From the latter there is a lovely panorama of the town and the surrounding countryside, and of the island of Brioni where Marshal Tito has a holiday villa. The Venetians used this island as a quarry, and most of the bridges and palaces of Venice were built from stone from Brioni. They also removed most of the steps of the amphitheatre for the same purpose. Pula has some excellent bathing beaches and many hotels, including the Lipa (category C) and the Miramare (category B). The latter is situated on the sea-front.

The eastern side of the Istrian Peninsula is generally of little interest and there are few villages along the coast until one reaches the stretch which is called the Kvarner Riviera. Here is found the popular resort of Opatija and also the smaller village of Lovran (with both of which I have already dealt, in the section on the coast from Rijeka to Split). Among the quieter resorts near here are Medveja and Mošćenička Draga. The latter is a beautiful village, with shallow beaches which are excellent for children and non-swimmers. The hotel Biser, category C, is on the sea-front and there are regular bus connections with the railway station of Opatija-Matulji, about thirteen miles away.

PART V

SOME SPECIAL INTERESTS

(i) WINTER SPORTS

THE MOST accessible ski-ing resorts of Yugoslavia are in Slovenia, easily reached on the Tauern Express route through Munich and Salzburg. The leading centres are Kranjska Gora, which has a ski-lift and Rateče-Planica, with a ski-jump used for international contests. Both of these are in the Julian Alps, and other well-known resorts in this range are Bled (which is, however, at a rather low altitude), Bohinj and Pokljuka. The Pohorje, farther to the east, is another attractive region.

Šar Planina, in Macedonia, is one of the highest ranges in Yugoslavia and enjoys excellent snow conditions. The best centre is the Tourist Hotel of Popova Šapka, approached from the town of Tetovo. The district south of Sarajevo is another good area for the ski-er, with several mountain huts.

Some travel agents organise winter sports parties to the northern parts of Yugoslavia, and a list of them can be obtained from the Yugoslav National Tourist Offices.

(ii) FISHING

The mountain torrents and the many lakes of Yugoslavia provide excellent sport for the fisherman. The River Drina in Bosnia is famous for its rainbow trout and the district around one of its tributaries, the Čehotina, is ideal for the man who wants to get right off the beaten track, going on a week's trip with tent and pack-mule. More accessible is the River Neretva, rich in huck and trout, through whose valley runs the railway-line between Dubrovnik and Sarajevo.

The River Kupa at Brod na Kupi, seven miles off the Rijeka-Zagreb railway-line, is also well stocked with trout, and inexpensive accommodation in this remote area can be found in small pensions and clean private lodgings.

Split, on the Dalmatian coast, is a less isolated fishing-centre, with trout in the River Jadro, four miles from the city. There are also trout in the Cetina river at Omiš, not far away.

Recommended for lake-fishing are the Lakes of Plitvice (in the National Park on the Split-Zagreb railway-line), Lake Ohrid in Macedonia, abundant in trout, carp and eel and the Lake of Bohinj in Slovenia, with trout and char. Slovenian rivers with good fishing include the Sava Bohinjska, Radovna, Soča and Krka.

The fishing is regulated on most waters and the angler can obtain full details of seasons, maximum permitted catches and fishing-licence charges (varying from a few coppers a day in the south to several shillings in Slovenia) from any Yugoslav National Tourist Office.

The Putnik offices at Zadar and Rijeka organise sea-fishing voyages, of about ten days' duration, along the Dalmatian coast. The boats are equipped with all kinds of fishing-tackle, such as lamps, spears, underwater guns, nets, etc. The voyage from Zadar is organised by an English-speaking sea-captain. Details are obtainable from the leading tourist agencies or from the Yugoslav National Tourist Offices.

(iii) WILD GAME

Three-quarters of Yugoslavia is occupied by hills and mountains and this accounts for the great variety of wild animal and bird life. The forests form game-preserves offering cover to the Red Deer and Roe Deer, and the mountain ranges of Slovenia and Bosnia and other areas are the playground of the Chamois and Bear. The Wild Boar abounds in the Deliblatska Peščara, a Serbian district of sand-dunes, whilst the Wild Cat is found in most forested districts. All these are hunted, but the rarer Lynx and Ibex are protected and their hunting is forbidden. Yugoslavia is also one of the few countries in Europe where the Wolf and Jackal still remain.

Among interesting birds are many types of Eagle, including the Golden Eagle, the Bustard, and several species of Vulture.

Hunting is regulated and there is a system of game-wardens. Further information can be obtained from any Yugoslav National Tourist Office—but readers are warned that shooting is expensive in this country, as elsewhere.

(iv) MOUNTAIN WALKING AND MOUNTAINEERING

The outstanding district in Yugoslavia for the strenuous walker and mountaineer is, without any doubt, the Julian Alps, in Slovenia. Here are the highest mountains, the finest system of mountain huts,

and the best maps at present available. This compara-
ively small range contains no less than forty huts, about
half of them open all the year round. They are mostly
under the direction of the Planinska zveza Slovenije, or
PZS for short, the Mountaineering Association of
Slovenia, which is also responsible for the system of
marked paths. It is seldom that there is more than
five or six hours' walk between one hut and another.

The huts are similar to those in other countries and
meals are provided at many of them. Most have a few
private rooms as well as the usual kind of common
dormitory. The following brief glossary of Slovenian
words will be useful to mountaineers:

Hut	koča (alternatively...dom)
Night's lodging in a room	prenočišče v sobi
Dormitory	skupno ležišče
Rope	vrv
Ice-axe	cepin
Crampons	dereze
Fixed iron bars	zavarovana
Snow	sneg
Rain	dež
Thunderstorm	nevihta
Thunder	grmenje
Avalanche	plaz
Mountain	gora
Summit	vrh
Lake	jezero
Glacier	ledenik
Rock	skala
Path	steza
Pass	sedlo
Scree	prod

The principal mountains in the Julian Alps are Škrlatica, Razor, Prisojnik and Triglav, the latter rising to a height of 9,391 feet, the highest mountain in Yugoslavia.

The best maps available are the PZS map on a scale of 1:75,000, and the Austrian Freytag and Berndt 1:100,000 series, sheet No. 14.

The nearby ranges of the Savinjske Alps and the Karavanken, along the Austro-Yugoslav frontier, are also very well provided with huts; and though their summits are not as high as those of the Julian Alps they provide excellent mountain-walking and climbing.

A list of all the mountain huts in Slovenia can be obtained from any Yugoslav National Tourist Office. The only guide-book available is the Priročnik za Planince, published by the PZS at Ljubljana. This is an excellent book if you have the patience to study it and extract the essential information—or if you can read Slovenian!

There are, of course, mountains almost everywhere in Yugoslavia but most are either barren (like the Dinaric Alps parallel with the coast), too wild and unmapped for the ordinary walker (as in Montenegro) or too long a journey from the north (for instance, the Šar Planina of Macedonia). Some reference to the mountains near Sarajevo has been made in the section on Bosnia and Hercegovina—see page 211.

(v) CANOEING—AND BY RAFT DOWN THE DRINA

Yugoslavia is a country which offers many attractions to the experienced canoeist, used to "wild water" conditions. The finest rivers are the Drina and Tara, the latter especially noted for the clearness of its water. There are canoeing clubs in most of the principal towns and cities.

An exciting and interesting week's journey down the River Drina, from Hum to Banja Koviljača, a total distance of 170 miles, is arranged each year by various student organisations. You travel on a lumber raft, camping out each night near the water's edge.

Further details of this unusual holiday, and addresses of canoeing clubs, can be obtained from Yugoslav National Tourist Offices abroad or from the Putnik office in Belgrade.

(vi) CHESS

Chess is one of the national games of Yugoslavia and you can see it being played everywhere. A common sight in the cafés is the chess-players; on a wet day in your hotel you will find groups gathered round men seated at the chessboard; you will even see chess being played on the decks of the steamers along the Dalmatian coast, the boards and chessmen being provided by the shipping concern.

You may well be invited to play if you show any interest and, if you accept, you will probably find that your opponent plays a fast, vigorous game. If you are not a good player you may find it embarrassing to have so many onlookers, all of whom seem to be thinking several moves ahead of you, but the Yugoslavs are generous winners and nobody minds how you play provided that you put up a good fight.

T

(*vii*) FOLK DANCING

The traditional dances of Yugoslavia are world-famous. The most common are of the Kolo, or Chain Dance, type and their origins are lost in the mists of antiquity. Homer describes this type of dance in Book XVIII of the Iliad and it is depicted in some of the ancient Byzantine frescoes. Today the Kolo is seen at any time that a few Yugoslavs meet together and feel the need to express their joy or comradeship in dancing.

It is, however, on special festival days that the finest dances can be witnessed. Some of them, like the Moreška on the island of Korčula, are miniature ballets with most interesting choreography. The dances of the women are generally lyrical in form, with measures of great intricacy, whereas the men often have fierce, warlike dances, with leaping movements which demand outstanding strength and agility.

The folk-dance festivals are, of course, occasions when costumes are seen at their finest. The old musical instruments, too, are very interesting.

(*viii*) SPAS

There are a dozen famous spas in Yugoslavia and a host of small ones. A list of the diseases which can be cured would take up many pages and make this holiday book read like a medical treatise. In former days, no doubt, they were much patronised by the rich Slavs whose diet consisted of too much meat and too few vegetables. Now most spas are holiday places and they are well provided with good and not very expensive hotels and excellent sports facilities.

The most beautifully situated of the spas are, in my opinion, Niška Banja in south Serbia and Rogaška Slatina in Slovenia. Lists of spas and of their hotels can be obtained from the Yugoslav National Tourist Offices.

(ix) YOUTH WORK CAMPS

One of the unusual features of Yugoslav life in recent years has been the voluntary work carried out during their vacations by thousands of students. Outstanding among their achievements has been the Youth Railway, an important new link between Doboj and Banja Luka. They have also been engaged, however, on the construction of hydro-electric plants and factories.

It is not all work and no play, for many sports are organised, amateur drama and discussion groups spring up and there is singing, folk-dancing and so on. Then, after a month's work the members of the work-brigades go on tours of the country or to camp in the mountains.

Many foreign groups and individuals have taken part in these schemes every year and further information can be obtained from the offices of the People's Youth of Yugoslavia, Milovana Djilasa 21, Belgrade.

APPENDIX A

PASSPORT INFORMATION FOR BRITISH SUBJECTS

Forms of application for passports can be obtained from any local office or employment exchange of the Ministry of Labour or from one of the following Passport Offices :

LONDON : Clive House, Petty France, S.W.1.
LIVERPOOL : Wellington Buildings, The Strand, 2.
GLASGOW : 14 Blythswood Square, C.2.

When the form has been completed, it must be returned to one of the above addresses, or to a Ministry of Labour local office or employment exchange, accompanied by two small photographs and a fee of £1. Personal application is advised, as it usually saves time, but applications may also be made by post.

It is also possible to obtain a passport through a travel agent, but a fee will be charged for their services in addition to the Passport Office charge of £1.

A husband and wife can be included on a joint passport, the charge of £1 then covering both of them. It should be noted, however, that a wife travelling abroad *alone* has to have her own individual passport.

A British passport is valid for a period of five years from the date of issue, after which it can be renewed for a further period of five years for a fee of 10s.

APPENDIX B

OUTLINE TOURS OF YUGOSLAVIA

TOUR A

Day 1 Arrive Ljubljana and overnight there.
2 Morning in Ljubljana. Afternoon train to Zagreb and overnight there.
3 Day in Zagreb. Night train to Split, with sleeper.
4 Arrive Split early morning. Visit the town, Diocletian's Palace, etc.
5 Excursion to Trogir and Salona.
6 Steamer from Split to Dubrovnik.
7 Explore Dubrovnik.
8 Half-day motor-boat trip to Lokrum and/or Cavtat.

9   Full-day coach excursion to Kotor, the Lovćen Pass and Cetinje.
10 Free day in Dubrovnik.
11 Rail to Mostar, overnight there.
12 Rail to Sarajevo.
13 Full day in Sarajevo.
14 Night train to Zagreb, with sleeper.
15 Travel home from Zagreb.

TOUR B

Day 1   Arrive Ljubljana and overnight there.
    2   Rail to Postojna, visit grottoes, continue by rail to Rijeka.
    3   Steamer from Rijeka to island of Rab.
    4   Free day at Rab.
    5   Steamer from Rab to Zadar.
    6   Steamer from Zadar to Split.
    7   Visit the town of Split, Diocletian's Palace, etc.
    8   Excursion to Trogir and Salona.
    9   Steamer from Split to Hvar.
    10 Free day at Hvar.
    11 Steamer from Hvar to Vela Luka and bus to Korčula.
    12 Afternoon steamer from Korčula to Dubrovnik.
    13 Explore Dubrovnik.
    14 Half-day coach excursion to Trebinje.
    15 Bus from Dubrovnik to Hercegnovi or Kotor.
    16 Bus from Hercegnovi or Kotor to Budva.
    17 At Budva.
    18 At Budva.   Visit Sveti Stefan.
    19 Steamer from Budva to Rijeka.   Night at sea.
    20 Arrive Rijeka.   Rail to Ljubljana and overnight there.
    21 Travel home from Ljubljana.

TOUR C

Day 1   Arrive Ljubljana and overnight there.
    2   Morning in Ljubljana.   Afternoon train to Zagreb and night train from there to Split, with sleeper.
    3   Arrive Split early morning.   Visit Diocletian's Palace and Trogir.
    4   Steamer from Split to Dubrovnik.
    5   Explore Dubrovnik.
    6   Half-day motor-boat trip to Lokrum and/or Cavtat.
    7   From Dubrovnik to Hercegnovi by bus or steamer.
    8   Bus from Hercegnovi to Titograd.

9 Bus from Titograd to Peć.
10 Visit to monastery of Dečani and return to Peć.
11 Bus and/or rail from Peć to Skopje.
12 In Skopje. Visit Nerezi in morning and Old Skopje in the afternoon.
13 Rail to Bitola and bus to Ohrid.
14 Free day at Ohrid.
15 Motor-boat trip to Sveti Naum, returning to Ohrid.
16 Bus from Ohrid to Skopje *via* Debar and Sv. Jovan Bigorski.
17 Rail from Skopje to Niš.
18 Rail from Niš to Prahovo and board Danube steamer.
19 Through the Iron Gates to Smederevo. Overnight there.
20 Rail or bus to Belgrade.
21 Day in Belgrade. Leave at night on Simplon Orient or Tauern Express.

APPENDIX C

HOW TO PRONOUNCE THE LANGUAGE

The languages of Yugoslavia are pronounced exactly as they are written and for the practical purposes of the tourist it can be said that the differences between one of the national languages and the others can be ignored. As soon as the visitor has mastered the contents of this appendix he should be able to pronounce any word in Yugoslavia with some semblance of accuracy.

Vowels

a ...	...	...	like the *a* in *Pa*
e ...	...	...	like the *e* in *let*
i ...	...	...	like the *e* in *me*
o ...	...	...	like the *o* in *go*
u ...	...	...	like the *oo* in *too*

Exceptionally, the vowel *a* at the end of a word is pronounced like the final sound of the word *umbrella*. If the letter *j* appears at the end of a word, or if it is preceded by a vowel, it is pronounced like the English *ee* but is kept very short.

Consonants

g is always hard, as in *get*.
j is pronounced like the *y* in *youth* (but see above for its occasional use as a vowel).
r is always strongly rolled.

254

s is pronounced as in *miss*.

h is a guttural sound, like the Scottish *ch* in *loch*.

c is pronounced like the *ts* in *hits*.

dj is pronounced like the letter *j* in *jump*. This combination of letters is sometimes written as the letter *d* with a horizontal stroke through the upright.

lj is like *lli* in *million*.

nj is like the *ni* in *onion*.

All other consonants are pronounced in the normal way in English, unless they have diacritical marks or "accents". The special series of letters with such marks is as follows :

ć is rather like the *tch* of *pitcher*.

č is pronounced like the *ch* of *richer*.

ž is like the *s* in *pleasure*.

š is like the *sh* in *sheet*.

dž is pronounced like the letter *j* in *jump*. It will be noted that this is the same as the pronunciation given above for the combination *dj*. *Dž* is, however, pronounced much more strongly.

Here are a few examples of the pronunciation of place names, using the above rules :

Name				*Pronounced like*
Cavtat	...	...	...	Tsavtat
Korčula	...	...	...	Korrrchoola
Baška	...	...	...	Bashka
Nikšić	...	...	...	Neeksheetch
Ilidža	...	...	...	Eeleeja
Jajce	...	...	...	Yaeetse
Džep	...	...	...	Jep

APPENDIX D

A FEW USEFUL WORDS AND PHRASES IN SERBO-CROAT

The days of the week, starting with Sunday : *Nedelja, Ponedeljak, Utorak, Sreda, Četvrtak, Petak, Subota.*

Morning : *jutro.*
Afternoon : *poslije podne.*
Evening : *večer.*
Today : *danas.*
Tomorrow : *sutra.*
Yesterday : *jučer.*
Tonight : *noćas.*
Later on : *kasnije.*

Where is my luggage ? : *Gde je moj prtljag ?*
Is this the steamer for — ? : *Je li ovaj parobrod za — ?*
When does the steamer start ? : *Kada polazi parobrod ?*
Some hot water, please : *Molim vas, vruće vode.*

Yes : *da.*
Thanks : *hvala.*
Please : *molim vas.*
No : *ne.*
Excuse me : *izvinite.*
Good-bye : *dovidjenja.*
Good morning : *dobro jutro.*
Good evening : *dobar večer.*
Good night : *laku noć.*
Good day : *dobar dan.*
Upstairs : *gore.*
Downstairs : *dole.*
Which is the way to — ? : *Koji je put za —?*
Which is the train for — ? : *Koji je voz za — ?*
When does the train leave for — ? : *Kada polazi voz za — ?*

Where is the W.C. ? : *Gde je nužnik ?*
Way in : *Ulaz.*
Way out : *Izlaz.*
No smoking : *Zabranjeno pušiti.*
Ladies : *Ženske.*
Gentlemen : *Muške.*
No admittance : *Zabranjen ulaz.*
What does this cost ? : *Koliko košta?*
That is too much : *To je previše.*
A stamp for England, please : *Molim vas, marku za Englesku*
Numbers : *jedan, dva, tri, četiri, pet, šest, sedam, osam, devet, deset.*

APPENDIX E

THE CYRILLIC ALPHABET

The ordinary Roman alphabet is in use in Croatia and Slovenia, but in Serbia, Bosnia and Hercegovina, Montenegro and Macedonia the Cyrillic letters are used. The following is the Cyrillic Alphabet (capital and small letters), with their equivalents in the characters used in Croatia and Slovenia :

Roman				Cyrillic		Roman				Cyrillic	
A	a	...	...	А	а	P	p	...	...	П	п
B	b	...	...	Б	б	R	r	...	...	Р	р
C	c	...	...	Ц	ц	S	s	..	...	С	с
D	d	...	...	Д	д	T	t	..	...	Т	т
E	e	...	...	Е	е	U	u	...	...	У	у
F	f	...	...	Ф	ф	V	v	...	...	В	в
G	g	...	..	Г	г	Z	z	...	...	З	з
H	h	...	..	Х	х	Dj	dj	...	...	Ђ	ђ
I	i	..	..	И	и	Dž	dž	...	...	Џ	џ
J	j	...	...	Ј	ј	Ć	ć	..	...	Ћ	ћ
K	k	...	...	К	к	Č	č	...	...	Ч	ч
L	l	...	..	Л	л	Lj	lj	...	...	Љ	љ
M	m	...	...	М	м	Nj	nj	...	...	Њ	њ
N	n	...	...	Н	н	Š	š	..	...	Ш	ш
O	o	...	...	О	о	Ž	ž	...	...	Ж	ж

APPENDIX F

A SPECIMEN MENU IN SERBO-CROAT

HLADNA PREDJELA	HORS D'OEUVRES
Jaja sa majonezom	Egg mayonnaise
Mješani hordever	Mixed hors d'œuvres
Hladne zakuske	Assorted cold meats
Dalmatinski pršut	Dalmatian ham
JUHE-SUPE-ČORBE	SOUPS
Juha od paradajza	Tomato soup
Jagnjeca čorba	Lamb soup
Govedja supa sa prženim grškom ...	Pea soup
Buljon sa jajetom	Beef soup with egg
TOPLA PREDJELA	HOT ENTRÉES
Voloven	Vol-au-vent
Melancani sos tartar	Aubergines with tartar sauce
Špageti na milanski način	Spaghetti à la Milanaise
Omlet sa šunkom	Ham omelette
Omlet sa sirom	Cheese omelette
Šunka sa jajem	Ham and eggs
RIBE	FISH
Sufle od rakova	Lobster in aspic
Kečiga	Sterlet
Jesetra	Sturgeon
Pržena pastrva na ulju	Trout fried in oil
GOTOVA JELA	MAIN DISHES ("Plats du jour")
Teleći rizoto	Veal risotto
Kuhana govedina	Boiled beef
Pečena patka	Roast duck
Pečeno pile	Roast chicken
Svinjsko pečenje	Roast pork
JELA PO NARUČBINI	MAIN DISHES (Made to order)
Svinjski kotlet...	Pork cutlet
Teleća šnicla	Escalope of veal
Ramstek	Rump steak
Pohovan mozak	Fried brains
Pile na žaru	Grilled chicken
Mešano meso na žaru	Mixed grill
Teleća jetra na žaru	Grilled veal liver

VARIVA				VEGETABLES
Špinat (or Spanač)	...	...	...	Spinach
Krompir	...	...	...	Potatoes
Karfiol	...	...	...	Cauliflower
Mrkva	...	...	...	Carrots
Riža ...	...	...	...	Rice
Kupus ...	...	...	...	Cabbage
Crni luk	...	...	...	Onion

SALATE				SALADS
Mešana	...	...	...	Mixed
Paradajs	...	...	...	Tomatoes
Cvekla	...	...	...	Beetroot
Zelena ...	...	...	...	Green salad

KOLAČI				CAKES
Torta sa šlagom	...	...	...	Cake with whipped cream
Torta Doboš	•••	...	...	Chocolate cake

VOĆE				FRUIT
Jabuka...	...	...	...	Apple
Trešnje	...	...	...	Cherries
Groždje	...	...	...	Grapes
Šljive ...	...	...	...	Plums
Kruške	...	...	...	Pears
Mješani kompot	...	...	...	Mixed fruit salad

SIR	CHEESE
SLADOLED	ICE-CREAM

APPENDIX G

DIRECTORY OF ADDRESSES

OFFICIAL INFORMATION, ETC.

Yugoslav National Tourist Offices

143 Regent Street, London, W.1.
816 Fifth Avenue, New York.
Chausée d'Antin Paris.
Tirgatan 6, Stockholm.
Ober Lindau 108, Frankfort.

TRAVEL AGENTS AND TRANSPORTATION

British Railways, Continental Enquiry Office, Victoria Station, London, S.W.1. *Phone :* WATerloo 5151.

Ramblers' Association Services Ltd., 48 Park Road, Baker Street, London, N.W.1. *Phone :* AMBassador 2495.
(This organisation plan holidays throughout Yugoslavia, chief interests being the lesser-known places and the mountains ; also winter sports.)

National Union of Students, 3 Endsleigh Street, London, W.C.1. *Phone :* EUSton 2184.
(Student travel.)

Eagle Aviation Ltd., 29 Clarges Street, London, W.1. *Phone :* GROsvenor 6411.
(Direct air services from London to Yugoslavia.)

CLUBS AND ASSOCIATIONS, ETC.

American Society of Travel Agents, 444 Madison Avenue, New York. *Phone :* PLaza 9-5610.

Automobile Association, Fanum House, New Coventry Street, London, W.1. *Phone :* WHItehall 1200.

Association of British Travel Agents, 10 Mayfair Place, London, W.1. *Phone :* GROsvenor 2920.

British-Yugoslav Society, 57a Queen's Court, London, W.2. *Phone :* BAYswater 3348.

Camping Club of Great Britain and Ireland, 38 Grosvenor Gardens, London, S.W.1. *Phone :* SLOane 5866.

Central Bureau for Educational Visits and Exchanges, Hamilton House, Bidborough Street, London, W.C.1. *Phone :* EUSton 3068.

Co-operative Holidays Association, Birch Heys, Cromwell Range, Fallowfield, Manchester 14. *Phone :* Rusholme 2887.

Cyclists' Touring Club, 3 Craven Hill, London, W.2. *Phone :* PADdington 8271.

Globetrotters' Club, BCM/Roving, London, W.C.1.

Holiday Fellowship Ltd., 142 Great North Way, London, N.W.4. *Phone :* HENdon 3381.

Institute of Travel Agents, 13 Conway Street, Fitzroy Square, London, W.1. *Phone :* MUSeum 1794.

Ramblers' Association, 48 Park Road, Baker Street, London, N.W.1. *Phone :* AMBassador 2495.

Royal Automobile Club, Pall Mall, London, S.W.1. *Phone :* WHItehall 4343.

For Maps of Yugoslavia

Barmerlea Book Sales Ltd., 10 Bayley Street, London, W.C.1.

Geographia Ltd., 68 Fleet Street, London, E.C.4.

Edward Stanford Ltd., 12 Long Acre, London, W.C.2.

Yugoslav National Tourist Offices.

Putnik and Other Tourist Offices in Yugoslavia

Chief Foreign Reception Offices

Belgrade ...	...	...	...	...	Bulevar Revolucije, 1
Dubrovnik	...	...	...	...	Pile
Ljubljana	...	...	...	...	Titova Cesta 2
Rijeka ...	...	...	...	...	Nebodar
Sarajevo ...	...	...	...	...	Vase Miskina 29
Skopje ...	...	...	...	...	Maršala Tita 22
Split ...	...	...	...	...	Ilićev Prolaz
Zagreb ...	...	...	...	...	Starčevićev Trg 6

Other offices in
Banja Luka, Bitola, Bled, Budva, Crikvenica, Hercegnovi, Hvar, Jesenice (frontier), Makarska, Mostar, Niš, Ohrid, Opatija, Peć, Postojna, Priština, Prizren, Pula, Rab, Sežana (frontier), Titograd, Zadar and many other towns.

British and American Representatives in Yugoslavia

British Consulates

Belgrade ...	...	...	Prvog Maja 42
Sarajevo ...	...	...	Nikola Tesla 5
Skopje ...	...	...	Ive Lole Ribara 28
Split ...	...	...	Titova Obala 7
Zagreb ...	...	...	Ilica 12

American

Belgrade ...	...	...	Ulica Kneza Miloša 50 (Embassy)
Zagreb ...	...	...	Kumičićeva 5 (Consulate)

INDEX

INDEX

INDEX

INDEX